"Charles Kniker harvests meaningful guidance from ancient wisdom, today's freshest writers, and the best of popular culture and melds it with his own tender life experiences to offer signposts that can lead the reader to a home of rich spiritual meaning. Written with openness, empathy, and insight."

—BARRY CYTRON,
Macalester College, emeritus

"A few years ago, I had fascinating conversations with Charles Kniker as we drove around central Iowa. If you never get to have this privilege, this book is the next best thing! Charles might identify himself as a geezer, but the stories, ideas, and activities in these pages will leave you calling him a wise elder, one who wants to ensure that younger generations know the value of spirituality. So hop in, buckle up, and prepare to be enriched as you travel down some spiritual roads with Charles."

—DAVID M. CSINOS,
Atlantic School of Theology

"*Spirituality That Makes a Difference* brims with wisdom and insight. In an age in which 'spiritual but not religious' has become almost a cliché, Charles Kniker provides much-needed ballast for navigating along the shoals of life."

—RANDALL BALMER,
Dartmouth College

"Reading *Spirituality That Makes a Difference* is like being in a good conversation. The mind is illumined with interesting stories, references, and anecdotes in ways that instruct and entertain. The heart is stirred by opportunities for reflection and introspection. The reader comes away informed and nurtured. A book practitioners will enjoy, and that offers a built-in curriculum for adult education and retreats, it will make a difference in congregations and people's lives."

—DEBORAH KRAUSE,
Eden Theological Seminary

"On a spiritual path where we journey with our ancient and urgent questions, Charles Kniker engages us in amicable conversations with humor, stories, and a searching heart. We hear the wisdom of faith traditions, lessons from personal experience, and insights from scholars focused on being human. We are fortunate to be welcomed into conversations where we and our deepest longings are the subject."

—LUTHER E. SMITH JR.,
Candler School of Theology, Emory University, emeritus

"This book, filled with poignant anecdotes, keen insights, and helpful advice, is about finding your spiritual home. If you're willing to have a conversation with someone who has learned a thing or two about home, wandering, and finally, going home again, settle in for a spiritual journey with someone who believes that we all need a spiritual home and that with effort, we all can find a place to call home once again."

—STEPHEN J. PATTERSON,
Willamette University

SPIRITUALITY
That Makes a Difference

"We may differ about the why and by whom the cosmos was created,
but the universe is home for all of us." – Charles R. Kniker

SPIRITUALITY
That Makes a Difference

CHARLES R. KNIKER

WIPF *&* STOCK · Eugene, Oregon

SPIRITUALITY THAT MAKES A DIFFERENCE

Wipf & Stock
An Imprint of Wipf and Stock Publishers
199 W. 8th Ave., Suite 3
Eugene, OR 97401

www.wipfandstock.com

PAPERBACK ISBN: 978-1-6667-1789-1
HARDCOVER ISBN: 978-1-6667-1790-7
EBOOK ISBN: 978-1-6667-1791-4

MARCH 28, 2022

Dr. William Theodore Kniker, 1929–2018, was an active and passionate pediatrician, allergist-immunologist, researcher, and professor who positively impacted at least 60,000 patients and hundreds of physicians throughout the course of his career.

He was a father and grandfather who remained a loving force in his children's and grandchildren's lives.

A colorful character, Ted was a curious and compassionate human being who shared his love with his friends, family, and anyone seeking an attentive ear. Joyful, he embraced life with neoteny—an adult who retained youthful qualities. There are so many stories to remember!

Ted was also an open-minded person who respected and explored many paths to spiritual fulfillment. He read, researched, and traveled extensively, hoping to one day express his deepening awareness of God's love for all people in the form of a book. In *Jesus: The First Psychiatrist*, he planned to discuss the answers he felt Jesus would have given to universal questions still unrecorded, yet Ted felt would still be asked today by people seeking spiritual enlightenment. Though Alzheimer's overtook him in the end, his quest inspired me.

Ted, the big brother whom I will never forget, this book is dedicated to you.

Charles

Contents

Preface—Listening

As I was about to take my granddaughter on a cruise, a graduation gift, a friend—a clinical psychologist—offered her wisdom. Listen, she said, don't give advice; it will be a better gift. It was! Later, I recalled observing famed anthropologist Margaret Mead "listening" while giving a presentation at the Chautauqua Institution, New York. Instead of lecturing, she had the audience of thousands write questions on 3x5 cards, instructing them to include their names. The entire hour she answered those questions, pausing after each, to ask the writer if her answer was sufficient.

After you read this book, I hope you feel that I listened to you, responding to questions you and others—young adults, mid-lifers, and seniors—would have asked. Questions I've been hearing say you are looking for something spiritual, not traditionally structured, that speaks to the world's erased moral boundaries and blurring geopolitical borders. Our homes, self-images, roles, and communities have changed. Beyond vocabularies and Band-Aids, questioners ask how can we be transformed into better people—individuals, neighborhoods, nations, and world?

The planet we live on now is a new world with a deadly virus that respects no geographical boundaries. The best scientific data, political speeches, economic plans, or religious prayers cannot guarantee that we, or our families and neighbors, will survive. For example, we debate the scientific consensus that social distancing and mask-wearing are the most effective strategies until most of us are vaccinated. We huddle in our homes, our safest sanctuaries. In the US, tribes debate liberty vs. common good, ignoring the fact that relatively few international neighbors have had the opportunity for any COVID remedy.

This book's message is that people need engaged spiritual sanctuaries that parallel family homes. A healthy spiritual home mirrors what a good home offers—walls and roofs of comfort, safety, and encouragement; windows and doors preparing us for life's challenges and confrontations. At their best, these similar but different homes prepare us for personal fulfillment, service to our neighbors, and a planet that survives.

Its eight chapters reflect what I hold to be universal: humans crave a home, a harbor from the world's storms, uniting in a love for each other. Such love is demanding, reflecting universal golden rules expressed more in deeds than in words, moral decisions, and actions taken or avoided. Is that being religious or spiritual? Theologian Paul Tillich asserts all persons are religious, worshiping or loving what they hold is of ultimate value. Do you agree? Sharon Daloz Parks and Father Richard Rohr believe that all persons are spiritual—determining meanings, acting on them. In either case, individuals must decide. A wise one quipped, "No one can take your bath for you." Therapists offer this perceptive truth: you can't fix someone else. That said, I believe each of us is a spiritual traveler, leaving a first home and needing others to guide us in our interpretation of and decisions regarding the steps and stones of life.

I hold that there are many varieties of spiritual homes. No one home has a corner on all the truth. As Barbara Brown Taylor asserts in *Holy Envy*, we enrich our spiritual lives by understanding the truths others derive from their faith explorations.

If we are to make a difference, humans need to engage with others beyond immediate families. Are you ready to see places and meet people who speak and act differently? That is part of the excitement of searching for your spiritual home. Be honest. Which cohort do you want or need now—a pious picnic, a social justice juggernaut, a community aloof, a clan actively subversive or aggressively neutral? These pages aren't a trap to return you to a mom-and-pop church, synagogue, or mosque, but a guide to finding your way to a world where you can engage in a transformative spirituality.

Why read this book? I'm a geezer; you're more likely a geek. Assume we've grown up in different eras, had distinct transformative events, and approached decision-making differently. Possibly, we have shared some of life's ups and downs, climbed similar fences, and felt we want to make a difference in the world that's coming. Odds are our neighborhoods are already new worlds.

I feel fortunate to have lived in diverse worlds. The first world was a town near San Antonio, Texas, in the post-Great Depression through post-World War II years. Sleepy, safe, Seguin was known for pecans, a golf course, small businesses, and farming. Its 10,000-plus residents had a decent high school for white and Hispanic students; black students attended separate schools. My parents' families had a lot of teachers, farmers, and ministers.

A second world began in the 1950s and 1960s in the Midwest—Chicago and St. Louis, for college and seminary. Throw in an intern year in Honduras, a first parish, then finishing the decade with graduate schooling in the San Francisco Bay area and New York City. More important than the geography was that world's personal events—the sudden death of my college sweetheart and wife of seven months, a second marriage, and the birth of our first son.

The worlds of higher education and theological education followed over the next thirty-plus years. Teaching was my calling, but in a research university, you publish, too. I founded the journal *Religion & Education* during my twenty-four years at Iowa State University. Then, Eden Seminary (Missouri), my alma mater, called me to be its president. That was followed by serving a loving congregation in Texas and returning to Iowa as a higher education administrator. During these experiences, I met many fascinating individuals. They differed in age, color, ideologies, faith perspectives, values, and agendas. I also became a father again; my wife and I had another son.

My last world is the one most likely to link us together. It began in 1998, when my wife of forty-five years, Eleanor, was diagnosed with a non-cancerous brain tumor. She survived two craniotomies, then grappled with double vision and diminished hearing. This former RN and nursing instructor lived until 2008 with a graceful ferocity. During those years, I learned again how precious life is and how supportive professionals, family, friends, and strangers can be.

Whether you call it my religion or my spirituality, these and new experiences transformed my life. A trip to Israel and Jordan in 2017 brought greater insights about world religions. A pacemaker increased appreciation of daily life. Learning became ever more enjoyable. The Chautauqua Institution is a periodic summer treat; my dissertation analyzed its pioneering book club, the Chautauqua Literary and Scientific Circle. It was a privilege to serve as moderator of an association of twenty-five congregations in central Iowa, in retirement, witnessing inspiring examples of healthy spiritual homes.

I hope these worlds and yours enrich our conversation about spiritual homes. As church historian Diana Butler Bass describes in *Strength for the Journey*, religious beliefs and practices of the past can become vital and vibrant in new forms. May your spiritual home reflect and support the voice and deeds you are called to share with the world.

Acknowledgments

The journey to help travelers find spiritual homes has been an adventure that now spans fifteen years. I was ending my professional career, becoming a caregiver for my wife. The drumbeat of woe about church decline was becoming louder. My adolescent dream of being a beloved pastor for fifty years like Grandfather Carl Kniker had faded long ago. It started well enough. The in-joke of my German Protestant heritage predicts: go to Elmhurst College, then Eden Seminary, then gain entrance to eternity. Crucible experiences—the sudden death of my first wife, a calling to educational ministry while in Honduras, a twenty-four-year diversion as a professor at a land grant university, the unexpected call to be a seminary president, and the devastating brain tumor and fatal fall for my second wife—have given me a bifurcated outlook on life.

On one hand, I am super-sensitive to the fragility of life. I am elated, to the point of tears, when I see the deep love, trust, and imagination of children. The enthusiastic love of young couples, the ideological concerns and commitments of emerging adults, and the gently gruff way that the elderly and their caregivers take care of each other make me speechless. Humor is my key to survival, and I appreciate loved ones who put up with my puns.

But many don't know that beneath my usual calmness, an engaged spirituality has become an enraged spirituality. It is more than our consumer-driven superficial lifestyles and simplistic acceptance of convenient ignorant solutions to life issues. Too often and easily, we demonize others, support legislation depriving minorities of civil rights, and casually ignore reasonable climate regulations. I am critical of religious institutions, from local houses of worship to bureaucratic minions and theological leaders. Too often, their laments focus on petty issues. Rather than transformative ministries, they protect their power and solicit perks.

I could not have imagined how much my own spiritual life has been enriched by others along the way. Some are old friends and colleagues while others, of various ages, near and far, have become dear and beloved acquaintances. I especially appreciate new friends who shared insights about various subjects found on these pages.

I'm deeply indebted to four readers who brought their knowledge and language arts skills to reading and editing each chapter: Anna Kniker and Dianne Prichard gave extraordinary time; Gene Larson and John Bolen offered key insights. Jane Zaring provided proofreading. Katie Tschopp was permissions coordinator and proofreader extraordinaire. Encouragement for publishing the book goes to Walter Brueggemann, fellow EC and Eden student, lifelong colleague, and friend. I cannot give enough praise to Sharon Daloz Parks, whose endorsement of the concept of *spiritual home* was inspiring; her classic work on big questions and worthy dreams, with examples of spiritual practices, is reflected throughout the book.

Those who provided expert advice for chapters—some, partners via Zoom—deserve accolades for their insights and support. Distinguished Iowa State University professors Diane Birt and Cornelia Flora; Dr. Michael Waggoner, University of Northern Iowa professor and my successor as editor of *Religion & Education*; Dr. Joyce Davidson, former director of Student Counseling Services, Iowa State University; Rabbi Barry Cytron, Macalester College, Minneapolis; Michael Surratt, organist at First United Church of Oak Park, Illinois; Dr. Lynn J. Zeigler, Iowa State University professor emerita of music; Dr. M. Franklin Dotts, curriculum editor, United Methodist Church; Rev. Dr. David Csinos, professor of education, Atlantic School of Theology; Rev. Hanna Hanover, associate pastor, Ames UCC; Rev. Maren C. Tarabassi; Rev. Dirk Ficca, Parliament of the World's Religions, Chicago; Barry Lynn, retired CEO of Americans United for Separation of Church and State; Dr. Robert J. Nash, professor emeritus, University of Vermont; Julia Rendon, professor, Des Moines Area Community College; and Rev. Dr. J. Jeffrey Means, Des Moines Pastoral Counseling Center.

Data and information, advice, encouragement, and support came from the following persons: Rev. Dr. H. Scott Matheny, chaplain, Elmhurst University, Illinois; Linda Mercadante, author of *Belief Without Borders*; Dr. Chuck Foster, formerly of the Candler School of Theology,

Georgia; Rev. John Thomas, former president, United Church of Christ; Luther Smith Jr., Emory University; Rev. Dr. Peter Schmiechen, retired president of Lancaster Seminary, Pennsylvania; Jonathan C. Page, minister of First Congregational Church, Houston, Texas; Dr. Larry Ebbers, Iowa State University professor emeritus of higher education; Rev. Dr. Deborah Krause, president of Eden Theological Seminary, Missouri; Dr. Sabrina MisirHiralall, professor at Montclair State University; Dr. Beverly Gelwick, director of several counseling centers; Byron Belitsos, publisher; Brent Walters, Garrett Theological Seminary; Jennie Norris and Dustin Ingram; author Scott Russell Sanders. Rev. Jo Hudson shared information about church development while Rev. Lillie Brock informed me about the spiritual location technique. Rev. Sarai Rice offered numerous insights regarding younger generations' interest in matters religious and spiritual. Dennis Eastin provided perspectives about spiritual formation. For several conversations about spirituality, faith traditions, mysteries, and music, including several resources, my deepest appreciation to V. V. Raman, Iowa State University professor emeritus. For insights regarding senior communities, Joel Nelson, CEO and president of Life Care Services; also Laura Beas Gutierrez of Green Hills. Angie Brown and Dan Coffey of the Iowa State University Library made it incredibly easier to access resources. Thanks to Dorothy, Judy, and Emily for words about your dad.

During my professional life, I have been privileged to be involved with two adult education programs that allowed me to have conversations with persons mentioned throughout these pages. I began attending the Chautauqua Institution in the late 1960s when it was the subject of my dissertation. With family, we've been to summer sessions numerous times since. Locally, the Ames United Church of Christ, Iowa, has sponsored a Theologian-in-Residence (TIR) program for over thirty years. TIRs have included Randall Balmer, Diana Butler Bass, Marcus Borg, Walter Brueggemann, John Dominic Crossan, Marva J. Dawn, Gary Dorrien, Ruth Duck, Amy Jill-Levine, Barry Lynn, John Selby Spong, Phyllis Tickle, David Vasquez-Levy, Ruth Duck, Cynthia Wilson, and Brian Wren. A discussion with Bass in 2008 about why some congregations thrive and a subsequent conversation with Richard Bass, then editor of Alban Institute publications, spurred my interest in factors that promote healthy spiritual communities. Emily Callihan, Rebecca Abbott, and Jonathan Hill of Wipf & Stock offered significant editorial assistance.

Finally, I've been molded by dear souls from congregations in Illinois, Missouri, California, New Jersey, Texas, and Iowa. Their memories, as well as those of colleagues at Iowa State and Eden Theological Seminary, give deeper meaning to the stories on these pages. For enrollees in Iowa State University's Osher Lifelong Learning Institutes class on Trends in Spirituality, a special thank-you for feedback on the early chapters of the book. Family members, many now in "that great cloud of witnesses," two women I was blessed to have married—Carrol and Eleanor—and my sons, Ted and Tim and their families, continue to help me complete several worthy dreams.

Introduction—Forming

Be happy for this moment. This moment is your life.

—Omar Khayyam (1048–1131 CE),
Persian mathematician, calendar designer

If you are open to it, let's have a conversation, a give-and-take about what it means to be spiritual or religious in this crazy world. Why? You may feel like a person who "travels the world over in search of what he [or she] needs and returns home to find it."[1] Or, if you are like the middle class who, in the 1950s, "left home, spiritually as well as physically, to take the vow of organization life" and became "the mind and soul of our great self-perpetuating institutions," are you now tired and want something more?[2] Perhaps you are at the other end of the spectrum, content but curious, wondering what lighthouses others use to chart their courses through the choppy waves and undertows on today's restless seas. Possibly, you're ready to take a trip to your selected destination, not needing a map or compass but eager to speak with previous visitors.

Why have a conversation with me? I'll admit it, I like to talk, and often, when seatmates and I finish our flights, the seatmates say they enjoyed the conversation. "Are you traveling for business or pleasure?" is my opening line, and I can tell if a person wants to talk or not. It's fascinating to hear inspiring stories of others as well as challenges they face and victories they've won. Sooner or later their stories revolve around their home situations. Quotations in the book I regard as gems of insights or provocation. As Roman Catholic sister and artist Corita Kent said, "If it is true, does it matter who said it?"

I've spoken with a rancher who auctioned a cattle sale for the Rockefellers, a FedEx driver arranging her mother's funeral, a college student

1. Attributed to George A. Moore, Irish poet (1852–1933).
2. Whyte, *Organization Man*, 3.

1

beginning a new job in a strange city, a software engineer's rushed trip to find a nursing home for his parents, the significant other of the author of a best-selling child psychology book, an Air India pilot proud of his daughter's accomplishment in her Canadian career. I've debated religious folk certain they knew the only way to heaven, guided by their sacred scriptures. The most surprising conversations have been with folks who were extraordinarily successful financially, politically, artistically, or academically. Well-respected, these men and women appeared to have it all but shared with me that something was missing. Many were struggling with severe problems that impaired their families' lives. A common thread was the little, or large, religious upbringing they had experienced had weakened or evaporated with the passage of time. What are they looking for? Social ethicist Brent Waters has shared that the word *transcendent* emerged in his similar conversations.

Another reason to talk. I'm told I'm a good listener and storyteller, a way of saying I'm a character. My "checkered past" stories go back to summer jobs working for a railroad, making slot machines, selling merchandise from children's shoes to Fuller brushes, and warehousing farm supplies. Professionally, I've been a minister, professor, seminary president, and higher education administrator. Two personal stories: late to preach at a rural house of worship because the car got stuck in the mud, I hastily put on a supplied robe. Following the service, a smiling parishioner said, "You were impressive in that robe, preacher, but seeing your muddy shoes and pants underneath it, I knew you were just like us!" More recently, a neighbor in my retirement community, a crusty, former career military veteran, and I had almost daily conversations because we both liked sports, music, and limericks. Unfortunately, we had another similarity: our wives died within several months of each other. He said to me one night, "You're not like any other minister I've ever known. I can really talk with you." I considered that a heartfelt compliment.[3]

Granted, some travelers clam up when they learn you are a minister. Other travelers ask for support in their lives or prayers for their loved ones. Some, because of their experiences, want logical answers for often unexplainable tragedies. In such circumstances, I feel a minister's function is to offer comfort but also to assist individuals in asking the right

---

3. Most ministers do well with spiritual and religious crises, in part because they have experienced one or more themselves. A seminary president once described the incoming student class as a "M*A*S*H unit" because of their medical or psychological histories. As in any profession, however, clergy differ in being good listeners.

questions rather than giving them some quick answers like an airborne Wizard of Oz. My theology appreciates God in nature, like Shakespeare, who saw "books in the running brooks, sermons in stones."[4] But I do not hold that God's will explains every single event. That's where spiritual homes come in. They can still be traditional houses of worship—synagogues, mosques, temples, shrines. Or attendees can meet in small or large homes, restaurants and bars, strip malls, or on mountaintops and seashores, anywhere that persons experience a real connection to a guiding higher force. Structure is secondary. What is key are spiritual homes that give souls tenacious support, while providing insightful information and practices that transform lives.

Were we to speak on a plane—mask or no mask—it would be a dialogue.[5] That's essential. To quote a professor who described his encounters with a highly opinionated colleague, "I had many conversations with him, but never a dialogue." I've tried to hone my listening skills as a minister, professor, seminary president, fundraiser, higher education administrator, and now, as a retiree—and let's not forget as a parent and a grandparent!

Over the years, I believe I've become more sensitive to the need to listen and understand when people share from their hearts. That's my hope, that you and I can communicate openly and honestly, regardless of our age, gender, race, or circumstances in this "new normal" world. Will it be easy? We are struggling now with what normal is or should be. As a friend reminded me, *normal* is just a setting on a washing machine. So, we are not a mentor and protégé, or college students shooting the breeze at a bar, but closer to what grad students call a bullpen, two new friends sharing, debating, questioning, coming from different experiences. Assertions are not proof! I'd like to listen to you, whether you are similar to my emerging adult granddaughter and her college friends dreaming about careers while dealing with nightmare college debts, parents struggling with a special needs child, or a single parent coping with a low-paying job. I have an image of some of you with a fireplace in the background, on a sofa watching a television. Perhaps you might be an empty-nest couple, hoping your families can weather the latest storm. Or you mirror a young, enthusiastic couple I know from the South, involved in politics, supporting candidates who will address the country's lack of

---

4. William Shakespeare, *As You Like It*, act 2, scene 1.
5. Nash et al., *How to Talk*, prefer the term *conversation*.

a moral compass. Under a reading lamp, there is a harrowed minister looking for strategies on church growth. Coming from the darkness are newcomers, suspicious of time and financial demands, joined by refugees from hurtful religious experiences.

We'll speak of possibilities that will enrich your life. I hope you will find some directions here to determine what is true and meaningful for a fuller life, for you and others close to you. As you navigate this moral/ethical/spiritual journey, somewhere along the road, you may find others willing to travel with you.

Past conversations convince me that wanting a home is in our DNA. Most of us also want a spiritual home. Catch that? A spiritual home. To repeat, it doesn't have to be a house of worship or tribe sharing unique, quaint doctrinal beliefs and religious practices. It should be a community bound by healthy values and practices. No one template will fit all, but I'll argue there are some common components. It would be safe and welcoming, have a spirit of belonging and unity, with a clear mission. Like any biological home, from time to time there will be arguments about what is healthy, proper, and the needed leadership. But we know any spiritual group's outlook that has meaningful outcomes will require commitment.

In the pages that follow, each chapter is structured around questions you might ask. I'll include a variety of stories and illustrations, both secular and saintly, that offer you comfort and challenge to help you and others address our individual and corporate struggles of the soul. I'll assume you are a traveler on a *spiritual* journey. That means at times I will use words associated with historical religions, such as disciple and discipleship, related to past faith leaders and movements. Please, don't get stuck in the mud about them. Much more, we'll review today's broader sociological context of choices about spiritual possibilities.

THE INTENDED READERS AND PURPOSES OF THIS BOOK

Years ago, when I wrote the first draft of this book, I assumed most readers had some exposure to a house of worship and were likely to have been young captives. Not now. I'm certain many are first-time searchers, looking to fulfill an individual or family's religious and spiritual needs.

What are the specific purposes of the book in that regard? There are four, encompassed by the belief that current world circumstances require us to be advocates for change. Poet Alice Walker has said, "Activism is my rent for being on this planet." The book purposes are:

1. Recognize voices that call us to live meaningful spiritual lives, not to be perfect, but to live as rightly as possible through spiritual growth.

2. Describe four key qualities/characteristics of spiritual homes that relate to new models of spirituality beyond changing borders and boundaries.

3. Provide examples of spiritual practices that allow communities to develop tangible dreams of caring, compassion, and justice for this world of neighbors.

4. Offer images to help you form a spirituality that makes a difference by becoming part of a spiritual home.

HELPING YOU BECOME A YEARNING, ENERGIZED, SPIRITUAL SELF

If you and/or yours want to find a new spiritual home, are you ready to begin the journey? If so, I will call you a traveler. I assume you want to answer such questions as what is the purpose of my life? What am I most passionate (excited) about? What do I want my legacy to be? Benjamin Franklin, a stretch to be called a spiritual authority, supposedly remarked: "He who knows only his own generation forever remains a child." Broaden that. A mature adult, spiritually speaking, needs a global perspective. Most of us, sooner or later, turn to formal education, civic organizations, support groups, and, yes, spiritual communities to find answers to life's essential questions. The chapter titles reflect ways our spiritual lives can be formed.

PART I: BECOMING A SPIRITUAL TRAVELER— FROM HOME TO HOME

Chapter 1, Home: Formed by Love—The Journey from Home Begins

Let me be clear about the trip you are about to make. It begins with understanding what you are looking for and what it is you want to avoid. David Campbell, in his best-selling book for counselors, concludes when you don't plan well, you will end up with fewer and less desirable choices.[6] Humans cherish good—healthy—homes. I believe we crave a parallel healthy spiritual home, a place where like-minded and like-intentioned individuals explore and act upon how they answer the meaning-making questions of life. How are spiritual homes like traditional houses of worship and yet different from them?

Chapter 2, Self: "In-Formed" by Others—The Spiritual Self You Are Called to Be

Homes are made up of individuals. As family therapists tell us, healthy homes have clear roles and rules for children as well as structured boundaries. Each member is respected; each child is encouraged to develop her/ his unique self. Spiritual homes should mirror our personal homes at their best. For some, the traditional terminology, images, and practices of organized religion, spirituality, and sibling rivalries are fine, but for others are detours and roadblocks. To be clear, these brief discussions will not be lengthy excursions into doctrinal debates. What does the expression "I'm spiritual but not religious" mean? Or do you have qualities of both? Everyone, I believe, is spiritual, with an innate sense that we are related as self to others, to our natural and material worlds, and to a greater, ultimate force. Religion is about the codification of beliefs and practices related usually to a divine being. Both religion and spirituality ask deep questions and promote dreams. Others may call it engaged spirituality; I call it transformative spirituality (formed, informed, reformed, conformed, transformed), or try this on: paradoxical piety!

Chapter 3, Voice: "Re-Formed" by Choice—Finding Your Voice (as Disciple, Friend, Moral Servant Leader)

The Abrahamic faiths—Judaism, Christianity, and Islam—and other traditions have founders. Christianity and Islam favored rigorous expansion. Their followers are called disciples who have beliefs and practices of discipline. What is discipleship in today's context? It is similar in some ways to what athletes and artists do. It is different in other ways, with

6. D. Campbell, *If You Don't Know*. Campbell was the president of The Center for Creative Leadership, a former professor of psychology at the University of Minnesota, and a friend.

transformed religious practices. The joyful outcomes are expanding our beings from disciples to friends and moral servant leaders. In short, finding your authentic identity.

Chapter 4, Community: "Con-Formed" by Comfort and Confrontation

What binds members of spiritual homes together is they share a special feeling; it is referred to as a calling or a commission. While that is different from biological homes, the homes are alike because both share two purposes. Both communities provide 1) various forms of *comfort* that make family members feel safe, welcomed, nurtured, and supported; and 2) deliberate challenges and, when necessary, *confrontations* to help members become mature adults, coping with issues related to love, work, and the wider society. All of us should strive to have healthy homes, meaningful lives, and dreams turned to deeds.

PART II: QUALITIES OF A SPIRITUAL HOME—YESS TO LIFE!

Geezers like me relish board games. Possibly during the pandemic of 2020, you played some with your family. Often, they involve taking a trip or building something. If this were a spiritual traveler game, Spiritual Home, it would begin by constructing the house's foundation with four key pillars. Each of the four pillars is represented by a letter: YESS. Chapter 5 gives you the *y* of yearning for something worthy, transcendent beyond human achievement. Chapter 6 provides the *e* of education or learning. Chapter 7 is the first *s*, where I deliberately merge the words *soul* and *care* to make *soulcare*—a special kind of self-care and caregiving for others. Chapter 8 is a second *s*, for service. Hey, there's even a mnemonic device for each chapter title!

Chapter 5, Yearning: "Trans-Formed" by Joy— Your Exploration through Scriptures and Songs (Yearning)

Spirituality believes in a higher power or living a full life. Traditional religious terms include divine being, creative force, God, Allah, or what Paul Tillich called the ultimate ground of being. In the Hebraic-Christian faith tradition, God is identified as YHWH. Here, *y* stands for Yearning. I believe humans have a DNA for meaning beyond simply living an "acceptable" day-to-day life. We humans yearn for a joy-filled relationship with a power or ultimate force. That is the first step toward discipleship, a systematic searching to fulfill that yearning. The word *worship* comes from an Old English word, *worth-ship*. This chapter reviews how that worth-ship has been expressed through words, music, rituals, and practices and also spotlights examples of creative trends. The result of this joy: a spirit of generosity that enriches daily life. An individual sacrifices self for a team. A soldier makes the ultimate sacrifice. Parents sacrifice for their children. Individuals provide for the common good. The chapter also discusses false worship, which essentially promotes unhealthy bodies and relationships.

Chapter 6, Education: "Trans-Formed" by Truth— Your Education of Self for Society (Learning)

Human nature has a drive to communicate with others, to be in groups, as the coronavirus demonstrated. Education is essential. This chapter discusses the when, what, and how we create and transmit the knowledge, skills, and dispositions needed for faith formation. Teachers in religious traditions tend to be "sages on the stage"; spiritual formation stresses "guides on the side." The emphasis is on lifelong learning about truth, which spurs courage.

Chapter 7, Soulcare: "Trans-Formed" by Trust— Your Everyday Soulcare and Support (Burning)

Do you feel you have "arrived" spiritually? Few of us do; throughout our spiritual journey, we are faced with doubts. The search for truth is never complete. Søren Kierkegaard, a Danish theologian, supposedly said, "I am not a Christian, I am always becoming a Christian." Spiritual communities encourage and assist their members in their soul searching. Another dimension of soulcare is a burning to care for others. This spiritual nourishment can be through a wide range of food-related ministries, support groups, interest groups, addiction-fighting organizations, and age-based social clubs. To be effective and long lasting, trust must be at its core, hope its outcome.

Chapter 8, Service: "Trans-Formed" by Love— Your Emphasis on Sharing and Service (Turning)

Authentic spirituality helps us see beyond our stained glass vision and doctrinal walls. Our talents, treasures, temperaments, and tenacity serve those in need. Sacred texts command disciples to offer witness to the intangible forces of joy and hope to desperate people tempted to give up. Faith without works, according to multiple faiths, is dead. What this chapter emphasizes is that your religious or spiritual search, with the support of a spiritual home, should move you from reaching an understanding of what your life means to developing dreams some of which encompass building a world of neighbors through Service based on love, with justice and peace resulting.

Final Conversation

When you are a yearning, energized, spiritual self who has said YESS to life, you can say you are home! What will make it even better is if you are part of a spiritual home that supports you. The pandemic has brought home (wordplay intended) the reality that daily life is fragile, not to be taken for granted. Even those of us favored by inheritance, race, class, age, or geography are not guaranteed a minimum number of days. As my brother, to whom this book is dedicated, said not long before his death, "I feel content with what I've accomplished." If you have led a disciplined, engaged spiritual life, you should be able to say that in your final days.

SOME QUIRKS AND SOME REASONS TO NOT READ THIS BOOK

In my checkered past, I made slot machines one summer (it's a long story). I learned how the slots are set to pay off at rates the house sets. This book's scope has been set by certain perspectives and experiences I've had with a variety of spiritual communities. You may disapprove or be disappointed I didn't include or exclude some traditions or practices. You might suspect that eventually I'll direct you back to a mom-and-pop church you've rejected or my personal brand. No. I will plead guilty to the evidence that I don't provide examples of all religious/spiritual traditions. I do take responsibility for errors of fact or interpretations about the traditions

I cite. I won't plead to subversively steering you to the "one holy road home." Why? Just as I've been in many natal homes—a bambooed hut in Honduras, the first homestead (National Park, Beatrice, Nebraska), prim colonial New England cottages, southwestern adobe casitas, midwestern ranch homes, swank New York City apartments, and McMansions in Florida—I've seen a variety of houses of worship. I can't match Diana Eck's descriptions of a mosque outside Toledo, Ohio; a Hindu temple in suburban Nashville, Tennessee; a Cambodian Buddhist monastery south of Minneapolis; a Sikh gurdwara in Fremont, California; a Hindu temple in Troy, Michigan.[7] Who am I to judge which of these households can or cannot meet the spiritual needs of their followers? I will share only what I believe are signs of a healthy spiritual home. You must choose.

A second reason is that our spiritual needs are based on what Sharon Daloz Parks calls the Big Questions, which require us to do meaning-making about the mysteries of life. The answers to those questions are often found in paradoxes. If you are into certainty, you will be frustrated, because I believe a healthy spiritual home will help you cope with life's paradoxes, not provide neatly packaged answers. Spirituality is "one's lived relationship with Mystery."[8] Also, I agree with the assertion *home* is the most powerful single word in the English language. Why? Our lived, tangible homes and dreams have intense meanings and consequences.

Put together, *spiritual home* is a paradox. A paradox is "a statement that seems contradictory, unbelievable or absurd but that may actually be true in fact." Reader, you may prefer to call it an oxymoron, described as "a figure of speech, sometimes acutely silly, in which opposite ideas can be true."[9] A warning. Throughout the book I will deliberately use familiar and new paradoxical expressions such as "the first shall be last" and "collective individualism" to remind us that we are in more than a traditional transition. We are in a new normal world. It is a world where conventional boundaries are blurred or broken or have vanished. Many of the world's current structures and buildings, beliefs and practices, traditions and freedoms, truths, and facts will change. Paradoxes alert us to alternatives we will face.

What then is a spiritual home? It is first a body of like-minded souls who contemplate and celebrate their personal experiences of the Mystery.

---

7. Eck, *New Religious America*, 1–2.

8. Parks, *Big Questions*, 26. See also H. Cox, *Future of Faith*, ch. 2.

9. *Webster's New World Dictionary*, "Paradox" and "Oxymoron."

Second, although not always agreeing, that household's members, will forge strategies and alliances with local and world neighbors, in actions required for the planet's survival.[10]

I don't want you to waste your time. My conviction, like that of Lillian Daniel, is that spiritual traveling is hard work, frustrating at times, and likely dangerous to the status quo.[11] To cope with that, I feel it is imperative to be part of a healthy spiritual home. Over the years, it will be beneficial to have several relay stations or home stations like pony express riders of the nineteenth-century needed. Challenging you at times, these way stations will recognize your hard choices and be close at hand when criticisms and attacks come.

If you expect to find any of the following in this book, you will be disappointed:

- Concrete certainty that there is only one way to do spirituality, and that true houses of worship have the right beliefs buttressed with inerrant scriptural references.

- Approval of the too frequently held view, often by mainline congregations, that the house of worship can be used as a credit card or insurance for social services such as baptism, weddings, and funerals, without dedicated involvement from its members.

- Trashing of the house of worship as a parasitic relic of the past, whose doctrines and dogmas have had only negative consequences.

- The perspective that individuals are victims and can't ever be held responsible for decisions/actions they make relative to life in general or faith development. (Exceptions are biological factors.)

- Scripture dictates that rulers and their social order are to be accepted and are above criticism, i.e., that the house of worship is not to be involved in politics. Such a position ignores accounts of historic founders and current members of various spiritual perspectives who confront leaders decisively when wrong is done.

---

10. Diana Bass, *Grounded*, chs. 5 and 7.

11. Daniel, *Tired of Apologizing*, 131.

ANOTHER PERSPECTIVE: SHARED AND DIVERSE GUIDELINES

If after reading this preface you are willing to continue, great! What I hope will follow is a mutual journey in which we will share questions as well as answers, doubts as well as certitude, and a civil commitment to seek a common ground.

Let's face it. Each reader will get something different from the book because each one brings her or his parental and familial rearing, schooling experiences, and life circumstances to bear. Over time, each of us operates with what we could call our internalized truths, i.e., observations we have made. Our actions are based on the era in which we grew up and the crucibles we encountered, in which we not only survived but thrived.

Because of my Protestant Christianity background, many examples I use are from the Hebrew Scriptures and Christian New Testament, often called the Holy Bible. I will cite other sacred writings and examples. I want to be inclusive. To be clear, there are no guarantees we will come to a consensus of what is best. Literature analysis and the field of hermeneutics (sacred text interpretation) make clear that each of us filters our interpretations through our experiences as well as training. Regarding texts, we will have different understandings of authorship, audience, and setting. We may disagree if these texts are divine words without error, human interpretation of divine covenants, good rule books, or simply great literature.

As you and I journey together we will have a real conversation. We should anticipate rest stops and breaks. In part I, others who have been past travelers will share their experiences and raise questions for you. In part II, voices from various spiritual traditions and communities and their critics will surface. You can have a conversation with them as you choose. I am, of course, referring to the footnotes as well as examples in the text. Call those voices a second dialogue. What is most memorable about a trip are often the characters we meet along the way. With that in mind, are you ready to begin?

PART I

BECOMING A SPIRITUAL TRAVELER—
FROM HOME TO HOME

Forma, a Middle English word, can mean a shape, image, or figure. Shape can describe our physical or emotional state. Image reflects our current or future perceived profile. A figure could offer an imaginative metaphor. Part I of this book describes the ways that various forces have molded or might mold you, especially as steps in your spiritual formation. Love should be the key ingredient in shaping everyone's life but sadly isn't. As you are reminded of the dramatic forces that formed your soul and self, I hope you will better understand why and how your spiritual being can be a difference maker for you and others. To do this, traveler, you begin at one home, and in time establish another.

Our first conversation, chapter 1, begins by asking you to remember the experiences and stories of your childhood. Hopefully, you were formed by love, yes, tough love at times. It sustained you. Continuing through your teen and early adult years, as chapter 2 chronicles, for days, weeks, and years, you were "in-formed" about life's values and choices. Your self began interpreting, charting meanings of life. During that time, you may have been challenged to "de-form" some of your behaviors or even body image. As you matured into adulthood, chapter 3 posits there were and still are many voices urging you to "re-form" your identity. You listen; you weigh; you decide. These forces, secular and sacred, benign to aggressive, are also seeking to "con-form" you. Chapter 4 ends part I by asserting that as a social and individual being you have the option of becoming part of a healthy spiritual community which will ask you to "con-form." You must discern which of its beliefs and practices you accept. Hopefully, it will assist you in making a positive difference in the world.

1

Home—Formed by Love

I had the feeling I was coming home,
and it was to a home I have never had before.

—Sam Baldwin, describing the relationship he had with his
deceased wife, in the movie *Sleepless in Seattle*

In East Asia, we speak of the human body as a mini-cosmos. The cosmos is our
home, and we can touch it by being aware of our body. Meditation is to be still:
to sit still, to stand still, and to walk with stillness. Meditation means to look
deeply, to touch deeply so we can realize we are already home. Our home is
available right here and now.

—Thich Nhat Hanh, *Going Home*, 45

A longing for homeland is one of the two great pulls in the tidal ebb and flow
that powers the development of meaning and faith . . . another powerful sen-
sibility that pulls as deeply and truthfully at the core of the human soul—the
call to dwell, to stay, to abide, to return home.

—Sharon Daloz Parks, "*To Venture and to Abide*," 62

The strength of a nation derives from the integrity of the home.

—Confucius

FORMED BY LOVE: BEGINNING A SPIRITUAL JOURNEY HOME

- ◆ Invitation: to remember your home and become a sheltered seeker

- ◆ Traveler, are you willing to go out on a limb?

- ◆ Ready to travel from home to home to back home?

- ◆ Why emphasize home first, then the self?

- ◆ What's a home? Imagine pieces of a homemade pie!

- ◆ What makes homes healthy? Unhealthy?

- ◆ How many homes are religious or spiritual?

- ◆ What's special about spiritual homes?

- ◆ How can we practice homefulness?

- ◆ Do spiritual families have benefits?

- ◆ Traveler: ready to be a sheltered seeker going out on a limb?

- ◆ Activities

- ◆ For Additional Conversations

INVITATION: TO REMEMBER YOUR HOME
AND BECOME A SHELTERED SEEKER

Who can disagree that the single most powerful word in the English language is *home*?[1] When the 2020 pandemic struck, "stay at home" became the coping mantra. Families rediscovered meals together, as well as ways to exercise and learn. They took "staycations." Parents, grandparents, and caregivers now exchange stories about the challenges as well as the rewards of this new paradigm. Religious organizations and social service agencies, like homes, created new ways to carry out their traditional roles and responsibilities.

Many prefer to cling to the past. Laura Ingalls Wilder's books and their television progeny, *Little House on the Prairie* (1974–1983), proclaim home the "nicest place there is." The film *Minari* (2020) paints a more honest but harder truth of family life as a South Korean American family grapples with farming in Arkansas and California. Wouldn't we rather retain memories of sight and smell such as Grandmother's canned pickles and rhubarb pies or neighbor Oma's crusty soft anise cookies? What can comfort us like the family rituals and special dishes at holiday observances? Are you ready to return to those family reunions, where we shared silly traits of siblings—such as rubbing their hands together after telling a joke—that make us smile? Is that past lost? With nostalgia, we recall how children behaved well, businesses and churches ran with integrity, and decorum prevailed.[2] Television eclipsed movies and radio;

1. Parks, *Big Questions*, 51. Elsewhere I'll quote several insightful articles Parks has written about home. See also Diana Bass, ch. 5, "Home," in *Grounded*, 163–92. With exquisite stories, quotations, and data, Bass describes the power, charm, beauty, and place of homes in our lives. I strongly encourage all to adopt her suggested practices in our natal and spiritual homes. Sanders, *Staying Put*, 29, offers several intriguing questions based on the etymologies of *house*—an Indo-European root meaning "to cover or conceal"—*home*, whose root is "the place where one lies." Sanders ponders: What are we concealed from? Does the lying down emphasize a place of safety, one to conceive our children, a shelter for rest?

2. Rohr, *Falling Upward*, "Home and Home Sickness," 87–96, speaks of nostalgia as a "desirous dissatisfaction" that looks both forward and backward at the same time. Sanders, *Staying Put*, 14, informs us that the Greek roots and German translation of

more convenient and easier on the eyes and ears, these technologies offered more utopian vistas than realities. Calls to a better life? Rarely. Today's social media focuses more on pleasant recollections than being a motivator for action. What is it we want: a mist vanishing with tomorrow's sun or a vehicle driving us toward a viable vision?

Will working at home continue to be part of the new norm? Will online learning forever change schooling patterns? Will houses of worship discover at-home worship services brought more benefits than deficits? Will responses to Black Lives Matter alter some citizens' descriptions of their hometowns?

What will never change is that the adults of our first or primary home are potters molding clay, shaping impressionable youth with knowledge, habits, and dispositions that transform their futures. Etched repeatedly into us is that while homes are places, they function as more than places.[3] Before and during our kindergarten years, we learn behaviors such as sharing, telling the truth, playing fair, cleaning up, washing hands, and flushing.[4] These behaviors reflect values and form the meanings we give to life's events. In the next chapter, I'll share a simple description of spirituality: it is meaning-making. It is our way of coping with life's mysteries, as Sharon Daloz Parks makes clear in her book *Big Questions, Worthy Dreams.*[5] For an interesting twist on the kinds of mysteries we'll be talking about, see **appendix 1A**. As these behaviors and values become embedded in us, as we repeat them in various situations, we gain confidence to face new worlds and begin to hone dreams. Homes become "the protector of our dreams."[6]

After mining images of our first homes, let's explore the rich veins of religious and spiritual training we might receive and how today's spiritual homes replicate, refine, or replace the gems of truth from the past. These events will impact how we "con-form" and "re-form" our later milestones. So, traveler, if you're ready to leave the shelter of your current home, I'll

---

nostalgia mean "return pain." The pain comes not from returning home but from desiring to return.

3. Bryson, *At Home*. A delightfully funny, documented, provocative account of how homes developed and why specific rooms in houses, such as kitchens, bedrooms, and halls, evolved.

4. Fulghum, *All I Really Need*.

5. Parks, *Big Questions*, 10, 30, 11–13, 67–69.

6. Bachelard, *Poetics of Space*, 6: "The house shelters daydreaming, the house protects the dreamer, the house allows one to dream in peace."

predict that you'll always have its stories with you and, in one form or another, return to it.

TRAVELER, ARE YOU WILLING TO GO OUT ON A LIMB?

Forgive me for a new metaphor—climbing a tree—but I think you'll soon understand why. I'm inviting you to be a traveler on a fascinating itinerary to explore what spiritual maturity involves. This path requires a willingness to take some chances and go out on a limb: be open to a big adventure that could change your life significantly. As an example of an out-on-a-limb experience, and as a way for us to get to know each other, I'll share something that happened to me. I'm not a mystic, but I believe it was far more than just a unique meditation. As a result, my life is certainly different now.

It began at 1:00 a.m. in the fall of 2017. I was in bed. I awoke suddenly. A voice was talking to me—not a distinct external sound but a definite presence. It said, "You cannot preach the sermon you're scheduled to give several Sundays from now—not the way you intend, anyway." "Why not?" I replied. "It's a good sermon! I'm recounting my trip to Israel and my favorite city, Jericho."[7] As if I needed to, I reminded the voice that the text was from the Christian scripture, Luke 19:1–10, the narrative of a "small" man, Zacchaeus, who climbed a sycamore tree to see Jesus because the crowd surrounding the popular rabbi blocked his view. The story's author, Luke, says Jesus notices Zacchaeus, a rich man. Unsavory, Zacchaeus was a corrupt tax collector, having colluded with the occupying Roman force. Locals despised him as a traitor, an outcast of his Jewish ancestry. Amazingly, despite protests from the grumbling crowd, Jesus goes to Zach's home. Later, Zacchaeus announces he has changed his life and will give back everything he has stolen, multiplied four times. Jesus says to the crowd, "Today salvation has come to this house because he too is a son of Abraham" (v. 19). Talk about a story of redemption and transformation! The short man became a moral giant, accepted in

---

7. Archaeologists consider Jericho, Israel, to be one of the oldest continuously occupied cities in the world. In the Hebrew Scriptures, Joshua led a successful attack in which its fortressed walls miraculously "fell down" (Josh 6:1–27). Jericho is mentioned in the parable of the good Samaritan (Luke 10:1). Tradition holds a mountain on the outskirts of the city was the site of Jesus's third temptation by the devil (Matt 4:1–11).

his hometown again. However, retelling that story wasn't enough for the voice.

Never in my fifty-plus years of ministry had anything like this happened. I resisted the way the voice instructed me to change the story's introduction. "Try it out," the voice commanded. Suddenly, I pictured the sanctuary in full color. I walked through a different approach. OK, it worked. Then the voice and I had a major argument. The voice asked, "What did Jesus and Zacchaeus talk about at lunch?" "I don't know! I wasn't there and there's no recording of it," I smartly argued. The voice chided me, "Come on, seminary graduate, make some educated guesses." I thought, "OK, Zach knew his power and money couldn't buy him happiness. An outcast in his historic hometown, stripped of his Hebrew heritage, was he upset that the revenge he had exacted on those who had teased and bullied him about his stature had not paid off? He was now an outsider. Jesus offered him the way to go home. Profoundly grateful, Zach was filled with compassion and returned the ill-gotten gains fourfold." "Tell the story that way," urged the voice, "but do it at the pew level with no notes." With a little edge, I said, "Is that all?" "No, as a matter of fact. You need to make that story relevant for those hearing you on Sunday. They will ask how it relates to them." That I had to think about. So, I got up from bed—at 3:00 a.m.—and wrote notes for an hour.

The next day, I redid the sermon, which I gave weeks later. Church members who had heard me preach before said this message was different. Since then, I have preached that sermon several times. Every time I do, I feel like I'm out on a limb, wondering if people will think I'm weird or being too dramatic. Instead, responses to that message are like none others I've received. Not the typical cheery "that was a great sermon," but a somber "that was genuine," with the unspoken "that challenges how far I go in witnessing to my faith." I'm not pretending that my experience would be anything close to costing you a job or loss of your popularity or status if you did something similar. You may wish to look at **activity 1.1** to consider ways you could go out on a limb.

That sermon has three meanings for me now. First, too many of us who inhabit safe homes take that setting for granted. Second, we need to be more sensitive to those who, for reasons like war, illness, climate change, or the economy have no homes or have unhealthy homes. Third, we who are blessed should become hosts, ministering to those homeless in body or spirit. For them, we should go out on a limb.

READY TO TRAVEL FROM HOME TO HOME
TO BACK HOME?

With all this talk about being a traveler, I don't want you to be misled. With the help of Sharon Daloz Parks, let's agree on a common understanding of your starting and end points. By reading this book, you are buying a round-trip ticket. That's speaking spiritually as well as geographically. As Parks has so clearly discerned, the English language associated with journeying needs to be clarified.[8] For many, the image of a journey is a one-way venture. We can support that with stories of past migrations and explorations, colored with tales of our own families who never returned to their place of origin. Recall the poignant musical *Fiddler on the Roof* (1964, film 1971). But there are just as many examples of explorers and travelers who do return, sharing dreams of a beckoning world.

A second reality is the gender gap. Literature on journeying assumes men travel; women stay home to tend to the children, cook, clean, garden—in short, to maintain the hearth and homestead. Conversations of men and women about travel are different. Men focus on the challenges of journeys, often picturing them as battles. Women reflect on new relationships developed, the languages and daily practices in new locations. In this world of changing and disappearing boundaries, all of us are travelers who need to be sensitive to what our tribes should retain, while also forming new loving communities that are open to diversity and working for justice.[9]

The spiritual journey I'm proposing is for any gender. That journey can be successful linearly with stops at *a*, *b*, and *c*, ending at *d*, or messy and non-sequential. With either approach, you will have experiences in several homes over a span of time. Your experience with a potential spiritual home may occur with a partner while you are both emerging adults (eighteen to mid-twenties). In that scenario, you may still be in regular contact with parents or siblings from your natal home. An alternate journey. Over one hundred years ago, the author of a best-selling book, *Acres of Diamonds*, described a youthful world traveler who returned home to find treasure in his back yard.[10] No guarantee, but possibly, your travel may take you back to your first home.

8. Parks, "Home and Pilgrimage" and "To Venture and Abide."

9. Daloz et al., *Common Fire.*

10. Conwell, *Acres of Diamonds.* Conwell, who founded Temple University, gave over six thousand lectures based on his book at what were called Chautauqua tent circuits.

The conversations we will have in this book reflect my personal observations, professional career experiences, secular work occupations, and the research findings of others. With the questions raised, my hope is that they also mirror your inner self's yearnings. I want you to live a fulfilled life. I believe that happens when your personal and spiritual homes are challenging and comforting—another way of staying healthy! What does that mean in everyday outcomes? I picture you having a clearer sense of what you believe is most important in life, participating regularly in activities, both physical and spiritual, that energize you. More than that, I hope your engaged spirituality will result in networks of support—for you and, in turn, for you to give to neighbors and global friends. If so, you have found your spiritual home.

WHY EMPHASIZE HOME FIRST, THEN THE SELF?

A great question. Some statistics give us a clue. By one estimate, the world in 2020 had 7.7 billion individuals. In recent years, annually and worldwide, there are 140 million births—a trend downward—and 55 to 57 million deaths. (The number of deaths is increasing.)[11] Most of us live with other people. China has 1.4 billion individuals in 456 million households, with an average of 3.0 members per household. India has 1.2 billion individuals in 245 million households, with 4.8 members per household. The United States has 327 million individuals in 138 million households, with an average of 2.6 members per household. The diverse profiles within households are fascinating.[12] Types of families include:

- Blended—remarried with children after divorce
- Unwed parents with children, including teenagers
- Same-sex couples with adopted children
- Multifamily communes
- Childless married couples[13]

11. Ritchie, "How Many People Die."

12. The highest percentage of these households or "families" according to the USCB is single persons living alone (33.9 percent in 2018). The second highest category is two adults without children (25.1 percent). More striking data are that more than 40 percent of the US's adults, over 87 million, are divorced, widowed, or always have been single; adults now spend more of their adult years single than married (DePaulo, *Singled Out*).

13. Woodward, *Getting Religion*, 317.

There are diverse family profiles, including many with children who are not blood related.[14] I'm assuming we can agree that "childhood is chiefly preparation for the all-important event of leaving home."[15] From my perspective, Zacchaeus became an exile whose dream was to be reunited with family and neighbors in their fabled walled city, not to find a geographical paradise in a far country. Are you his modern-day equivalent—a Zach, Zoe, or Zelda—wanting to plant roots for a tree of life in your current hometown rather than start a foreign forest?

Ironic, isn't it? The coronavirus of 2020 has exploded interest in home baking, family bike riding, gardening, and involvement in local civic matters. At the same time, we are witnessing an increase in what one sociologist calls "vanishing" neighborhoods and another calls "the big sort, with deliberate groupings by class and race."[16] Are both trends accurate? What are the most important trends of natal homes and families? Do these trends apply equally to spiritual homes, or are there different trends that are more significant?

WHAT'S A HOME? IMAGINE PIECES OF A HOMEMADE PIE!

When I return from a trip, my GPS voice announces, "Arriving at home." Ah, home sweet home. Is home sweet for you? Is it filled with Hallmark card memories of the smell of brewing coffee or the taste of a favorite cookie? The sound of a brother's teasing? A late-night parental conversation? My sons now cherish their late mother's perceptive grilling sessions. Do you remember special rituals at family reunions? Have you emulated favorite meals and rituals in the homes you later established or joined?[17]

14. Kulgowski, "How Many Orphans." In the US, 443,000 children are in foster care. She cites the Dave Thomas Foundation estimate that there are 140,000,000 orphans worldwide. I have an adopted grandson from Russia.

15. Bellah et al., *Habits of the Heart*, 57.

16. Dunkelman, *Vanishing Neighbor*, notes technology and other forces have increased isolation. We focus more on our "inner-ring" family and close friends, with "outer-ring" social media contacts, but are losing contact with "middle-ring" neighbors and community members. B. Bishop with Cushing, *Big Sort*, describe how Americans are living increasingly in "like-minded" and economically similar conclaves. Diana Bass, *Grounded*, 193–231, offers evidence of booming trends in farmers' markets and gardening prior to COVID in 2020.

17. M. Cox, *Book of New Family Traditions*. The subtitle says it all: *How to Create Great Rituals for Holidays and Every Day.*

Let's have some fun now. Imagine a homemade pie. Cut it into six pieces. I can think of five qualities found in homes, each one represented by a piece of pie. Can you think of another quality or role of a home? That would be the sixth piece of pie for you to enjoy.

1. Home is a place.

The award-winning 1982 film *E.T.* was about an extraterrestrial risk-taker who desperately wanted to go home. What motivated him to explore a different world but ultimately return to his home? Does his yearning parallel your feeling? Think of phrases from famous songs, boasting of "the land of the free and the home of the brave," pining for a "home on the range." Do you identify with John Denver's wistful "Take Me Home, Country Roads" and country singer Joe Diffie's "Home," which evokes images of a fishing pole, a swing, and words of wisdom heard on a porch? We, too, see ourselves as the souls who can return to a home five hundred miles away. Poet Robert Frost put it this way: "Home is the place where, when you have to go there, they have to take you in."[18] That echoes the biblical parable of the prodigal son (Luke 15:11–32), which inspired one of Rembrandt's most famous paintings.[19] Home is the welcome place where we may be abundantly forgiven, embraced, celebrated, and fed.[20] Despite these assertions, a caveat is that this specific "home and pilgrimage"[21] does not guarantee welcoming souls will greet us.

2. Home offers an accepting, safe environment.

In the classic movie *The Wizard of Oz* (1939), Dorothy wants to return to her safe and comfortable Kansas home, where she will be surrounded by loving family and caring neighbors. Maya Angelou writes in *All God's*

18. Frost, "The Death of the Hired Man," lines 118–19, as cited in Platt, *Respectfully Quoted*, 165.

19. Nouwen, *Return of the Prodigal Son*. M. Robinson, *Home*, offers a modern parallel story.

20. Diana Bass, *Grounded*, 166–67. Place means more than a geographical location; it connotes a heritage, an outlook on life, persons, a system of "moral and social values." There is some historical evidence that many "tyrants" as youth had done little travel outside their countries.

21. Daloz, *Common Fire*, 31. Home is also understood to be a neighborhood, a community, a nation, a homeland, and more.

Children Need Traveling Shoes, "The ache for home lives in all of us. It is
the safe place where we can go as we are, and not be questioned."[22] The
1973 hit song "Tie A Yellow Ribbon Round the Ole Oak Tree" embodies that sentiment. We will discuss later that some homes are so unsafe
that children's spirits are crushed or their teen years obliterated.[23] In such
homes, what therapists call "intimate terrorism" occurs. In Toni Morrison's *Home*, a veteran of the Korean War returns to Georgia and angrily
pronounces his hometown "worse than any battlefield."[24] Residents, he
finds, are killing time, not interested in learning, simply waiting for the
next death. Only through his sister's illness and death is he able to find
redemption. Kudos to those who salvage what they can from unhealthy
homes and resolve to make their new homes wholesome.

3. Home is about relationships.

In *Anna and the French Kiss*, Stephanie Perkins muses, "Is it possible for
home to be a person and not a place? . . . [speaking of her boyfriend] This
is home. The two of us." Robin Hobb, in *Fool's Fate*, echoes that sentiment: "Home is people. Not a place. If you go back there after the people
are gone, then all you can see is what is not there anymore." Novelist
Thomas Wolfe's book *You Can't Go Home Again*, published posthumously
in 1940, reflected relationships he had lost or changed.[25]

James Baldwin opined in *Giovanni's Room*, "Perhaps home is not
a place but simply an irrevocable condition."[26] In that pioneering gay
literature set in Paris and Europe, Baldwin portrays "home" as a place
of positive reinforcements and debilitating rejections. Home helps some
thrive because of its atmosphere of peace, well-being (*shalom*), love, and
respect, while homes filled with negative circumstances motivate others to survive and succeed against great odds, as in the story of Andrew
Bridge in *Hope's Boy*.[27] In *David and Goliath*, Malcolm Gladwell describes

22. Angelou, *All God's Children*, 196.

23. Sacks, *Not in God's Name*. Sacks was the chief rabbi of the Jewish Orthodox
congregations of Great Britain. He concludes many of the "brother" stories of Genesis
show the violence between siblings is not God-intended; the narratives result ultimately in forgiveness and reconciliation.

24. Morrison, *Home*, 83.

25. Perkins, *Anna*, 250; Hobb, *Fool's Fate*, 720; Wolfe, *You Can't Go Home*.

26. Baldwin, *Giovanni's Room*, 86.

27. Bridge, *Hope's Boy*.

modern-day underdogs who parallel the legendary boy David who kills the giant Goliath. A driving force for many is proving their parents' and peers' pessimistic assessments wrong.[28]

4. Home emphasizes activities done together.

British poet Edith Sitwell (1887–1964) underscored the importance of being together: "Winter is the time for comfort, for good food and warmth, for the touch of a friendly hand, and for a talk beside the fire; it is the time for home."[29] If you are like me, you salivate about food and conversations around the table! It is no coincidence that the most lived-in room in a home is the kitchen—at churches, too. In *Strength for the Journey*, Diana Butler Bass reflects that at a Virginia congregation, she spent more time in the kitchen than the sanctuary. It was there she learned "how to let down my guard, let go of my pretenses, and be myself."[30]

In movies and real life, home revolves around vacations. Do you have vivid memories of being stuffed into a car or station wagon, with or without a trailer, going on camping trips or sight-seeing tours? Chevy Chase and several of his vacation movies come to mind. Did your family have a second home, like a cabin on a lake? Fishing and boating experiences linger for eternity. Yearly, a senior friend regaled listeners by extending his arms as wide as possible, and with much drama, boasted, "I caught a fish that . . . [pause] . . . far from my dock." In some families, sports activities reign supreme. Memories abound of trips to baseball or football stadiums to root for a favorite team.

5. Home is where we learn to take risks.

Scientists in many disciplines agree that a primary function of a home is to prepare the child for leaving. As an African American parent poetically put it, "The job of parents is to provide both roots and wings," echoing what Kahlil Gibran (1883–1931), a Lebanese American poet/philosopher, advised parents decades ago:

28. Gladwell, *David and Goliath*.
29. Sitwell, *Taken Care Of*, 228.
30. Diana Bass, *Strength for the Journey*, 146–47.

You may house their bodies but not their souls, for their souls dwell in the house of tomorrow, which you cannot visit, not even in your dreams. You may strive to be like them but seek not to make them like you. For life goes not backward nor tarries with yesterday . . . . You are the bows from which your children [who] are living arrows are sent forth.[31]

Parents need to expose their offspring to a healthy mix of the familiar and the unfamiliar, the reliable and unexpected.[32] Perhaps you can think of another facet of home for the sixth piece, or something else that that could be the "à la mode." Together, it is no wonder one of the warmest feelings we can get is when a family member, a relative, or a friend offers us a piece of pie. It says "welcome home."[33]

WHAT MAKES HOMES HEALTHY? UNHEALTHY?

To be honest, for too many home has been a negative experience. Recall the 1994 movie *The Lion King*. The young cub, Simba, has mixed feelings about returning to the place of his origin and says, "Home is an empty dream."[34] Pastoral counselor and minister J. Jeffrey Means posits that homes should be where children can speak, be heard, and be held, so that their souls are whole—rather than homes where, as Joan Borysenko asserts, too often children are left "adrift in a sea of strangers."[35] With Mary Ann Nelson, Means provides numerous examples of children and youth who had inappropriate treatment in their homes and the therapies they needed.[36] Few of us can claim we had no dysfunction in our homes. I do not want to diminish the difficulties some readers may be overcoming due to harm they suffered at home.

---

31. Gibran, *Prophet*, "On Children," 17–18. He claimed appreciation of Judaism, Islam, and Christianity but was open to many religious traditions. The book continues to be a bestseller, worldwide.

32. Daloz, *Common Fire*, 28.

33. For a song text I've written, "Welcome Home," the refrain repeats, "Come home, come home, we're here for you, with open arms and love that's true. A welcome home we have for you, a love that's old and always new."

34. Allers and Minkoff, *Lion King*.

35. Joan Borysenko, *A Woman's Book of Life*, as cited in Means with Nelson, *Trauma and Evil*, 64.

36. Means with Nelson, *Trauma and Evil*, part 3, "Healing the Self and Soul," 97–158.

Despite negatives, the dream persists: humans crave homes, stable healthy homes. What are healthy homes and examples of practices within those homes? The words *health* and *wholeness* have similar meanings to the word *holy*.[37] Call adult responsibilities sacred duties. Consider these four tasks identified by a seminary professor: protection, permission (guidelines), potency (learning independence), and prayer. To him, prayer incorporated wanting the best future for the family's children. A more specific description of a healthy household is:

◆ a *safe environment* that provides reliable shelter and nourishment

◆ at least *one trustworthy adult* who sees the child, adolescent, or young adult as precious, unique, lovable, capable, and worthy of respect

◆ opportunities to learn that one can *make a positive difference*, first in small ways, later in more significant ways

◆ *time and space to express and heal* the inevitable pain and hurt of life—including rage and bereftness—in a way that strengthens the spirit and deepens the capacity for compassion toward both oneself and others[38]

HOW MANY HOMES ARE RELIGIOUS OR SPIRITUAL?[39]

With the diversity of families, it is difficult to identify the precise number of homes in any country that are considered religious or spiritual. [One estimate in 2019 stated that the United States had over 138 million house-holds—compared to 456 million in China and 245 million in India.]

How many of these homes or households are religious? Surveyors' answers focus on concrete matters such as membership, attendance, and prayers. A representative study in 2019 reported only 12 percent of Americans report being raised outside a formal religious tradition. The most significant finding of the changing family patterns is by generation. While only 3 percent of seniors say they were not raised in any religion,

37. Gehman, *Dictionary of the Bible*, 401–2.

38. Daloz, *Common Fire*, 219.

39. Data included are from "List of Countries" and "Marital Status by Religious Group."

22 percent of young adults answer the same. Another striking statistic is that young adults (eighteen to twenty-nine) who have always been religiously unaffiliated are nearly as large a segment as those who have chosen to become unaffiliated.[40]

A different study provides us with a profile of religious affiliations of those American families who reported they belonged to specific traditions. A Pew Research Center survey of more than 35,000 American from all fifty states ended with these broad categories of religious homes:

Table 1. Families by Religious Group[41]

Christian	70.6%	Non-Christian Faiths	5.9%	Unaffiliated (None)	22.8%
Evang. Protestant	25.4%	Jewish	1.9%	Atheist	3.1%
Mainline Protestant	14.7%	Muslim	0.9%	Agnostic	4.0%
Black Protestant	6.5%	Buddhist	0.7%	Nothing in particular	15.8%
Catholic	20.8%	Hindu	0.7%	Don't know	0.6%
Mormon	1.6%	Other world religions	0.3%		
Orthodox Christian	0.5%	Other faiths	1.5%		
Jehovah's Witness	0.8%				
Other Christian	0.4%				

40. Cited in D. Cox et al., *Decline of Religion*, 1–2.

41. "Marital Status by Religious Group." The percentages are not exact.

WHAT'S SPECIAL ABOUT SPIRITUAL HOMES?

Tilden Edwards, a poet, has observed about modern life, "Yet the beast ever lurks near; our hearts yearn for a fuller Home."[42] Do you agree that humans crave something more than physical well-being and a safe, comfortable personal home? Diana Butler Bass does. Humans want a spiritual home, a place where they wrestle with the mysteries of life. Some find such a home in one of the world religions, which integrate corporate practices with other practices that can be observed privately. Buddhists consider they are home when they have found enlightenment. Muslims face toward Mecca, their home, to pray. Adherents speak of going home with death rituals, regardless of whether they are buried in the earth or at sea or cremated. Some traditions speak of finding the divine home in nature.[43] To bring it down to earth:

> Home is where we figure out primary patterns of nurture and productivity, habits of needs and desire, forms of rage and forgiveness, ways of "taking time" and discovering the people who "count" for us. Our households are anchoring places.[44]

In the Abrahamic traditions—Hebrew, Christian, Islam—as in many other religious faiths, the roles of the home and family are highly significant in everyday life. A variety of texts in Hebrew and Greek describe what in English we call homes (Hebrew: *mishpachah* for family; *bayith* for family dwelling or house). There are also phrases such as "house of David," "house of God," or "house of prayer." Related words include *ohel*, tent; *maqom*, place of dwelling; *shub*, to return home; or *navah*, to keep oneself at home. In Greek, *oikos* is the most common word for home, house, or household. In Christian Scriptures such as Ephesians 2:19, the early church is "the household of God." There, persons formerly estranged—Jews and Gentiles—can be mutual members; in the next verse, for its second-generation Christian disciples, they should "like loving stones, let yourselves be built into a spiritual house."

---

42. Cited by Parks, "Home and Pilgrimage," 1.

43. Diana Bass, *Grounded*, 169.

44. Parks, "Household Economics," 43.

HOW CAN WE PRACTICE HOMEFULNESS?

Before we go any further, we must recognize that not all people live in homes. As will be discussed in greater detail in chapter 8, there are those in the US who are homeless—567,719 in 2019. There are over 250 million international migrants in the world.[45] In 2020, due to the coronavirus, laws were passed that prevented persons from being evicted in the short term. There is also another category, one where people don't feel at home or feel that they don't belong. Theologian Walter Brueggemann suggests this is a different kind of homelessness, not physical but spiritual. His analysis of Jewish and Christian Scriptures likens those who are unfaithful to God as orphans. Actually, that descriptor comes from the book of Hosea. Brueggemann describes the process and ingredients of how the nation of Israel can establish what he calls "homefulness" to counter its homelessness.[46] In part, it involves those in power restoring homes to those individuals who have been forgotten, cheated, or evicted or who have lost homes due to war. Sound timely?

Homes that are religious or spiritual have developed practices related to their beliefs. The more formalized practices are called rituals and done in communal celebrations, while others, like prayers, are also done at home. Tish Warren, an Anglican—Episcopal—priest, describes how she and her family do some "down-to-earth" practices while at home: making the bed, brushing teeth, eating leftovers, calling friends, and sleeping.[47] Using the five descriptions of home previously discussed, here are some more conventional practices that spiritual homes could consider doing.

Place

Many traditions erect buildings for religious rituals and practices, ranging from simple cabins to extravagant megachurches, temples, and

---

45. Statista Research Department, "Estimated Number of Homeless." See also Haass, *World*, 193, who estimates 70 million persons of them are refugees. More recent estimates project 80 million refugees.

46. Brueggemann, *Practice of Homefulness*, 1, citing Hos 14:1–3. He notes Ps 109 is the angriest; its author calls for vengeance against a neighbor who has mistreated him, cursing that the neighbor not only be killed but that his family be stripped of their home.

47. Warren, *Liturgy of the Ordinary.*

cathedrals. John Bell, the Iona colony hymn writer, shared a powerful ritual he witnessed when tour groups stopped at various places of a house of worship (the doors, the altar, the pulpit) and offered prayers for what the places mean. These specific places come to have special memories for members: how they worship, instruct the young, welcome the stranger, and live out the congregation's shared values.

However, studies in the 2010s to 2020s of new spiritual groups found a common theme. Members do not want to be bound by problems associated with owning buildings. The mission of the congregation can be overwhelmed by the costs of maintenance, for example. As meaningful as buildings can be, faith traditions have admonitions that the structure is not as important as what is in the hearts of the believers.

Safety

Strange then, after years of declining attendance at worship services, that in 2020, during the pandemic, there were heated debates about holding worship services rather than accepting the Zoom service alternative. A wise expression is that humans have "skin hunger." That is, we need to touch, hug, be close to other humans. Even as COVID restrictions are reduced or eliminated and services are beginning again, I hear many religious leaders comment that online services will remain in one format or another. Spiritual communities are making growing efforts to welcome those estranged because of handicaps, sexual orientation, mental illness, addiction, or a prison record. Their new message that all are children of God and need welcoming in safe environments is comforting to many.[48]

Relationships

Nomadic faith cultures robustly sing of the importance of families, offering accolades for fathers and mothers who carry out their responsibilities and warnings for those who fail. Children, too, are expected to be respectful of their place in families. Because many of these societies have experienced hardships as immigrants or aliens, their sacred scriptures

---

48. Chapter 7 will discuss the lack of safety for children. There are too many stories about sexual abuse, too many tales of cult leaders luring gullible converts to commit suicide, too many preachers becoming wealthy promoting schemes of self-elevation rather than of servanthood.

instruct them to welcome strangers. Past hostilities are transformed into hospitality.[49] In spiritual communities today, newcomers are genuinely welcomed to the household of faith, not merely tolerated as spectators.

Activities Together

A frequent criticism of religious organizations, especially their worship services, is that they are boring. According to research studies and anecdotal accounts, thriving congregations do a variety of meaningful activities that participants find memorable.[50] I can testify to that! Churches I grew up in or served often had a women's quilting group. Meeting regularly, their sewing turned out quilts that changed jigsaw-like puzzle pieces of different colors, patterns, and sizes into litanies of beauty. Those hours of stitching included snippets of gossip, spools of concern for the pastor, and dishes to take to grieving families. How about sports? We Texans didn't have basketball courts, but sweaty outdoor volleyball games were a favorite of my youth group. Later, I saw pioneering programs of mentorship for youth in Illinois and Texas and witnessed an Indiana church institute a music festival, a California congregation sponsor an art fair, and a Florida spiritual home—it was more like a college campus—offer an annual curriculum of courses for seniors. In the Midwest, churches sponsor summer camps, including a week for grandparents and their grandchildren. More frequently, you will find spiritual homes of various traditions celebrating major secular as well as religious holidays.[51]

Some years ago, working with K-12 teachers in a values education course, I created an easy and fun way to get a handle on the core beliefs and values, or major meanings, of individuals and families. I asked class members to create an object called a centerpiece. You might consider doing that. See **activity 1.2.**

49. Nouwen, *Reaching Out*, "Reaching Out," 62–109; Doucleff, *Hunt, Gather, Parent* offers numerous examples from ancient cultures.

50. Searcy and Thomas, *Activate*; Baskette, *Real Good Church*; Sparks et al., *New Parish*.

51. M. Cox, *Book of New Family Traditions*, for example, includes ideas related to Kwanzaa.

Taking Risks

As chapter 4 asserts, spiritual homes should challenge us to ask what Sharon Daloz Parks calls "big questions" and to create "worthy dreams." Lillian Daniel phrases it similarly: "A good religious community is . . . both comforting and discomforting. God loves us exactly as we are, and God loves us too much to let us stay that way."[52] Nouwen offers this paradox. To be receptive to friend and stranger is one side of hospitality; being truthful is another. "Receptivity without confrontation leads to a bland neutrality that serves nobody. Confrontation without receptivity leads to an oppressive aggression which hurts everybody."[53] Risk-taking alerts us to our boundaries and challenges us to expand into finding the home where we truly belong. Because economic justice issues often pit the haves against the have-nots, they can be contentious and therefore need to involve special concern for the well-being of all parties.[54]

DO SPIRITUAL FAMILIES HAVE BENEFITS?

The consensus of scholarly research is that participation in spiritual homes is more helpful than harmful—to both personal health and the development of spiritual values.[55] For example, studies show that children in religious families may have better discipline, hold honor higher, have a greater sense of pride, have a clearer sense of right and wrong, and handle emotional stress better. Consider **activity 1.3**. Adults who regularly attend church may live longer than non- or infrequent attenders, and religious couples are likely to have fewer divorces.[56] To be fair, some scholars believe there is no proof that family cohesion is better in religious homes or that prayer changes negative things for the better.[57]

52. Daniel, *Tired of Apologizing*, 131.

53. Nouwen, *Reaching Out*, 99.

54. Brueggemann, *Practice of Homefulness*, 41–42.

55. Dollahite et al., "Why Religion Helps"; Miller-Wilson, "How Religion Affects Family"; "Religion and Spirituality" in "Religion and Health"; Milam, "How Religion and Spirituality."

56. Dollahite et al., "Why Religion Helps"; Miller-Wilson, "How Religion Affects Family"; Milam, "How Religion and Spirituality."

57. Barber, "Are Religious People Healthier"; C. Smith with Lundquist, *Soul Searching*, 263, indicates better social outcomes for religious vs. nonreligious teens; Professor's House Staff, "Does Religion Have Positive Impact."

One more interesting statistic that relates to American families and their belief or non-belief in God is that most persons hold similar images of God or beliefs about God as their parents.[58] Which one of the four images described in note 58 best fits you and your primary family?

TRAVELER: READY TO BE A SHELTERED SEEKER GOING OUT ON A LIMB?

How were you formed spiritually? Do any of these descriptions fit your current self-image? "I have lost my faith." "My family, community, and I believe I am immoral." "At times, I feel like telling others to go to hell, so leave me alone. Other times, I really want to be part of a spiritual community." That last description sounds like Zacchaeus, who went out on a limb primarily because his life's dream—to be rich, powerful, and travel to other parts of the world—was ending in a nightmare. His revenge for being teased and bullied for his small size, the wealth and power garnered through collaboration with the occupying Romans, had gained him wealth but no respect. Rabbi Jesus discerned Zach wanted a homecoming. I imagine in their private conversation he told Zach his spiritual home required sacrifice, a public confession, and the return of funds he had corruptly gained.

To you, reader—Zach, Zelda, or Zoe—your spiritual journey will likely not be that dramatic. You can do it on your own, but my recommendation is that it will help if you are part of a spiritual community that parallels a healthy first home. Interviews with persons who consider themselves Spiritual but Not Religious (SBNR) or Not Religious reveal many believe that their interaction with their families is the most spiritual thing they do. We, like Zach, want to be accepted and validated. Paradoxical, isn't it? Sharon Daloz Parks challenges us to be what I call sheltered seekers: "The formation of adequate forms of meaning and faith—and perhaps the future of our small planet home—is dependent, in part, upon the liberation, reappropriation, and renewed companionship of the metaphors of detachment *and* connection, pilgrims *and*

58. Froese and Bader, *America's Four Gods*. Based on their Baylor Religion Survey and Interview project, they found Americans believe in what they call the Authoritative God (engaged in the world and judgmental), the Benevolent God (engaged yet nonjudgmental), the Critical God (judgmental but not engaged), or the Distant God (nonjudgmental and disengaged).

homemakers, journeying *and* homesteading."[59] While difficult in an era of social distancing, consider making efforts to communicate with your "home bodies" a frequent spiritual practice. That may require you need to go far out on a limb if family relations that need to be reconciled. Traveler, I'll leave ("leaf" if you are punny) it up to you.

---

59 Parks, "Home and Pilgrimage," 5.

Chapter 1 Activities

ACTIVITY 1.1: OUT ON A LIMB

This is a two-part activity. The first part is to reflect upon your childhood home and the home you are in now or hope to have. Ask yourself:

- What was meaningful about your home?

- What was difficult about that first or primary home?

- Have you ever had to experience a time when you either had to choose to take the side with your family or go against them? How did that change your relationship with the family?

- What aspirations do you have for your present home? Future home?

- Now for the second part. If you have a current spiritual home, how would its members feel about your stance? Is your decision made easier or more difficult if you are a member of a faith community?

- Here are specific possibilities for going out on a limb:

  - Would you make a difficult decision about a job or school? Would the decision be more difficult based on who would know about it?

  - Would you be willing to be a foster parent? Adopt a child?

  - Would you stand up to a bully in school for a friend?

Suggestion: keep a journal of these questions and your answers.

ACTIVITY 1.2: CENTERPIECE

With other family members, create a centerpiece that reflects your family's identity and values. Since it will take some time for thought and gathering objects, set a specific deadline, perhaps at a time when there will be family gathering or holiday get-together. You want to have everyone contribute to this. The emphasis is not on doing something that must be polished and complete or a work of art. The emphasis is to create a centerpiece that reflects what your family values.

- It could be like a floral arrangement or a collection of photographs. It might be a series of drawings, a piece of pottery, or a shadow box with compartments of trinkets, jewelry, and tools.

- Key items: magazine clippings, tickets from concerts or theme parks, a piece of clothing, a school notebook.

- After creating mementos and gathering items, put them into a dish, box, or special container. One family used an aquarium! Make it exotic or funny. Have each family member secretly select his or her object or creative item. Bring them together.

After your centerpiece is created, take time to discuss it. Do the stories of the items need to be shared? After viewing what was included, was there something left out that truly describes your family?

ACTIVITY 1.3: HOUSE RULES

Families, faith communities, and even casinos have "house rules." Growing up, you were instructed by your parents, guardians, and/or relatives on how you should live your daily life. The first chart, from various religious traditions, is called the Golden Rule. The second list is from Marian Wright Edelman, daughter of sharecroppers in South Carolina. She became a lawyer, founder of the Children's Defense Fund, and adviser to presidents and civil rights leaders like Martin Luther King Jr. She addresses her book to her three sons and their families. The third list is recalled by United States Congressman

(Activity 1.3 continued)

Jamie Raskin of Maryland, the lead trial manager of the 2021 impeachment of President Donald J. Trump.

Did you receive similar or different advice? Would you disagree with or modify some of these? What additional pieces of advice would you give to children today? Do you see these as values? Moral statements? How do they relate to your spirituality, i.e., meaning-making?

The Golden Rule

Here are classic versions of the Golden Rule found in major religions.

- Christianity: "In everything do to others as you would have them do to you; for this is the law and the prophets" (Matt 7:12); "Do to others as you would have them do to you" (Luke 6:31).

- Judaism: "You shall love your neighbor as yourself" (Lev 19:18); "What is hateful to you, do not to your fellow man" (Talmud, Shabbat 31a).

- Islam: "None of you [truly] believes until he wishes for his brother what he wishes for himself" (Number 13 of Imam Al-Nawawi's Forty Hadith).

- Buddhism: "Hurt not others in ways that you yourself would find hurtful" (Udana Varga 5:18).

- Confucianism: "Do not do to others what you do not want them to do to you" (Analects 15:23); "'Is there one word that can serve as a principle of conduct for life?' Confucius replied, 'It is the word reciprocity. Do not impose on others what you yourself do not desire'" (Doctrine of the Mean 13.3).

- Hinduism: "This is the sum of duty: do not do to others what would cause pain if done to you" (Mahabharata 5:1517).

From Marian Wright Edelman, *The Measure of Our Success*, 35–78

(Edelman's book goes into much greater detail on her father's rationale for each piece of advice.)

1. There is no free lunch: don't feel entitled to anything you don't sweat and struggle for.

(Activity 1.3 continued)

2. Set goals and work quietly and systematically toward them.

3. Assign yourself.

4. Never work just for money or for power. They won't save your soul or help you sleep at night.

5. Don't be afraid of taking risks or of being criticized.

6. Take parenting and family life seriously and insist that those you work for and who represent you do.

7. Remember that your significant other [original: wife] is not your mother or your maid but your partner and friend.

8. Forming families is serious business.

9. Be honest.

10. Remember and help America remember that the fellowship of human beings is more important than the fellowship or face and class and gender in a democratic society.

11. Sell the shadow for the substance.

12. Never give up.

13. Be confident that you can make a difference.

14. Don't ever stop learning and improving your mind.

15. Don't be afraid of hard work or of teaching your children to work.

16. Slow down and live.

17. Choose your friends carefully.

18. Be a can-do, will-try person.

19. Try to live in the present.

20. Use your political and economic power for the community and others less fortunate.

21. Listen for "the sound of the genuine" within yourself and others.

22. You are in charge of your own attitude.

(Activity 1.3 continued)

23. Remember your roots, your history, and the forebears' shoulders on which you stand.

24. Be reliable. Be faithful. Finish what you start.

25. Always remember that you are never alone.

Representative Jamie Raskin's "Lessons I Learned from My Father"[60]

1. My father taught us that, when a situation seems hopeless, then you are the hope. When everything looks dark, you must be the light.

2. Spoil children with love and wisdom, not with things.

3. Whatever the background noises, follow the music in your head and the dreams in your heart.

4. Go to school to teach as well as to learn, and never let your schooling interfere with your education.

5. Bring your full intelligence and ethics to work every day, and if you can't, you may need to find a new job.

6. Hate war, and work as citizens for peace and justice.

7. Act pragmatically, not in the degraded sense of doing what powerful people want you to do, but in the [John] Deweyan sense of promoting experiments to advance the ideals of freedom and the common good.

8. Never give up on anyone, never hate anyone, and act with love whenever you can.

9. No good act in life is ever wasted.

60. This is a summary from the remarks Congressman Raskin (MD-08) gave at the memorial service for his father in Jan. 2018. Used with permission.

FOR ADDITIONAL CONVERSATIONS

Want to dive even deeper before we continue our conversation? The following books are a great place to start.

- On meaning-making and spirituality issues for emerging adults (18–29), Sharon Daloz Parks, *Big Questions, Worthy Dreams: Mentoring Emerging Adults in Their Search for Meaning, Purpose, and Faith.*

- On a non-Western understanding of spirituality and the concept of home, Thich Nhat Hahn, *Going Home: Jesus and Buddha as Brothers.*

- On a religious interpretation of family dynamics and an analysis of a famous Rembrandt painting, Henri J. M. Nouwen, *The Return of the Prodigal Son: A Story of Homecoming.*

- If you want theological insights into such issues as homelessness, nurturing forgiveness, and addressing world neighborliness, consider Walter Brueggemann, *The Practice of Homefulness.*

- To gain insights, with a large dash of humor and trivia, into the structure of the houses we build, Bill Bryson, *At Home: A Short History of Private Life.*

- For a delightful collection of essays from a prize-winning author, himself a committed builder and do-it-yourself carpenter, Scott Russell Sanders, *Staying Put: Making a Home in a Restless World.*

2

Self—"In-Formed" by Others

In the course of life, we never "graduate" from working on identity; we simply rework it with the materials at hand.

—SHERRY TURKLE, *ALONE TOGETHER*, 158

I can only answer the question "What am I do ?" if I can answer the prior question "Of what story or stories do I find myself a part?"

—ALASDAIR MACINTYRE, CITED BY MARTIN E. MARTY, *THE ONE AND THE MANY*, 9

The only questions that really matter are the ones you ask yourself.

—URSULA K. LEGUIN, *THE WRITER*

When the 18th-century Hasidic rabbi Zusya reaches the next world, God will not ask, "Why were you not Moses?" but "Why were you not Zusya?"

—CITED BY STEPHEN PROTHERO, *GOD IS NOT ONE*, 333

I believe God gives us our soul, our deepest identify, our True Self.

—RICHARD ROHR, *FALLING UPWARD*, IX

We see things not as they are, but as we are.

—H. M. TOMLINSON (1873–1958)

SELF: THE SPIRITUAL SELF
YOU ARE CALLED TO BE

- Invitation: to become an authentic self, possibly a wilderness guide

- You're distinct! What are your big questions?

- Do you want to make a difference? (How about stopping a bank robbery?)

- How will you plan your self trip?

- Who can I turn to? Where should I go?

- How would you identify yourself now? Are you religious?

- Are you spiritual?

- Are you both spiritual and religious—a Hybrid or a None?

- Return to the scene of the crime: what would you have done?

- Traveler: ready to become your authentic self, possibly a wilderness guide?

- Activities

- For Additional Conversations

If chapter 1's descriptions of home gave you the impression that you are in for a sweet, sentimental journey about spirituality, time out for some plain talk. No moonlight and roses—no, you can't be anything you want to be.[1] Let's talk about you and your potential. Not a guilt trip, but I want you to be honest. Will you be truthful as you search for a life with more meaning? If you've grown up in a rigorous religious tradition, you know that to live faithfully is not easy. An engaged spiritual perspective is a path that demands structure. I believe you're fooling yourself if you believe you can be spiritual but not religious, if you minimally observe spiritual practices. Wishing isn't magic; things don't automatically appear. You could be destined for great things.[2] But a worthy life includes our responsibility to become fully "in-formed" about ourselves and the world.

INVITATION: TO BECOME AN AUTHENTIC SELF, POSSIBLY A WILDERNESS GUIDE

The purpose of this chapter is to help you—the self you are—prepare to go on a rewarding journey of meaning-making. That meaningful trip will require planning, a good map, and tenacity. Consider me a travel agent who alerts you to the trip's pleasures as well as its perils, its treasures as well as its trash heaps. Know that the itinerary will require you to be in good mental and physical shape. That's another role I embrace: to be a spiritual trainer, pushing you to tone your beliefs and sharpen your gains from practices. Consider the footnotes. They represent other trainers supporting your spiritual formation, who, can "in-form" you.

Those guides and I know that you are unique. I emphatically agree with one of the house rules discussed in chapter 1: you should love others as you love yourself. Do you really know and love who you are? If so, you will truly be serious about your journey, viewing it as a venture filled

1. Sandel, *Tyranny of Merit*, argues that despite one's merit, if societies have developed other priorities, one won't necessarily achieve one's goals through hard work. He asks readers to reconsider what is the common good.

2. Howard Thurman, it is alleged, said that if only one chapter in the Bible could be saved, he would want it to be Ps 139. It is an affirmation that the divine knows individuals intimately. Columnist David Brooks asserts in "Rise of Haphazard Self," it is especially difficult for working-class men to develop a clear self-image.

with planned and unplanned trips, some frivolous, some life-changing. On a long journey, you will change from time to time. It will benefit you to learn from the experiences of previous travelers. Why? Humans are about making sense and meaning.[3] Simply stated, we are meaning-making creatures. We do that by asking and answering big questions, such as "Who am I? What is the purpose of life and my role? How can I make a difference? Is there a God, or is life just an unsolvable mystery?"[4] Recall the movie *It's a Wonderful Life* (1946) with James Stewart, who learned what a difference one person can make. Or the 1971 song, "I Am . . . I Said," by Neil Diamond, whose lyrics, as with other songs, nudge us to find meaning in our lives.

The way you shape the questions and frame your answers is related to the memories and stories you've heard at home, the education you've obtained, and the work and social experiences you've compiled. What stories are you in currently? What visions are you projecting? What successful adventures have you already achieved? In this era of rapidly expanding social media, where unscrupulous persons spread misinformation and disinformation, you must be alert. It is a major task to evaluate all this information you are receiving.

Have you been met head-on by a crucible event in your family or personal life that changed your life's direction, positively or negatively? Are you at a place in life where you need help achieving a worthy dream? Traveler, how you choose to go forward is part of *your* meaning-making journey. If you were asked now to be a survey respondent, what label would you choose: religious, spiritual, spiritual but not religious, or none of the above? How open are you to changing

3. Phenix, *Realms of Meaning*. Phenix, a philosopher, describes four ways we find meaning: through personal experiences, the power to reason, diverse cultural memories, and changing cultural expressions. Our self is determined by what we accept or reject as meaningful or meaningless. Our "truths" come from tribes, relatives, religious and educational institutions, media, politics, and other forces. See also Rohr, *Immortal Diamond*, 127–38.

4. Parks, *Big Questions*, 10, 52, 94, 191–92. Heschel, *Moral Grandeur*, 54, has more questions: Will anything on earth be impaired by my disappearance? Is it incumbent upon me to fulfill a purpose in this life? Do I exist that I might build or restore? Hunter, *Servant*, asks: How did the universe come into existence? Is the universe a safe or hostile place? Is there anything after death? Regarding mystery, Daniel, *Tired of Apologizing*, quips, "God didn't give us a paperback, *Divine Knowledge for Dummies*" (127). See **appendix 1A**, "Three Kinds of Mysteries."

your journey? My role is to assist you with rest stops and pitfalls along this exciting path, not give you a route that is the one and only true destination. I'll give you many sources of "in-formation." Let's begin by assessing where you are currently.

YOU'RE DISTINCT! WHAT ARE YOUR BIG QUESTIONS?

Recall your role in the family. Were you the model child? The trouble-maker or mischief maker? Naughty monkey? Laugh generator? The fa-vored or ignored child? If the firstborn, did you become an adult at a young age? Were you the pensive middle one, or the fawned-over, spoiled baby? How you answer those questions will color the way you ask the big questions of life. I'm assuming you could be an emerging adult—an-other one of those paradoxical terms—or a later-stage adult struggling to answer or reconsider your earlier answers to the big questions.[5] A fair question to ask here is, "Are these questions the 'self' or the 'soul' asks?" We'll discuss the differences in chapter 7.[6]

Most travelers want to explore these three big questions:

+ Is there a greater Power?

+ Why am I here?

+ How can I, alone or with others, contribute to a better world?

To help you develop your answers, it should be no surprise that I will cite others in this chapter who hold that your life will be more trans-formative if you have a relationship with a religious or spiritual com-munity. I believe the prime responsibility of any home, natal or spiritual, is to want what is best for each member. Don't be conned or forced into losing your uniqueness. Don't become locked into replicating the role(s) you played in your birth family or feel compelled to go to your parents'

---

5. Jeffrey Arnett, *Emerging Adulthood*, as cited in Denton and Flory, *Back-Pocket God*, 4. The ages eighteen to twenty-nine years old have these five characteristics: 1) identity explorations, especially in areas of love and work; 2) experiences of instability; 3) intense self-focus; 4) feelings of being in between adolescence and adulthood; and 5) feeling they have opportunities to transform their lives. See Parks, *Big Questions*, 7, 96, 114, on ambiguities of the term *emerging adult*.

6. See Boyd, *Reclaiming the Soul*, xxi, for his comparative table on differences be-tween soul and self.

house of worship. If you wear a mask that projects a false image to please any current spiritual home, you can't be your true self.[7]

DO YOU WANT TO MAKE A DIFFERENCE? (HOW ABOUT STOPPING A BANK ROBBERY?)

Will you make a difference? No guarantees, but you never know when an opportunity might strike. Consider this story about a bank teller in a small town near San Antonio, Texas. When this happened, the teller was in his late 40s or early 50s, bald, a school board member, active in a Lion's Club, and the Sunday School superintendent at his church. Non-athletic, a medical exemption barred him from World War II service. We'll consider later: did his behavior reflect his religious and spiritual roots or simply the secular norms of his time?

His family didn't learn of this incident until the 1960s. The man's youngest son, who had moved to Missouri, had taken his new bride to Texas. On the final day of their visit, they picked out souvenirs at a local shop. Ready to leave, the son discovered he didn't have enough cash, only his out-of-state checkbook. He assumed his check would be rejected. The shopkeeper overheard the couple. Recognizing the family name, he accepted it, whispering, "Your father saved my life."

"How could that be?" The shopkeeper explained he had dropped out of school, plunged into alcoholism, and become so desperate he decided to rob the bank when it first opened. He had a gun hidden in his waistband. "Your father unlocked the door, then welcomed me with, 'How are you doing?' I mumbled, 'Things are bad.' He simply responded, 'God bless you,' but those honest words expressed care. That was it, I couldn't do it. I turned, wandered the streets, went to a church . . . cried for hours. I knew I had to change. That's how he saved my life."

Why did this exchange of a few words—I'm not saying the banker's exact words are a magic formula—make such a difference? Family background?[8] Some psychological cause? The bank teller was the son of a

7. Rohr, *Immortal Diamond*, 191. The book is an insightful gem that compares the true and false selves. In the movie *My Fair Lady* (1964), Eliza Doolittle, played by Audrey Hepburn, rebukes her mentor, Professor Henry Higgins, shortly after her triumphant ruse at a ball, for not recognizing her as a person rather than a role player.

8. A therapist might surmise that as the youngest of seven children, this banker likely felt he was never as good as his accomplished sisters and brothers. One sister became world famous in her field, micropaleontology. Attending the University of Texas

minister. Considered friendly, he privately arranged to cover home loan repayments for African American families.[9] He was my father. Our family is convinced he died without ever knowing what he had done. What a difference this self made!

HOW WILL YOU PLAN YOUR SELF TRIP?

Ready to begin your spiritual trip now? As St. Francis de Sales (1567–1622), a French Roman Catholic priest and bishop (not the famous St. Francis), advised, "Be who you are and be that well."[10] With the 2020 coronavirus travel limitations, do you remember what it is like to plan a long trip? If it's to an exotic location, you typically gather data on the destination, like its climate, citizenry, and tourist sites, and solicit comments from friends who have visited. When I went to Israel and Jordan, I needed special clothes and shoes. If you were going to a mountainous or jungle area, that would demand physical conditioning. Spiritual journeying can also be strenuous.

If it will be a challenging trip, we need to convince ourselves we have the stuff to succeed. Perhaps I'm overemphasizing what any one person or self can do. Most of us echo the song "I've Gotta Be Me" made famous by Sammy Davis Jr. in 1968. It reflects our culture of rugged individualism. Admit it: we like to be tough. While my perspective holds that selves make a difference, you and I must be sensitive to some techniques, as well as religious traditions, that downplay the significance of selfhood.[11] What faith traditions believe about the self varies tremendously. Reminiscent of the opening quotation, Sam Harris, a popular atheist writer, posits from a Buddhist perspective that being a self is an illusion.[12] As a pun puts it,

---

from 1910 to 1915, she graduated with three undergraduate degrees and a master's degree. She and he were decidedly different in personality. Quite bluntly, she, my Aunt Hedwig Kniker, commanded me the night of my high school graduation to not "get homesick," knowing I would attend a college 1200 miles away.

9. As the only son who did not become a minister, did he experience pressure to be nice to everyone or to be an achiever like the biblical story of Joseph (Gen 37:1–11)? What would Sulloway, *Born to Rebel*, think of his actions?

10. Kielsmeir-Cook, *Blessed Are the Nones*, quotes this adage. A conservative Evangelical, she found involvement with a group of nuns was most helpful in her spiritual journey.

11. Gergen, *Saturated Self*, describes the forces of technology that are causing "the postmodern erasure of the self."

12. S. Harris, *Waking Up*, "The Riddle of the Self," 81–118.

"What did the Buddhist say to the hot dog vendor? 'Make me one with everything.'" You're not the same person you were as a child, teenager, or younger adult—correct? Will there be any evidence, a billion years from now, that you existed? No, because you are merely a part of one great Self.[13] Harris concludes the best you can do about it is to enjoy the moment. My theological, philosophical, historian's bones say, too shallow.[14] I agree with Dorothy West that "there is no life that does not contribute to history."[15] Or as author Nancy Abrams once quipped, "If I didn't write this book, who did?"[16] An inspiring true story is that of Homer Hickam, the son of a coal miner in West Virginia, who, despite many odds, achieved his dream of becoming a NASA engineer.[17] Mahatma Gandhi said, "The strength of numbers is the delight of the timid; the valiant in spirit glory in fighting alone." Cherish yourself! Let's admit it; we all want to have places, from homes to bars to restaurants to clubs and houses of worship, where everybody knows our name.

To assist in this process of preparing *your* self for this spiritual trip, I believe three steps are involved. Step 1: engage in a rigorous self-study, focusing on your positives. In addition to some self-help resources described below and elsewhere, try one or two activities per chapter in this book; consider them a self-study or journaling. Step 2: ask tough questions of yourself. Where do I fall short? How well do I handle criticism?

13. A somewhat similar Hindu perspective is that you are part of the one Self, which means you have unique, authentic gifts. In the *Upanishads*, a section on the universal self states, "In the beginning this was Self alone, in the shape of a person. He, looking round saw nothing but his Self. He feared, and therefore anyone who is lonely fears. He thought, 'As there is nothing but myself, why should I fear? . . . Verily fear arises from a second only'" (as cited in Ballou, *World Bible*, 39). The editor adds, "What is here is the universal soul or self which is in each of us, that 'self' which existed before all else, akin to the Western conception that 'God is within us.'" See Rohr, *Immortal Diamond*, for a Christian, specifically Roman Catholic, perspective.

14. Diana Bass, *Christianity after Religion*, 173–98, challenges the Western Church's assumption that people would relatively easily answer the questions "Who am I?" and "Whose am I?" theologically. Dated by gendered language, but surprisingly relevant for self-understanding, is psychotherapist Rollo May's *Man's Search for Himself.*

15. Dorothy West (1907–1998) was an African American who wrote extensively about middle-class life during the Harlem Renaissance. Her most famous work was *The Living is Easy.*

16. Abrams, *God That Could Be.*

17. Hickam, *Rocket Boys.* The story is retold in the movie *October Sky* (1999). The stories of African American women who were instrumental in NASA flights is told in *Hidden Figures* (2016).

How will I confront the evil, yes, evil forces in today's world? Step 3: find one or two trustworthy travel companions. Then, become part of an action group.[18]

Step 1: Self-Study and Personality Tests

We all know our family's size, birth order, and home location influence our self-perceptions.[19] Too many television shows, from *Leave It to Beaver* and *Father Knows Best* to *The Jeffersons* and *The Modern Family*, give us blurred or distorted images of parental influence. We learned more from the Black Lives Matter movement and coronavirus vaccination data from 2020 regarding the impact that race, economic background, gender, and geography make or do not make in our personal lives.[20] Koppelman's multicultural textbook is an excellent resource for the impact of race, gender, and religious differences.[21]

As much as we think we know ourselves, psychological instruments can give us additional insights. I suggest you consider either taking the Myers-Briggs test or exploring the enneagram of personality.[22] You might also consider a Spiritual Locations instrument described later.

Perhaps we easily fool ourselves about our independence. Two theologians, Walter Brueggemann and Henri Nouwen, speak of the illusion of independence. What freedom we think we have, Brueggemann argues, is, in fact, too often, "a seductive form of conformity," while Nouwen warns our illusions "can turn dreams into idolatry."[23] While we may not believe

18. Means with Nelson, *Trauma and Evil*, 53. "The self requires the continuing presence of others in its life." The self has a series of needs that can be met only by others (Means with Nelson, *Trauma and Evil*, 63).

19. Rosling, *Factfulness*, 84. What size family did you come from? In America in the 1800s a typical family had six children. By the 1940s, the average was four; in recent decades it has dropped to 2.5 children per family. Norris, *Dakota*, chronicles significant life changes in a rural state after living in New York City.

20. See Ritchie et al., "Coronavirus Pandemic," and "United States COVID-19 Cases."

21. Koppelman with Goodhart, *Understanding Human Differences*, has chapters on cultural pluralism, racism, sexism, classism. See timely information in ch. 8 on racism. Chapter 1, "Understanding Ourselves and Others: Clarifying Values and Languages," relates to our discussion here.

22. In this area I'll assume you can contact a counselor or spiritual representative. For background information on these instruments, see Wikipedia.

23. Brueggemann, *Practice of Homefulness*, 95; Nouwen, *Reaching Out*, 120.

a person can be brainwashed as depicted in the film *The Manchurian Candidate* (1962, remade 2004), we may concur with Kenneth Gergen that the postmodern world has tried to erase the self or certainly mold it.[24]

Here are some self-help resources. The first is David Richo's *How to Be an Adult*.[25] The second is on authentic selfhood, *Self Matters* by Phillip McGraw. Dr. Phil, as he is known, suggests that each of us has several defining moments/events in our lives that require our critical choices. Another point he makes is that many of us paint ourselves with a "gray" image; our goal should be to provide a more colorful personhood. What is your worldview? Here are resources to answer that question.[26]

Step 2: Tough Questions about Yourself

Ultimately, you must make the choice to be honest about yourself and to be responsible for your actions.[27] You might begin by reading a remarkable essay, "Finding Oneself."[28] It provides multiple perspectives on what others have done when they took on this task. The focus moves from positive to negative. What are you not pleased with about yourself? What can't you do because of a physical, mental, or emotional condition or circumstance? Do you accept your limitations? Have you conquered them? Working on it? What happened when you were given certain responsibilities that were or became burdensome?

A reality of life is that each of us is likely to face at least one possibly life-shattering event. It could be an illness that threatens a loved one or you or, worse, results in a death or permanent handicap. It might be something you brought on, like a traffic accident, cheating on an exam, or a mistake with opioids. On the other hand, this crucible could be a positive opportunity—a job offer in a new location, a scholarship, or a

---

Another Brueggemann book, *Journey to Common Good*, addresses the problem that individual striving and achievement is not always rewarded or should be rewarded.

24. Gergen, *Saturated Self*.

25. Richo, *How to Be an Adult*, contains a treasure trove of activities.

26. Smart, *Worldviews*. Raman, "Worldviews." Waggoner, "Religion and Spirituality," speaks of a "tournament of worldviews." See also Taylor, *Holy Envy*, 77. Here and elsewhere she discusses college students' worldviews of religions other than their own and strategies for discussing differing worldviews.

27. H. Niebuhr, *Responsible Self*, and Kegan, *Evolving Self*.

28. Bellah et al., *Habits of the Heart*, 55–84.

romantic relationship. Label it a shipwreck, or recall it as a crucible. Did you handle it well or poorly?[29]

Beyond grappling with your tough personal events, are you willing to speak and act out against what are truly evil behaviors? Would you agree there are some actions so morally repugnant, repeatedly harmful, deliberately destructive, and disaster-causing that they must be opposed?[30] If that word *evil* sounds harsh, consider the reasoning of a past saint, William of Ockham (c. 1283–1347 CE), who claimed "failed obligations"[31] should be included under the umbrella of evil. Someone who fails to live up to a sacred oath or constitutional pledge commits evil, and those enablers who see it but habitually fail to respond are also evildoers. How do you respond to that definition of evil?

Step 3: Finding Those Who Will Help

Most of us aren't brave or courageous as individuals. But if we become part of a group, we are more likely to act. It made a difference in the civil rights movement of the 1960s. The odds are that you, like most seekers, will join a spiritual community for a short period of time, then drop out or move on to another one.[32] One reason membership in religious faith communities fluctuates is that fighting issues such as gender, sexual orientation, or patriarchy is draining in terms of energy, time, and good will.[33]

Use the journey analogy, or compare yourself to an athlete: you can move forward. Building upon what you know and believe, engage in new practices that promote your strengths and eliminate deficiencies. You must do these yourself, but coaches and teammates can help you grow spiritually by working on your meaning-making questions. See **activities 2.1 and 2.2.**

29. Parks, *Big Questions*, 108; Bennis and Thomas, *Geeks and Geezers*, "Crucibles of Leadership," 87–120.

30. Means with Nelson, *Trauma and Evil*, 12–17. See also p. 26 for reasons against being a bystander when evil occurs.

31. Reese, *Dictionary of Philosophy*, 161.

32. Kegan, *Evolving Self*, as cited in Parks, *Big Questions*, 62.

33. Gilligan, *In a Different Voice*, was a groundbreaking text speaking to how women face moral issues differently than men. More recently, Gilligan and Snider have authored *Why Does Patriarchy Persist?*

WHO CAN I TURN TO? WHERE SHOULD I GO?

Personal Spiritual Journeys

You can make your spiritual search a rather calm, sedate, minimally challenging journey. That minimal effort might include a few versions of traditional religious practices. If you are like many respondents in recent interviews and survey data, you will only infrequently think of your religion or spirituality. One description of that approach: God will be like a smartphone in your back pocket, an infrequently used GPS.[34] Another researcher states that for some SBNRs, spirituality has become a commodity rather than a lifeboat.[35] If that is your level of involvement, it won't transform your daily life. I concur with the late twentieth-century mystic Rabbi Abraham Joshua Heschel's view: "One who thinks that one can live as a Jew in a lackadaisical manner has never tasted Judaism."[36] Other faith traditions have similar outlooks—namely, that you can't be lukewarm about your spirituality. What kind of a commitment are you willing to make?

Wilderness Stories

Wilderness narratives are typically stories of individuals.[37] The 2020 coronavirus, paradoxically, has created an international wilderness experience. Involuntarily, we are all isolated and disoriented, searching for new meanings. In religious literature, significant changes in perspective often follow a time of isolation from a wilderness experience. Stories abound regarding African explorations, nomadic treks, and American wagon trains. Christians recall Jesus's forty days in the wilderness after his Jordan River baptism.[38] Similar accounts of spiritual exile, sometimes spent in caves, are told about Muhammad, the Buddha, Confucius, and

---

34. Denton and Flory, *Back-Pocket God*.

35. Mercadante, *Belief without Borders*, 228–229.

36. Heschel, *Moral Grandeur*, 55.

37. Young, *James Baldwin's Understanding*, 79, cites Baldwin's fear of "the wilderness of himself."

38. See Gospel accounts in Matt 4:1–11, Mark 1:12–13, Luke 4:1–13. "Forty days" is a colloquialism meaning "a long time." Other accounts are of Moses and the refugees from Egypt (Exod 12–17); Saint Paul's blinding vision on the Damascus Road (Acts 9:19); and, later, saints like Augustine (see his *Confessions*).

famous saints.[39] Here's a more recent story. Jim Autry, a retired CEO of a publishing company, describes his unhappiness with a Southern Baptist upbringing and how he later, "hitchhiking" with others, made some "oddly reverent observations" in his wilderness days.[40] If you've had a similar experience, I'd say you qualify to be a wilderness guide.

I labeled 1960 my wilderness year. My college sweetheart and I were married for just seven months when she was diagnosed with acute leukemia and died three weeks later. Carrol and I had spoken about becoming missionaries, so I took advantage of an opportunity to serve in Honduras for the 1960–1961 academic year. During that span, with much reflection and a bevy of experiences, I received a second calling to be a teacher.

Turning to Others

Perhaps you are thinking, "Charles, get real. I don't have the time, money, or energy for a wilderness experience." I agree with the sentiment that "one thorn of experience is worth a whole wilderness of warning."[41] For many, going off to college, doing a tour of military service, or being assigned abroad provides the springboard for examining one's big questions, finding some answers, and forming dreams. Fine. The bulleted list which follows offers multiple possibilities for what I believe is the heart of your task: to become more capable of meaning-making. I suggest the person or group with whom you engage should be competent in knowing the history of and literature associated with that tradition and have demonstrated integrity, compassion for learners, and, if the person or group

39. Freedman and McClymond, *Rivers of Paradise*. Similar "wilderness" accounts can be told for Joan of Arc (c. 1412–1432 CE), a young girl who became a military leader; Mahatma Gandhi (1869–1948 CE), a Hindu, returned from legal studies to India and led his country's break from Great Britain; Albert Schweitzer (1875–1965 CE), who could have become a theologian or professional organist, chose instead to be a medical doctor in Africa; Mother Teresa, an Albanian (1910–1997 CE), changed her planned career to instead assist the poor and ill in India. Earlier, a rich young man felt called to minister to the poor and gave up his wealth to do so. Saint Francis (1182–1226 CE) founded the Franciscan order. Taylor, *Learning to Walk*, describes her unique cave experience, 112, 127–28.

40. Autry, *Looking Around for God*. Heschel offers readers a more formal approach for exploring a relationship with God in *God in Search for Man*.

41. James Russell Lowell (1819–1891), an American writer and diplomat, *Among My Books*, 223.

is not a member of that faith/tradition, then a commitment to teaching about it with fairness regarding its strengths and weaknesses.

◆ **Family and friends:** If your family has a member or two who is steeped in a tradition you wish to learn about, great. If you learn that a friend, a teammate, a fellow camper has had a "religious experience," it's fine to learn more.[42] My concern is what is the other person's agenda? Is it to "save" you? When you hear their group is "perfect," beware.

◆ **Religious bodies:** There are so many shades of religious faith. It's been said that each of the world's religions represents a great mansion with countless rooms. No wonder there are over two thousand denominations in the United States alone. An oft-quoted assertion is that half of them believe you will go to hell if you don't belong to their group. I'm familiar with the other half, mostly mainline ecumenical bodies who openly and honestly share what they believe and practice; they'll share their warts and all. A concern is that their ministers and teachers typically don't have much knowledge of other traditions. Until the early 1900s, most church-related institutions were "defenders of the faith," their own. Granted, about that time, many gradually put science on knowledge's throne.[43]

◆ **Spiritual homes:** You'll notice I am making a new category. Phyllis Tickle spoke often of small, informal groups that may begin meeting in bars, homes, or rented spaces. A concern in higher education by student affairs staff and chaplains at religiously related campuses and even public institutions is to find spaces where small groups of non-Christian students can meet.[44] These informal groups tend to avoid tangible connections with any traditional faiths and spiritual movements yet may feel a linkage to one or more of their inherited beliefs and practices.[45]

42. Drescher, *Choosing Our Religion*, 42–44. The Nones she interviewed believed that they had the most spiritual experiences with their families and friends. Similar statements are found in Oakes, *Nones Are Alright*.

43. Sloan, *Faith and Knowledge*.

44. According to Elmhurst University Chaplain H. Scott Matheny and *Convergence's* H. Cody Nielsen, finding spaces is difficult on some campuses. For example, Muslim students require prayer rugs. Storage is difficult with multipurpose rooms. Faith differences require sensitive accommodations. See Seligmann, "Making Space."

45. Tickle, *Great Emergence*. Her analysis, with many examples, is found in

+ **Spiritual gurus or non-theistic organizations:** On this point, I defer to Harris's extensive experiences and detailed descriptions of the best and worst about gurus.[46] If you have grown up without any religious trappings—that's one out of four Americans—and you feel comfortable in the atheist or agnostic camp, you might consider the approach Harris advocates.[47]

+ **Educational institutions:** My days as a university professor with research areas in teaching about religion and values education permit me to speak confidently about this group of helpers. I concur with the college chaplains, student affairs administrators, and world religion scholars who assert that while job preparation is the siren call of higher education institutions today, a prime focus of the collegiate experience should be on spiritual exploration.[48]

+ **Therapists, spiritual directors, and pastoral counselors:** If you bring up big questions with secular therapists, they will guide you to find the answers from within yourself and possibly urge you to meet with proponents of traditions you favor. While some pastoral counselors have specific traditions they favor, many will respect alternate paths for you. Joseph Stewart-Sicking provides an excellent example of what a spiritual director can provide for a seeker.[49]

HOW WOULD YOU IDENTIFY YOURSELF NOW?

Since 2000 there have been several major surveys of the religious and spiritual attitudes, beliefs, and practices of adults, especially emergent

---

Emergence Christianity. She offered additional examples when she was the theologian-in-residence at Ames, Iowa, in 2014.

46. S. Harris, *Waking Up,* 151–200.

47. S. Harris, *Waking Up,* 32–33. He views the Bible and the Qur'an as "worse than useless," urging people to gain "contemplative insights . . . without accepting metaphysical ideas inspired by ignorant and isolated peoples of the past." One of his "ancestors" would be Sigmund Freud, who argues that religion is a human illusion, seeking assurance from father-figure. See Freud's *Future of an Illusion.*

48. Astin et al., *Cultivating the Spirit,* 1–7; Chickering et al., *Encouraging Authenticity;* Parks, *Big Questions,* 9; Stoppa, "Becoming More a Part," 154–79. See also Waggoner, "Religion and Spirituality."

49. Stewart-Sicking, *Spiritual Friendship after Religion.*

adults.[50] SBNRs (Spiritual but Not Religious) or Nones will acknowledge they periodically engage in what they identify as a religious event or a spiritual practice. While I will cite the categories or labels used in different surveys, my concern is how do you approach your meaning-making? What do you mean when you say you are religious or spiritual? How should others interpret your response if it is "I'm spiritual but not religious" or "I'm a None"?[51]

ARE YOU RELIGIOUS?

I grew up in a mainline Protestant church. Although critical of the wider church throughout my adult professional life, I've remained a "stayer." Frankly, I'm surprised to see how many college students have maintained their religious heritage.[52] Although some of us persist, I respect the choices others make regarding religion/spirituality.

The word religion is from the Latin *religare*, meaning to bind fast. Historically and sociologically, it refers to an organization or institution that had a founder and a recognized body of followers or communicants who gather for a worship service on a regular basis. Believers may worship God or a group of gods. They observe rituals and institute "holy habits" or practices. From faith traditions to denominations, even cults, members hold and act on a set of doctrines or beliefs.[53] Chapter 3 and chapters 5–8 will give many examples of practices.

50. The results of a major ten-year study, the National Study of Youth and Religion (NSYR), are reported in a series of books, beginning with C. Smith with Lundquist, *Soul Searching*; C. Smith with Snell, *Souls in Transition*; and Denton and Flory's *Back-Pocket God*. Also, books by C. Smith, *Religion*; Drescher, *Choosing Our Religion*; and Mercadante, *Belief without Borders*, cite these and other studies. The Pew Center is well respected for its periodic studies on the religious landscape of the United States.

51. See Drescher, *Choosing Our Religion*, 18–26, 28–120, for extensive descriptions of persons from these categories. Burge, *Nones,* offers extensive data and trends

52. Schmalzbauer and Mahoney, *Resilience of Religion*, 1–19; Astin et al., *Cultivating the Spirit*, 83–100. The authors report on large-scale surveys and interviews with students over decades. See also C. Smith with Lundquist, *Soul Searching*, 260–62.

53. Reese, *Dictionary of Philosophy*, 488–89; Dorothy Bass, *Practicing Our Faith.* Nash, *Spirituality, Ethics, Religion*, posits that religion and spirituality represent two related but different perspectives—the institutional and the personal or transcendent. For the reader who wants to explore diverse explanations of and opinions about religion, see Pelikan, *World Treasury.*

The simplest definition I've found is "being religious connotes belonging to and practicing a religious tradition."[54] German philosopher and theologian Friedrich Schleiermacher (1768–1834) defined religion in terms of *feeling* rather than *reason* or morality—the feeling of absolute dependence. An individual, feeling dependent upon the Almighty, develops a proprium, that is, his/her place in the universe.[55] Want a more academic definition? "Religion is a complex of culturally prescribed practices, based on premises about the existence and nature of superhuman powers, whether personal or impersonal, which seek to help practitioners gain access to and communicate or align themselves with these powers, in hopes of realizing human goods and avoiding things bad."[56] Ninian Smart (1927–2001) believed the scope of religion is covered by seven dimensions.[57]

Andrew Greeley offers this pithy, provocative description: "Religion . . . is the result of two incurable diseases from which humankind suffers: life, from which we die; and hope, which hints that there may be more meaning to life than a termination in death."[58] Paul Tillich, a theologian, defined religion as what is ultimately "the ground of being apart from daily life."[59] Huston Smith, considered the preeminent world religions scholar of his day, referred to the "religious sense" that many traditions have. The first of four parts is that human beings ask ultimate questions (see footnote); the remaining steps concern how we approach answering them.[60] An error for religious adherents and their critics might be to

---

54. Wayne Teasdale, *The Mystic Heart*, cited in Chickering et al., *Encouraging Authenticity*, 7.

55. Reese, *Dictionary of Philosophy*, 513.

56. C. Smith, *Religion*, 22. Smith goes into detail discussing "practices" as well as the "superhuman," noting how it is different from the supernatural. Smith, a sociologist of religion, is a professor at Notre Dame University.

57. Smart's seven dimensions include: 1) practical and ritual; 2) experiential and emotional; 3) mythic or narrative; 4) doctrinal and philosophical; 5) ethical and legal; 6) social and institutional; and 7) material (J. Bishop, "Ninian Smart's Seven Dimensions").

58. Greeley, *Religion as Poetry*, 26. An excellent summary of the concept of religion and major religious traditions is Holloway, *Little History of Religion*.

59. Tillich, *Systematic Theology*, 1, 155–58.

60. H. Smith, *Why Religion Matters*, 274–76. Questions include: What is the meaning of existence? Why are there pain and death? Is life worth living?

assume that these steps—call them traditions and practices—are permanent; but they are not. To remain vital, they will change over time.[61]

Organized religion is under siege. Surprise, surprise: it's always had critics. Recent criticisms include clergy abuse, outdated beliefs, disagreements with the pastor, irrelevance (won't deal with social issues), too much political involvement, and dysfunctional management. Retired Episcopal Bishop John Shelby Spong once characterized those still attending mainline congregations as "the church's alumni association." Nones and SBNR interviewees have labeled houses of worship as "social clubs" or "moral finishing schools."[62]

These definitions may promote more confusion than clarity. Sorry. Let's try Stephen Prothero's practical approach. He holds that religion(s) began by noticing what was wrong with the world and then offering the best way(s) to solve those problems. Their proponents proclaim what they believe is the truth, what gives meaning to life. The issue is that some traditions claim their religion is the only truth or the only way to truth.[63] They do not agree with the Hindu position that truth is one, though people speak of it in many ways. The only-we-have-the-Truth stance is deadly serious, as too many historical accounts reveal. One argument for the decline of religion is that people find that the truths that religions proclaim are flat out false or not relevant for daily life.[64]

Karen Armstrong remarks that "religion is not about accepting twenty impossible propositions before breakfast, but about doing things that change you." However, I disagree with her comment that ends "I have discovered that the religious quest is not about discovering 'the truth' or 'the meaning of life' but about living as intensely as possible in the here and now."[65] One interesting debate is whether religion includes those who claim that certain outcomes are due to superhuman rather than

---

61. Eck, *New Religious America*, 9.

62. Drescher, *Choosing Our Religion*, 31, 69.

63. Prothero, *God Is Not One*, 11; Borg, *Speaking Christian*, 171–74. Borg interprets the familiar passage of Jesus being the only way in a manner that holds Christianity is *not* the exclusive way for salvation. See also Taylor's *Holy Envy*, on truths in world religions.

64. Diana Bass, *Grounded*. Her thesis is that the worldview of a three-tiered world—God in heaven, humans on earth, an underworld—an "elevator faith"—has been rejected for a "God is in the world with us" theology.

65. Armstrong, *Spiral Staircase*, 270–71.

supernatural powers.[66] An example: some will say that the rapid spread of the coronavirus was caused by God, i.e., a supernatural or religious reason. Others conclude it was remarkable, superhuman, but not divine.

Having read these definitions and descriptions, do your beliefs and practices put you in the religious cohort, or do you think the next option, spirituality, is more appropriate?[67]

ARE YOU SPIRITUAL?

This commonly used word has some uncommonly interesting roots.[68] Let's start with the dictionary: *spirit* may be defined as the "animating or vital principle held to give life."[69] Some combine the root word, *spiritus*, Latin for breath, and the Greek word *enthousiasmos*, "the God within," to stand for "the breath of God within." Other descriptors say spirituality is an emphasis upon self-exploration or consciousness, reliance on self for problem-solving, holistic or non-rational thinking, flexibility, connectedness with others or a source greater than self, transcendence, reluctance to harm others, tendency to ask why and what if questions, and an ability to work against conventional thought. Whew! Try this out: "Our inner subjective life, as contrasted with the objective domain of observable behavior and material objects that we can point to and measure directly . . . our affective experiences as least as much as our reasoning or logic."[70] Some descriptors focus on what spirituality isn't. It is more flexible; there is no need for a religious framework, i.e., following specific rules and practices, but has an identity that is authentic.[71] Too academic? Here are some down-to-earth descriptions: "It is heart knowledge." Kinetic

66. C. Smith, *Religion*, 136.

67. Wuthnow, *All in Sync*, 33, has a brief but insightful paragraph on the difference between religion and spirituality: "*Religion* conjures up words such as organization, institution, structure and dogma; spirituality evokes phrases such as *believing in God, walking the walk, surrendering, actively searching*." He tends to use them interchangeably, making his main point that the arts, especially music, are a force in generating new interest in churches.

68. See Kniker, "Spirituality." Although Adler, *Essentials of Spirituality*, 2, admits that "spirituality" might be thought of as "muddy thought and misty emotionalism," he describes it as the system of ultimate morality.

69. Kniker, "Spirituality," 431.

70. Astin et al., *Cultivating the Spirit*, 4–5.

71. Astin et al., *Cultivating the Spirit*, 5.

energy levels. Equanimity. Authenticity. Purpose.[72] Researchers define some who have joined spiritual communities as persons who "believe in belonging" or want social action projects.[73] Consider **activity 2.3** for further exploration.

There are observers—OK, some are critics—who use a barrage of oxymoronic terms to describe spirituality negatively. They call it a jacuzzi of beliefs, hot tub religion, a tournament of worldviews, grassroots religion, or spiritual intelligence (SQ). One critic quipped, "Spirituality is a code word for flake." Another, Lillian Daniel, a minister in a progressive denomination and author of When "Spiritual but Not Religious" Is Not Enough, describes an SBNR person as somebody who feels connected to the divine in some way but does not practice or worship with any community.[74] Academic critics target three shortcomings of being SBNR: adherents are tempted to create God in their own images, to fail to see that there is something bigger in life than one's world, and to avoid the rigors of scholarship.

A second perspective comes from historians, sociologists, and anthropologists. They note that Native Americans have a rich tradition of spirituality. Roman Catholic priests and missionaries of the 1600s and 1700s either incorporated Indian spiritual traditions into their religious rituals or suppressed them. As researcher Diane Eck notes, white settlers of New England, and later the Midwest, established formal religious practices located in houses of worship that, while linked to specific doctrines and dogma, also incorporated some local spiritual practices.[75] Robert Wuthnow, a sociologist of religion, identified clusters of practices that lasted until the 1950s as "a spirituality of dwellings," i.e., an emphasis upon buildings.[76] A "spirituality of seeking" emerged during the 1960s, fueled by criticisms of the Vietnam War. A flood of new ways to ask questions of ultimate meaning and personal enlightenment emerged as businesses and government, religion, and educational systems were found wanting. American Spiritualities, edited by Catherine Albanese, provides a helpful summary of movements. Some final comments on spirituality: many of

72. See Chickering et al., Encouraging Authenticity; Chickering and Reissner, Education and Identity; Parks, Big Questions, 40–41.

73. Drescher, Choosing Our Religion, 122, citing sociologist Abby Day's findings.

74. Merritt, "Why Christians Need;" Daniel, When "Spiritual but Not Religious," 3–17.

75. Eck, New Religious America.

76. Wuthnow, After Heaven.

my references relate to the spirituality of emerging adults. A *Christian Century* article summaries their outlook; you might want to compare your beliefs with theirs.[77] I'll say more in chapter 6 on the spirituality of children and older adults in the educational process.[78]

ARE YOU BOTH RELIGIOUS AND SPIRITUAL— A HYBRID OR A NONE?

Do religion and spirituality overlap? It's debatable. Surveys and interviews by Wuthnow concluded many people draw a sharp distinction. For them, religion embodies organization, institution, structure, dogma, history, and culture. Spirituality, conversely, reflects spontaneity, freedom of belief, a sense of surrendering, or actively searching.[79] Robert Nash holds a similar position: religion is institutional, while spirituality is personal or transcendent.[80] A growing movement, credited to Buddhist Thich Nhat Hanh, is "engaged spirituality." Its proponents say its two foci are immersing oneself in nurturing resources—i.e., teachings, readings, and practices—and actions of compassion and justice.[81]

Does one or the other offer true faith, or is a hybrid more fitting? Some authors conclude that a person can be both religious and spiritual, with spirituality the goal to find self and a higher power and religion the road to that goal.

By contrast, therapist and life coach Pamela Milam argues that religion and spirituality should be used in tandem. Her model contends that religion provides a set of rules and beliefs that guide behavior, while spirituality offers methods for managing emotions internally and regulating the experience and expression of those emotions. She concludes that "those who combine routine religious practice with a committed spiritual

---

77. Denton and Flory, "DIY Religious Outlook." The basic tenets of emerging adults are karma is real, everybody goes to heaven, just do good, it's all good, religion is easy, morals are self-evident, and live with no regrets.

78. Coles, *Spiritual Life of Children*; Cully, *Education for Spiritual Growth*; David Csinos's work on spiritual formation of children (see ch. 6).

79. Wuthnow, *All in Sync*, 33. Several studies he cites indicate over 70 percent of respondents agree that religious beliefs are very personal and private; for them, spirituality does not depend upon belonging to any organized religion.

80. Nash, *Spirituality*.

81. Parachin, *Engaged Spirituality*, 2; Nangle, *Engaged Spirituality*.

practice are more likely to achieve both healthy outward behavior and healthy inward experience."[82]

What do survey results tell us? Some evidence suggests that as many as 50 to 60 percent of adults think or believe they have some spirituality. A common finding in emerging adults, supported by interview data, is that the SBNR and the Nones categories are growing rapidly. What does that mean? Respondents feel God is more remote, distant from daily life. God is to be called upon or may crop up in small ways when we are with our families, friends, dining, or playing with pets.[83] Unlike Sam Harris, who trashes religion, there are others who are trying to reconcile their religious heritage with the science of today and the future of the planet. An example is Nancy Ellen Abrams's *A God That Could be Real.*

Others, however, argue that their processes and purposes are significantly dissimilar, so a person can be spiritual but not religious, or vice versa. I tend to disagree. The current trend toward SBNR echoes a seventeenth-century religious movement called pietism. Historian Roland Bainton describes it as a rebellion against stale dogmatism and stagnant practices, yet it did not reject a need for education. It emphasized feelings, especially a personal relationship to Jesus. Pietists expected believers to do good deeds, providing healthcare, orphanages, and assistance for the marginalized.[84] Let me suggest the following. It expected more than an informed life; it mandated transformation.

If you accept the premise that roughly every five hundred years, there is a major attic-to-basement cleaning of houses of worship (the major traditions), wherein beliefs, traditions, practices, and architectural styles are pitched or modified, assisted by cultural mores and technology changes—transportation and communication mostly—then I'm suggesting that what is occurring now is a similar global phenomenon. We are witnessing a rejection of traditional religions as non-scientific, irrelevant, and impotent to speak to daily life. Traditional spiritual practices are tolerated because they offer a shell of respectability without demanding too much effort. Example: the DIY or moralistic therapeutic deism that is popular is a substance more like popcorn than like rock.

82. Milam, "How Religion and Spirituality Affect."

83. Mercadante, *Belief without Borders*, 228–29; Denton and Flory, *Back-Pocket God*, 7, 64, 66. Drescher, *Choosing Our Religion*, 24–25, reports 88 percent of Nones disagree with the statement that they "are looking for a religion that would be right for you."

84. Bainton, *Christianity*, 332–36.

The alternative that is emerging which can be a difference-maker is what I call transformational or eclectic spirituality. Its ingredients are modeled by some described in Diana Butler Bass's *Christianity for the Rest of Us* and *Grounded* as "spiritual revolution" or "spiritual awakening" and in stories told by Parachin and others.[85] Difference-making, in personal, social, government, and corporate worlds, is demanding. The key building blocks for positive change require individuals working collectively in communities committed to giving time to a thoughtful determination of what is truthful[86]—testifying through communication and modeling to what is authentic and needed today; developing their tools (honing personal gifts and creating new techniques and instruments); being willing to spend time and treasure to bring about needed common good changes. Religion or spirituality that is a second thought, a minimally used commodity, a form of social acceptability, is absurd.

It is easy to say that you are willing to search for a religious or spiritual home. Don't let me or anyone else push you into mouthing that testimonial to earn a few brownie points. You must decide when and how to make the journey. You only will decide when and if you will visit a variety of faith communities. Not I, nor others, should judge your state of spirituality. We won't be your decider. Use a resource called Spiritual Locations to find out where you are now.[87] It is **activity 2.4**.

RETURN TO THE SCENE OF THE CRIME: WHAT WOULD YOU HAVE DONE?

Recall the story at the beginning of this chapter, of the bank teller whose few words with a prospective bank robber changed that man's life. Imagine that you are standing with that young adult. First, recall you didn't know his intent. How would you have greeted him? Second, what if you

85. Diana Bass, *Christianity for the Rest*, 77–218, on practices; *Grounded*, 216–21, for examples of hospitality in our neighborhoods; Parachin, *Engaged Spirituality*; Nangle, *Engaged Spirituality*; Heschel, *Moral Grandeur*, "Analysis of Piety," 305–17.

86. Your behaviors must square with your beliefs, or you will suffer cognitive dissonance. The essential beliefs I submit are a God/Higher Power, image of self, relationship with neighbors, perspective about the world, and afterlife; see Diana Bass, *Christianity after Religion*, 145–50, for overview of spiritual actions and practices.

87. Lillie Brock developed this Spiritual Locations resource for use in MCC congregations. For information, contact Trinity MCC, Sarasota, FL 34243, https://www.trinitymcc.com. Outline provided in **activity 2.4**.

did happen to notice the gun in his waistband? Would your words or actions have changed? What if he pulled the gun? Would you be willing to sacrifice your life for others? Your answer to those questions will reflect your religious or spiritual orientation. Return to them later, through practices of reflection, meditation, or prayer.

TRAVELER: READY TO BECOME YOUR AUTHENTIC SELF, POSSIBLY A WILDERNESS GUIDE?

Whether your self is religious, spiritual, or a combination, I believe somewhere, sometime, you will receive a message to lead a life that has more meaning with fulfilled dreams. A theme of C. S. Lewis's *The Lion, the Witch, and the Wardrobe* is that "finding yourself" is a matter of learning who you have always been but hidden. As indicated early in the chapter, you may need to have a wilderness experience. If you have survived a wilderness experience, and are the better for it, consider whether you would be willing to be a guide assisting another person as she or he faces going to a wilderness.

May that higher power or spirit within you respond to that voice or mystery with a chant like this refrain:

> *Take, O take me as I am; summon out what I shall be;*
> *Set your seal upon my heart and live in me.*[88]

---

88. John Bell, "Take, O Take Me as I Am," in *Singing Thing Too*, 114. Bell is with the Iona Community.

Chapter 2 Activities

ACTIVITY 2.1: BEFORE I TRAVEL: WHO AM I?

Do you agree with the high school biology teacher who said, "The only permanent thing in life is change?" Perhaps not, but you will likely acknowledge that you have changed over time.

Today, _____ (add date), provide a brief answer to the following questions. At a future time of your choosing, review your answers and note any changes.

* What is the purpose of my life?

* What am I most passionate (excited) about?

* What do I want my legacy to be?

* What is one of my worthy dreams?

ACTIVITY 2.2 SWEATER STATEMENT (OR T-SHIRT TESTIMONY)

To do: create a sweater or T-shirt design that contains a message representing your stance on an issue that you strongly favor.

1. Do you feel so passionate about it that you would be willing to have it printed?

2. Are you willing to wear it? Would you be willing to have additional copies made to distribute to others?

3. How comfortable do you feel explaining the issue and your stance to those who agree with you? Those who would disagree with you?

4. It could be a humorous message. Would people laugh? Be offended? Understand?

5. Bottom line: are you willing to go public for what you believe in?

Alternative: rather than design a sweater or T shirt, create a design for a button (like a political button). Or a bumper sticker. You don't have to be super serious about this but do send a message such as: "Live your life so that the preacher doesn't have to lie about you at your funeral."

ACTIVITY 2.3: AM I RELIGIOUS? SPIRITUAL? A PLURALIST? NONE OF THE ABOVE?

Consider this activity a practice you should return to periodically. It centers around two questions: What is the meaning of the truth? Is there only one truth about God?

Begin with a statement from Harvard religion scholar Diana Eck, who has said that religion—and let's add spirituality—is never a finished product. It is never passed fully intact from one generation to another.

To begin this activity, I suggest you use a technique that Boston University Professor Stephen Prothero developed in his world religions course. To study a major religious faith or spiritual tradition, he has his students approach it this way: the problem the religion proposes to solve, the solution to the problem, its techniques or practices, and an exemplar of that path.[89]

For example, in Christianity, the problem is sin; the solution or goal is salvation; the technique for achieving salvation is some combination of faith and good works; the exemplars who chart this path are the saints in Roman Catholicism and Orthodoxy and ordinary people of faith in Protestantism. In Buddhism, the problem is suffering; the solution or goal is *nirvana*; the technique for achieving nirvana is the Noble Eightfold Path, which includes such classic Buddhist practices as meditation and chanting; and the exemplars who chart this path are *arhats* (for Theravada Buddhists), *bodhisattvas* (for Mahayana Buddhists), or *lamas* (for Vajrayana Buddhists).

First, read more about a religion and/or spiritual tradition, using the four-step approach described above. From that, determine what truth(s) the traditions offers. If you grew up in another tradition, or learned of others, can you accept those truths?[90]

Diana Eck states in *A New Religious America*, 23, that she is a "Christian pluralist." What do you think of her approach to discerning the truth? "Through the years I have found my own faith not a threat but brought in and deepened by the study of Hindu, Buddhist, Muslim, and Sikh traditions of faith. And I have found that only as a

89. Prophero, *God Is Not One*, 14–15.
90. Thangaraj, *Relating to People*.

(Activity 2.3 continued)

Christian pluralist could I be faithful to the mystery and the presence of the one I called God. Being a Christian pluralist means daring to encounter people of quite different faith traditions and be finding my faith not by its borders, but by its roots."

Truth to me is:_____

ACTIVITY 2.4: SPIRITUAL LOCATION

This is an outline of an approach developed by Rev. Elder Lillie Brock to assist persons in assessing where they are. For more specific details, contact www.trinitymcc.com in Sarasota, FL. (Verbal approval was given to share this material.)

1. Starting Point: right where you are now—use movies, TV shows, books as a way to identify how you feel

2. Inner Compass: Spiritual Types: which best describe your personal "spiritual navigation systems"?—reflective/thinking, heart/feeling, mystic/being, activist/doing

3. Spiritual Location Strategies: right where God is—what are you doing or want to do?—searching, changing, connecting, listening, serving, preparing

4. Chart Your Path: open-ended space to write your thoughts.

FOR ADDITIONAL CONVERSATIONS

If you have looked at the footnotes and still want to explore more about the self, religion, or spirituality, these books are excellent sources.

◆ If you want to delve into the meaning of self and take time to ponder what is most important at this stage of life and what is less significant, consider Richard Rohr, *Immortal Diamond: The Search for Our True Self*. Some would consider it a devotional book.

◆ An eye-opener if you are wrestling with weighing personal autonomy in a digital age as well as how one can meaningfully engage with others, is Sherry Turkle, *Alone Together: Why We Expect More from Technology and Less from Each Other*.

◆ For a resource that provides a readable but meaningful introduction to world religions without being overwhelming, I recommend Jim Willis, *The Religion Book: Places, Prophets, Saints, and Seers*.

◆ Pondering why and how spirituality is a growing force in the world? With depth and down-to-earth examples, turn to Diana Butler Bass, *Grounded: Finding God in the World—A Spiritual Revolution*.

◆ If you want specific examples of persons impacting others through their daily lives, try Janet W. Parachin, *Engaged Spirituality: Ten Lives of Contemplation* and *Action*. If you want to learn more about the fastest increasing category of religion/spirituality—Nones—consider Ryan P. Burge, *The Nones: Where They Came From, Who They Are, and Where They Are Going*.

3

Voice—"Re-Formed" by Choice

This is the true joy in life, the being used for a purpose recognized by yourself as a mighty one; the being a force of nature instead of a feverish, selfish little clod of ailments and grievances complaining that the world will not devote itself to making you happy . . . . I want to be thoroughly used up when I die, for the harder I work, I rejoice in life for its own sake. Life is no "brief candle" for me. It is a sort of splendid torch which I have got hold on for the moment, and I want to make it burn as brightly as possible before handing it on to future generations.

—GEORGE BERNARD SHAW, *MAN AND SUPERMAN*

From quiet homes and first beginning,
Out to the undiscovered ends,
There's nothing worth the wear of winning,
But laughter and the love of friends.

—HILAIRE BELLOC, "DEDICATORY ODE,"
SONNETS AND VERSE, STANZA 22

If it is true we are made for community, then leadership is everyone's vocation . . . when we live in the close-knit ecosystem called community, **everyone follows, and everyone leads** [emphasis added].

—PARKER PALMER, *LET YOUR LIFE SPEAK*, 74

We are here to be loved by God, and we are here to love because of God.

—EMILY C. HEATH, *GLORIFY*, 122

VOICE: FINDING YOUR VOICE AS TRAVELER, DISCIPLE, FRIEND, MORAL SERVANT LEADER

- Invitation: to "re-form" your identity and become a listening voice

- What about discipline?

- Who is a disciple? What is spiritual discipleship?

- What is the cost and joy of discipleship?

- Who calls us to be disciples and travelers?

- What do disciples believe? What do disciples practice?

- Can you be perfect?

- The first benefit: new friends!

- The second benefit: a moral servant leader

- Traveler: ready to "re-form" your identity and become a listening voice?

- Activities

- For Additional Conversations

The voice of the interviewee on the National Public Radio program was tense. She was describing her problem in maintaining a relationship with her mother and friends who wanted to visit her new baby. She had listened to why her mother had chosen not to get a COVID-19 vaccination, then had to explain why she and her husband refused to let her mother visit their home. Similar conversations between family members, workers, classmates, friends, with many other voices, are often tense today. Clergy, columnists, and commentators chide politicians for either being too bipartisan or not compromising on needed legislation. Could we agree that for too many of us ideology borders on or has become idolatry?

INVITATION: TO "RE-FORM" YOUR IDENTITY AND BECOME A LISTENING VOICE

It is time for spiritual voices. Yes, spiritual voices. Parker Palmer believes we each possess one. Really? We're spiritual beings, he asserts, and as such, our assignment or vocation—it's full-time for only a few of us—is to enrich that voice.[1] He proposes we think of it this way. We possess an inner voice that keeps trying to tell us how to speak out in life and an outer voice that too often is a quiet witness to what we value. Don't we need more exceptions like the following? A reserved neighbor in my retirement community was an internationally known research veterinarian. After his death, I learned of his longtime spiritual practice of visiting prisoners. It was no pious ornament he wore to gain attention but a quiet voice that resulted in life-changing action.

How does that relate to the concepts of home and self, described in chapters 1 and 2? Your inner and outer voices were being formed and groomed in your natal home. If you've been participating in a faith community or non-profit agency, your voice has been "in-formed" and "con-formed" in many ways. Carol Gilligan's *In a Different Voice* explains

---

1. Palmer, *Let Your Life Speak*. The word *voice* is related to the root word for vocation. In ch. 4, we'll discuss *commission*. Other sources include Muller, *Latin and Greek Theological Terms*, s.v. "*vocatio*," and Mendenhall, "Call, Calling."

why and how women's voices were silenced for such a long time.[2] The question now is: are you speaking up and acting as a spiritual self? Will what you do, as well as what you say, reveal who you are spiritually and reflect you as a disciplined traveler? Chapter 3's purpose is to sharpen what you believe and practice so you can gain insights to better express your inner and outer voices. Put another way, there are many who want you to change who you are, to "re-form" you into a role that benefits them. To be a voice that is heard requires passion, integrity, and tenacity.[3] That is gained when you practice what you preach, when your life's rhythm, melody, and harmony have been formed through what has been experienced. In my view, such traits are especially important for spiritual travelers.

Consider the parable of the pedal. Years ago, two bike enthusiasts, columnists of the *Des Moines Register*, organized an annual ride from one side of the state of Iowa to the other. Called RAGBRAI (*Register*'s Annual Great Bike Ride across Iowa), participants began the trip dipping their rear wheels in the Missouri River and, seven days later, baptized the front wheels in the Mississippi River. Over time, annual participation grew from hundreds into thousands. Now it is one of the largest recreational bicycle rides in the country, attracting riders from all over the country and world. It was once jokingly described as a slowly moving parking lot. To participate fully requires discipline—biking skills, endurance for hill climbing, and battling wind—and commonsense culture for interacting with other travelers and town hosts. Benefits? You bet: new friendships, goodies at stops, and stunning landscapes. Ultimately, should you participate in a similar event, you will gain insights into both your inner and physical selves.

Picture those pedaling together through towns and cities, gazing at fertile farm fields, puffing up hills, stopping for water and rest breaks, debating out-of-staters about who has the best whatever. Imagine the munchies and meals provided by local faith congregations. (Over the years, it seems different congregations have been linked to certain dishes—Catholic churches for spaghetti and meatballs, Lutherans for salads, Unitarians and UCC for exotic dishes.) Evenings are filled with drinks

2. Gilligan, *In a Different Voice*, "Letters to Readers, 1993," ix–xxvii, explains her unique understanding of *voice* and *different*.

3. Coles, *Lives of Moral Leadership*, provides two vivid examples of the sustained efforts needed: Robert Kennedy for political action and Dorothy Day for services to marginalized persons.

and dances. Always there is conversation, on the road or in the cornuco-
pia of tents and ingeniously converted vehicles providing comfort against
the elements. Heard enough? Would you accept an invitation to ride?

Your spiritual voice will tell you. It will move you, but you will always need to weigh the costs and benefits, then determine if you would
be a courageous cosmic explorer or a contented couch potato. Spirituality
does require discipline.

Anything worth doing well has costs as well as benefits. A healthy
home, like a marriage, doesn't happen magically. Its values, joys, loves,
and delights reflect a disciplined commitment. In spiritual homes, the
parallel is discipleship. In a healthy spiritual home, travelers are true
friends who help you develop your voice—how you express yourself, in
deeds as well as words. That home will not be perfect; it will reflect the
paradoxes of life, supporting you in times of crisis but also challenging
your actions from time to time.

WHAT ABOUT DISCIPLINE?

Likely, you are thinking, "Charles, why hammer us with the word
discipline?"[4] Answer: I was a cranky, control-freak teacher. Seriously,
it's a big part of life. Yes, you may have negative memories of spankings,
mindless rules with unfair consequences, and self-righteous relatives
touting their stringent, perfect piety.[5] You likely rejected or are suspicious of discipline in organized religion. You're disturbed by accounts of
cults making converts grovel under the weight of preposterous claims or
church pastors fleecing naïve disciples and abusing members. If it continues to bother you, use the word *commitment*, which a serious traveler
certainly needs to make.[6]

---

4. While the word *disciple* is associated with many faith traditions, it is frequently linked to Christianity. A reminder is that Jesus did ask his followers to be disciples,
not church members! One of the chief benefits is that they would learn the truth that
would "set them free" (John 8:31–32).

5. Doucleff, *Hunt, Gather, Parent*, describes a fascinating array of discipline techniques of ancient cultures she believes are relevant today.

6. Daloz, *Common Fire*. C. Smith with Lundquist, *Soul Searching*, contains many
statistics describing the religious practices of teenagers. One trend cited here and in
other books is the decline in attending religious services. Another excellent source on
spiritual commitment through diverse practices is Dorothy Bass, *Practicing Our Faith*.

Three positive examples of discipline offset the negatives for me. Bicycle riding is the first. It's not natural for most of us. Do you know the hardest thing about learning to ride? It's the pavement! My children and grandchildren can attest to the need to put up with bumps, bruises, and prodding before the joy of cycling wins out.

Second, to be successful at a sport, you need discipline. That requires you to 1) learn the rules; 2) gain the big picture of the individual and team skills needed; 3) master the skills, typically following a process of learning in steps, moving from the basic to the more complex; and 4) function in a culture based on trust in coaches, guides, and teammates who challenge you to do things that may seem illogical and beyond your skill level but end with success.

These analogies not working for you? Try this one: baking. After my wife died in 2008, I decided to continue what she had begun, teaching our granddaughter how to bake. First, I devoured cookbooks and clues from classmates and neighbors who were good bakers. Second, I became familiar with ingredients and measuring tools. Then, the baking began. Mistakes, plenty. I substituted ingredients that made stomach-pumping concoctions, set off smoke alarms, and ended with expensive garbage contributions. Today, I can make a mean sloppy joe sandwich, concoct salted nut bars that garner recipe requests, and produce a strawberry-rhubarb pie that brings smiles and hearty grunts. The secret ingredients? Discipline and love. Bottom line: commitment has more positives than negatives.

Let's sprinkle in, for spice, some definitions of discipline: "training that develops self-control, character, or orderliness, and efficiency" or "treatment that corrects or punishes." This third one relates to religion: "a system of rules for the conduct of members of a group, such as a monastic order."[7] The point is that engaged spirituality is more than being a tourist, bringing back a few trinkets from visiting Mecca on Monday and Jerusalem in July. Two realities raised in the surveys of the Spiritual but Not Religious (SBNRs) and emerging adults is 1) their casualness about beliefs and 2) the irrelevance of the practice of their "faith" in daily life.[8]

7. *Webster's New World Dictionary*, "Discipline." A. Robinson, "Follow Me," 23–25, describes a renewed focus on discipleship in the early years of the twenty-first century.

8. Wilfred Cantwell Smith, *Faith and Belief*, 12, as cited in Parks, *Big Questions*, 52: faith is at its best "a quiet confidence and joy which enables one to feel at home in the universe." I hold with Parks that this description of faith offsets the often held view that faith primarily reflects a person's formally held religious doctrines.

If you agree that you want an interactive rather than a superficial spirituality, and that just wishing for a meaningful moral life won't get you one, then what must you do?[9] A spiritual voice seeking positive outcomes doesn't operate from "benign neglect."[10] The voice will seek remedies to sensitive and difficult issues. See **activity 3.1**.

WHO IS A DISCIPLE? WHAT IS SPIRITUAL DISCIPLESHIP?

Have you ever heard the phrase, "I would take a bullet for . . ."? Whether it's for a military leader, a mob boss, or the president of a country, it signals complete loyalty to a person or a cause. A disciple has another dimension: emulating the path of beliefs and practices modeled by a guide. The Old English word *discipul* (fem. *discipula*) means "one who follows another for the purpose of learning." Here's a summary of what a spiritual disciple or voice is about: "There is a sense of a self that is the single, distinct, integrated body; there is the agent of actions, the experiencer of feelings, the maker of intentions, the architect of plans, the transposer of experience into language, the communicator and sharer of personal knowledge . . ."[11] Historic examples abound in the Islamic Sufi, Buddhist, Judaic, and Christian traditions.[12] The word *disciple* comes from the root words to learn (from the Greek *mathētēs*), from the Hebrew (*talmid*, from *lamad*), and from Latin (*discipulus*, from *discere*). A disciple is a learner, scholar, someone who discerns, who follows given doctrines or teachers.[13]

9. Oakes, *Nones Are Alright*, "Belonging without Believing," 33–46; Mercadante, *Belief without Borders*, 7–13, 52–53, 71–72, 227.

10. In 1969, *benign neglect* was a term from an infamous report written by later US Senator Daniel Patrick Moynihan, "The Negro Family: The Case for National Action," that became widely repeated. The report was both attacked and defended for offering some strategies to reduce systematic racial poverty while withdrawing from addressing other concerns. Active religious communities are known for producing "community belonging, social solidarity, and social support; moral order, cosmic and life meaning, . . . artistic creations; opportunities for aesthetic expression . . . political legitimacy, and the legitimation of dissent" (C. Smith, *Religion*, 246). These outcomes are not brought about just by talking about them.

11. Daniel Stern, *Interpersonal World of the Infant*, 5–6, as cited in Means with Nelson, *Trauma and Evil*, 51.

12. Jaffee, "Discipleship."

13. Parker, "Disciple"; J. Campbell, "Disciple," 69. Campbell adds that the root

In some traditions, disciples retreat from or totally reject the social world. In others, like Judaism and Christianity, disciples are to be committed learners, with their purpose to be transformed into a new life for themselves and the world they inhabit. That happens through repentance, *teshuvah* (Hebrew, "to turn back") or *metanoia* (Greek, "to change one's mind"). Why turn back? It is to return home. The goal of discipleship is "to return home by deciding our faith in a loving God will not be peripheral to the rest of our life."[14]

WHAT IS THE COST AND JOY OF DISCIPLESHIP?

Earlier, I made clear that engaged or transformative spirituality requires discipline: building stamina, scoping out the terrain, preparing for the unexpected. Other costs come from speaking truth to power and persisting against the odds of failure when promoting what is right but unpopular. Eck cites studies that concluded only 2 percent of emergent adults are seriously spiritual. Engaged spiritual discipline requires tenacity to complete the "mission" successfully.[15]

While bike rides like RAGBRAI rarely result in accidents or fatalities, the legacy of spiritual discipleship is marked with martyrs. Take, for example, Dietrich Bonhoeffer, a German minister and theologian who chose to oppose the Nazi regime of the 1940s and was executed. He wrote extensively on discipleship.[16] He dismissed those who believed God's grace absolved disciples of living their faith in a half-hearted way. God offers a "costly grace," not a cheap grace—another paradox! Discipleship brings joy, but it also has costs.

Perhaps the biggest cost of being a disciplined traveler is that it requires you to be alone in study, reflection, and prayer from time to time.[17]

---

word can be understood as "apprentice." The Pashto word, taliban, means "students."

14. Heath, *Glorify*, 48. See 39–51 for context. Hindus have similar words that call adherents to come back home or to Hinduism.

15. Wuthnow, *All in Sync*, 43–44, 52–55, speaks of spirituality being driven by a consumer mentality, wanting things as quickly as possible, with as little effort as necessary. In another context, Eck, *New Religious America*, wonders if we expect our shopping malls to replace our public squares as places where we discuss religious issues.

16. Bonhoeffer, *Discipleship*. An excellent biography is Metaxas, *Bonhoeffer*.

17. Kielsmeier-Cook, *Blessed are the Nones*, 102–14. The author and her husband asked each other at the end of each day these two questions: Where did you give or receive the most love today? Where did you give or receive the least love today?

Spiritually, you can be alone together with others. Psychologist Bruno Bettelheim (1903–1990), observing young children in classes, described the scene as one of "collective individualism." That will be the joy of your spiritual bike ride, the love and care of those who coach and teach you, the concern of those who organize and oversee the day-to-day travels, and interactions you will have with fellow travelers, who model discipleship and friendship for you and with you. Look at **activity 3.2**.

WHO CALLS US TO BE DISCIPLES AND TRAVELERS?

Historically, people have found "masters" whom we remember as founders of world religions. Although Hinduism has no single founder, its Indian founders proclaimed all people are part of one reality. In India, the Buddha (563–c. 483 BCE) was a teacher who offered an approach to life that emphasized forces of good and evil striving to separate humanity but who urged all to strive for unity. His contemporary Confucius (551–479 BCE) offered teachings that were not so much a theology but ethical instruction on self-fulfillment, in part by reaching out to other people. In the Western world, Judaism traces its roots back to such leaders as Moses (c. 1355 BCE). Moses led a nomadic people from servitude to an Egyptian pharaoh to freedom, which includes a fabled tale of a dramatic exodus. The people later became the nation of Israel. A Jewish Israelite teacher, Jesus of Nazareth (born c. 6 BCE), is regarded as the founder of Christianity. In 570 CE, a prophet named Muhammad founded Islam, interpreted as searching for peace. Judaism, Christianity, and Islam are sometimes referred to as the Abrahamic faiths because all three claim Abraham as one of their founders.[18]

I could continue describing other religious founders, but that becomes a non-chemical sleeping pill. My point is that you must be incredibly careful about the leadership in a spiritual community. Don't go just by someone's favorable reputation. Take the time to find out if the master is more concerned about his or her own well-being or the community's future. Describe your leader preference in **activity 3.3**.

---

18. The Islamic view of Christians is that they are People of the Book. Boyett, *Twelve Major World Religions*, presents easily understood descriptions of various faith traditions' beliefs and rituals.

Grandpa talking here: I'm not the first and won't be the last to warn you that there are phony, manipulating hustlers out there posing as spiritual mentors. As you read this section, you will find some descriptors of those who should be avoided. Granted, some fit the stereotypes of a master: a hermit in a mountaintop cave, a Greek philosopher, a guru from India, or a mysterious sage. From another perspective, masters include political leaders, from Caesar on a throne to the twentieth century's Adolf Hitler, who skillfully used his rhetoric to call for a pure race that would control Europe and the world. Past and present, tyrants' voices decimate governments for their evil purposes.[19] The uncertainty of today is fertile ground for despots and autocratic rulers, as well as secular and spiritual hucksters. Be especially wary of those who say they alone possess the truth or can provide a better way.

Too often, charismatic leaders and cults have devastating consequences. In a cult, the leader controls the truth, teachings, and rulings on members' behaviors. Limits on communication and frequent testing of loyalty are red flags. A colleague demonstrated this for his class by placing a Bible—an old, tattered one—on the floor and then stomping on it repeatedly. To his shocked students, he declared what a cult leader would proclaim, "I'm more important than the Bible. My interpretation is all you need to know. Trust me as the source of everything."[20]

WHAT DO DISCIPLES BELIEVE? WHAT DO DISCIPLES PRACTICE?

You'll need nourishment if you go on a spiritual bike ride. I'll make a special BLT sandwich for your sustenance. Ingredients: beauty, love, and truth, with a side order of humor. Consider it a tasty treat with more time and space in later chapters to slowly relish the complete tastes. Feel like you're too busy now to make that bike ride? What are your priorities?

19. Levitsky and Ziblatt, *How Democracies Die*. Pages 23–24 describe four key indicators of authoritarian behaviors that destroy democracy: 1) rejection of (or weak commitment) to democratic rules and norms, 2) denial of the legitimacy of political opponents, 3) toleration or encouragement of violence, and 4) readiness to curtail civil liberties. They warn that the United States of America's democracy has serious challenges.

20. Recall the stories of the fire in 1993 of the Branch Davidian cult of Waco, Texas, led by David Koresh or the earlier 1978 murder-suicide of 900-plus followers of Jim Jones's Peoples Temple in Guyana.

Make time for it. In *Falling Upwards*, Richard Rohr posits there are two halves to adult life: in the first half, we focus on essentials such as finding jobs or establishing homes; and in the second, we *should* focus on our spiritual selves.

Beliefs

Humans are belief machines. We use beliefs to develop our meanings and values. Examples: we believe the sun comes up every morning. Because of science and technology, most of us believe in vanity products, vaccines, and our vehicle's bells and whistles. Other types of belief include the testimonies of ancients and contemporaries regarding sacred scriptures and practices. Multiple types of beliefs blend to become our faiths.

Most spiritual realms develop beliefs about an ultimate power (god or gods), the universe, the significance of a founder or principal teachers, the goodness or evil of humans, relationships to others, and what happens after death.[21] In some traditions, like Christianity, the beliefs became formal dogma or doctrines and were made into creeds. Episcopal Bishop John Spong became famous in the late twentieth century for wanting to terminate the creeds.[22] Diana Butler Bass more recently posits, somewhat similarly, that younger generations and church alumni are abandoning the ancient three-tiered worldview of God in heaven, the sky, and the earth in favor of a spiritual revolution that recognizes God as active in the world and humans invited to be God's partner.[23]

Studies suggest that boomers, post-boomers, Gen-Xers, millennials, and emerging adults in their twenties are looking for something more substantive than entertainment. Granted, megachurches with newer religious music, casual services, and extensive programming attract a fair share of attendees. But what do younger generations believe? A ten-year

21. Prothero, *God Is Not One*, describes eight major religions, describing each in terms of offering a "way of . . . " They are Islam: submission; Christianity: salvation; Confucianism: propriety; Hinduism: devotion; Buddhism: awakening; Yoruba: connection; Judaism: exile and return; and Daoism: flourishing. He adds a chapter on atheism as the way of reason.

22. Spong, *Why Christianity Must Change*. A similar stance is offered by Cook, *Christianity beyond Creeds*.

23. Diana Bass, *Grounded*. Raman, *Deus Ubiqutius*, has in-depth coverage of beliefs about God and examples of spiritual practices from many traditions. See also Matlins and Magida, *How to Be a Perfect Stranger*.

study followed teens through their late twenties (officially, the National Study of Youth and Religion). It concluded they held, somewhat loosely, a spiritual outlook that could be described as do-it-yourself (DIY) spirituality. Its key propositions: karma is real, everybody goes to heaven, just be good, it's all good (do anything you want, but don't hurt anyone), religion is easy, morals are self-evident, and live with no regrets.[24] An underlying finding from these studies is that while younger persons may hold these beliefs, for most they aren't easily articulated and are infrequently referenced in critical decision-making.[25]

Practices

Sticking with my BLT sandwich image, I'm saying your beliefs are the condiments that give your spirituality its unique flavor. The practices you follow are the bread slices that keep the sizzling bacon, juicy tomato, and lettuce from being a delicious but spilled mess. Some will be individual or personal, others public or communal. For the Abrahamic faiths, attending worship, praying, and reading Scriptures are the primary practices.[26] Typical non-theistic spiritual practices include meditation, yoga, breathing exercises, and, in some traditions, study. Literally, there are hundreds of practices.[27] Interestingly, some studies suggest that even those who claim to have no religion or have minimal interest in spiritual matters acknowledge that in some of their ordinary events they recognize something spiritual. Drescher calls these the four *f*s: family, friends, food, and Fido (for pets).[28]

24. Flory and Miller, *Finding Faith*, and Denton and Flory, "DIY Religious Outlook." See also Drescher, *Choosing Our Religion*, and Denton and Flory, *Back-Pocket God*.

25. These studies also found that most teenagers remain in their parents' religious traditions.

26. Dorothy Bass, *Practicing Our Faith*; Drury, *Spiritual Disciplines*; Diana Bass, *Christianity for the Rest*. McLaren, *Finding Our Way Again*, and Putnam et al., *American Grace*, provide extensive analysis of current practices

27. Harvey, *Direct Path*, and C. Smith, *Religion*, 29. Reprinted as **appendix 5B**. This is a chart listing over one hundred practices.

28. Drescher, *Choosing Our Religion*, 43–44. A sharp contrast to this "loose" interpretation is found in Manskar, *Accountable Discipleship*. Bender, *Heaven's Kitchen*, offers a sociologist's description of spiritual practices and religious conversations at a food kitchen.

You may feel these four indicators are too broad or non-traditional. One 2007 list of practices and attitudes of spiritually mature persons included a daily time of private prayer, a sense of God's presence in their lives, and religion as a source of strength in healing conflicts. In attitudes, they experienced a sense of inner peace, were joyful, felt humbler, and were less racially prejudiced. In terms of action, they were more favorable toward their spiritual community's involvement in social justice, more open to reconciliation efforts, and became more engaged in compassionate projects.[29]

In other chapters, we'll revisit some of those claims. For now, spiritual persons—disciples—claim their voice is powered by what they consider the ultimate mystery.[30] They find, although not always, more satisfaction with their family and personal lives, careers, and involvement with others. But be cautious. Some traditions have stories about those who seem to have followed the prescribed laws out of duty rather than love or concern for others.[31]

Wait a minute. Aren't disciples expected to be perfect?

CAN YOU BE PERFECT?

Can anyone be perfect? Sounds like a *duh* question. Unfortunately, racists, past and present, believe certain groups can never be perfect because of color. With tribalism and nationalism festering, dare we laugh at Mark Twain's introduction of Winston Churchill at a banquet, when he joked Churchill was perfect because his father was English and his mother American?

29. H. Miller, "Do We Help People." See also Gallup and Jones, *Saints among Us.*

30. Parks, *Big Questions,* 26. Prothero, *God Is Not One,* closes with an epilogue noting that the beliefs and practices, while different, all tell us that this world is not our home, but in the end "work not so much to help us flee from our humanity as to bring us home to it." Chapters 5 through 8 of this book describe a variety of spiritual practices. Richard Rohr, in such sources as *Immortal Diamond* and *Falling Upward,* asserts that spiritual journaling is work and that all religions offer sympathy, empathy, and connection. Rohr believes we are all made for union with one another, expressed through different rituals, doctrines, dogmas, or beliefs. The goal is always union with the divine.

31. See Bonhoeffer, *Discipleship,* 74, 128, 145, 206, 278, for Bonhoeffer's interpretation of a conversation Jesus had with a man who asked about living a righteous life (Matt 19:16–22). His answer could be an answer to who are "perfect," or of one mind with God (see Matt 5).

In some things, we want perfection. In baseball, a pitcher celebrates a perfect game when he gets all twenty-seven batters out. You hope to facilitate a perfect meeting. We compliment loved ones for cooking a perfect meal. Couples may recall their wedding was perfect. We hope for perfection in our mates, but the ironic truth is, as a minister's story puts it, a bachelor who thought he had found the perfect woman to marry later informed the minister there would be no wedding because she was looking for the perfect man!

Some Christians are hung up on perfection because of their interpretation of one of Jesus's instructions to disciples in the Sermon on Mount.[32] "Be perfect, therefore, as your heavenly Father is perfect" (Matt 5:48). Early church founders buttressed that with the belief that God is perfect, and Jesus Christ is "the perfecter of our faith" because of his sacrificial love (Heb 12:2). The author of Hebrews therefore admonished readers, "Let us go on toward perfection" (6:1).

Ball game over. No way I'm perfect. I wrestled with that, too. Here's what I found out . . . and it is good news. That understanding of perfection is based on Greek thinking about good and evil that concluded that the body, because it decays, is imperfect; only the soul could be perfect. The philosopher Aristotle (384–322 BCE) defined perfect as "lacking nothing in respect of goodness or excellence,"[33] which led Christians to believe the goal is to strive for a life without flaws. The counterargument from Hebrew language scholars is that a better translation of the Matthew 5 phrase is "Be merciful, even as your Father is merciful." Other possible translations for perfect are "having integrity," "being mature in the faith," or "being righteous."[34] The scriptural intent is clear: in gratitude for God's love for us, imperfect as we are, we do our best as individuals to lead a good life, loving neighbors and strangers as well as ourselves and

32. Many scholars believe these instructions for his followers were compiled over time. The Gospel of Luke offers a similar collection of comments called the Sermon on the Plain (Luke 6:20–49). Psalm 15 suggests a blameless lifestyle ought to be sought.

33. Aristotle, *Metaphysics* 5, as cited in J. Campbell, "Perfection."

34. Borg, *Speaking Christian*, 131–41, argues "be righteous" is a better translation than "be perfect." J. Campbell, "Perfection," offers "upright" or "blameless" as other interpretations. Campbell argues that in both the Hebrew Scriptures' and the Greek New Testament's descriptions of perfection, there is no expectation that humans are expected to be without flaws. Closer to our time, John Wesley, founder of Methodism, wrote "A Plain Account of Christian Perfection." Wesley spoke of a quest to be more than Christ, but he did not believe in flawlessness. Norris, *Amazing Grace*, 57, opts for perfection as meaning growth or maturity.

ourselves and our families. Recalling St. Francis, Richard Rohr provides an appropriate closing thought: "The demand for the perfect is the greatest enemy of the good."[35]

To return to the bicycle analogy, assume you really want to participate in a parallel spiritual journey. You hire someone as a trainer or mentor, scope out the challenges of the moral terrain, reserve accommodations (attend some meetings), and spend hours involved in study and social action projects. What benefits can you expect from these efforts?

THE FIRST BENEFIT: NEW FRIENDS!

First and always, disciplined spiritual travelers are learners. In time, in natal homes and healthy spiritual homes, siblings can become best friends. *Friend* is a powerful word. It can be much more than a pal, buddy, acquaintance, classmate, or colleague, as the television series *Friends* (1994–2004) and the movie *The Shawshank Redemption* (1994) reveal. Out of shared intense experiences, silly to serious, friends reveal innermost thoughts, improper behaviors, and improbable dreams to each other. Because true friends trust each other, heartfelt disagreements, tough criticisms, and fundamental differences are out in the open, dealt with, and fade into the shadows.[36]

Centuries ago, a Greek philosopher and a spiritual founder, miles and years apart, offered similar benefits of friendship. Aristotle (384–322 BCE) observed, "We need friends when we are young to keep us from error; when we get old to tend upon us and to carry out those plans which we have no strength to execute ourselves, and in the prime of life to help us in noble deeds."[37] The Buddha (563–c. 483 BCE) noted, a friend "guards you when you are off your guard and does not forsake you in trouble; he even lays down his life for your sake; he restrains you from doing wrong; he enjoins you to do right; . . . he reveals to you the way of heaven."[38]

---

35. Rohr, *Falling Upward*, xxiii. See also Kurtz and Ketcham, *Spirituality of Imperfection*.

36. Daniel, "Insights of Isolation," describes how we separate ourselves from friends. Prothero, *Religious Literacy*, 147, describes how the Secular Left and the Religious Right could avoid culture wars and loss of friendship if a middle path were used regarding Bible study and discussions.

37. Aristotle, *Nicomachean Ethics*, 7.1.1.

38. Suttanta, *Dialogues of the Buddha*, 177–79. Cf. Howard, "Fellowship of Love,"

Hebrew Scriptures speak of a friend as one "who is as your own soul" (Deut 13:6 NKJV) or "one who sticks closer than one's kin" (Prov 18:24). Jesus, a Jew, would have known these sayings.[39] At the end of his earthly life, the soon-to-be-departed Jesus tells his disciples that he is not their master; they are not his servants but friends.

> No one has greater love than this, to lay down one's life for one's friends. You are my friends if you do what I command you. I do not call you servants any longer, because the servant does not know what the master is doing; but I have called you friends, because I have made known to you everything that I have heard from my Father.[40]

Are such friendships present in today's spiritual homes? I hope so. They should mirror as much, if not more, than the messages of such popular songs as "Lean on Me" and Carole King's "You've Got a Friend." Fred Rogers, the gentle host of the mythical television neighborhood, is a model for a child's adult friend. Granted, it takes time to get to know newcomers in a group. A key is that friendship involves a genuine interest in the other person, a willingness to offer support, a guarantee of trust and dependability based on time with that person. Martin Buber described it as an "I-thou" rather than an "I-it" relationship, a fancy way of saying you treat the person you are speaking with as a person, not as an object, by listening purposefully and intently, to understand what he/she is saying.[41] In friendship, one believes in the other, commits to working together without reservation, and, like the military, is willing to sacrifice his or her life for the other. **Activity 3.4** recommends some suggestions for how to begin conversations with possible new friends.

723.

39. Drescher, *Choosing Our Religion*, 123, cites the adage "Tell me who your friends are, and I'll tell you what you believe." See her section on communities, 93–144.

40. John 15:13–15. Searcy and Thomas, *Activate*, contend that one is more likely in small groups to develop new friendships than intimate relationships. A different interpretation of John 15:13–15 is "Love one another the way I loved you. This is the very best way to love. Put your life on the line for your friends" (*The Message*).

41. Buber, *I and Thou*; see also Buber, *Between Man and Man*.

THE SECOND BENEFIT—A MORAL SERVANT LEADER

Why call leadership a benefit? Whether it is that bike event, a business, factory, civic organization, or home, a person or group will lead or manage the changes in life that occur. That applies to our spiritual lives as well. You know that there are always those who want change and those who want the security of the status quo.[42] Whom do you picture as leaders or changers?[43]

Rack your brain for images of servants. Do the same for leaders. Now try to picture someone who is a superb blend of both. It's hard! That paradoxical reality is difficult to visualize. Most movies depict strongwilled generals rallying reluctant troops to overcome terrible odds. Conversely, *Mr. Roberts* (1955) and *The Caine Mutiny* (1954) depicted flawed commanding officers overcome by others with integrity. A powerful image of servant leadership is an artist's depiction of the Last Supper, when Jesus, with a towel symbolizing servanthood, washes the disciples' dusty feet before their meal.[44]

Why bring this paradox of servant leadership into the discussion about discipleship? In Western cultures, leaders in business, politics, even religion, are authority figures. Usually outgoing and often charismatic, even confrontational, these leaders expect their employees, customers, clients, members to support their visions. Yet, sometimes they forget when and how to lead! The story is told of two churches that merged at a Sunday service. The congregations scheduled a celebratory parade to their suburb's downtown. But after the service, the ministers became so engrossed in a conversation that the members grew impatient and started the parade. In their robes and stoles, the clergy were soon in hot pursuit, shouting, "Wait for us! We're your leaders!"

---

42. Kegan and Lahey, *Immunity to Change*, point out on occasion, there are legitimate reasons to resist change. They emphasis needed changes don't occur until "big assumptions and assertions" are successfully challenged.

43. You may be familiar with the Myers-Briggs instrument. Somewhat similar is the enneagram of personality, mentioned in ch. 2. Some advocates believe they can give you insights into your personal strengths, including leadership.

44. John 13:4–10. In the religious traditions where clergy wear robes and stoles, the stoles are a symbol, like the towel, of servanthood. Some Christian traditions follow Jesus's example of washing feet as a ritual of humility; see Fryholm, "Strange, Humble Ritual," 22–25.

In government, corporations, denominations—with few exceptions—hierarchical structures keep the systems going. In the American secular world, a new leadership philosophy emerged in the 1970s. Robert K. Greenleaf proposed businesses adopt servant leader attributes.[45] In this model, leaders share power, staff well-being is stressed, and a primary goal is better customer service. I add the term *moral* servant leadership, borrowing from Robert Coles, whose long list of insightful qualities concludes, "To be a moral leader is, then, to call upon moral passion within oneself, set it in motion among others"[46] and to do so resourcefully, pointedly.

Ironically, this model has been available in world religions for several thousand years.[47] Eboo Patel, the founder of the Interfaith Youth Core organization, recalls those who motivated him were servant leaders from various traditions, including Dorothy Day, the Roman Catholic, lay founder of a workers' movement; the Dalai Lama; Mahatma Gandhi; and Malcolm X.[48]

"So what?" That's a legitimate response. What does it mean today for me? You may say, "I'm not a leader type; leave it to the professionals." Parker Palmer responds, "If it is true we are made for community, then leadership is everyone's vocation . . . when we live in the close-knit ecosystem called community, everyone follows, everyone leads."[49] If you still don't believe you should be a moral servant leader, talk with others you trust and discuss your passions, values, and causes. Would you be willing to be a leader for some of them?

45. Greenleaf, *On Becoming a Servant Leader*, and Hunter, *Servant*. Servant leaders are said to have ten capacities: listening, empathy, awareness, healing, persuasion, conceptualization, foresight, stewardship, commitment to the growth of people, and building community. See also Kea, "Skills That Make."

46. Coles, *Lives of Moral Leadership*, 191–92. Verbs Coles uses include exhort, remind, reprimand, reprove, stir, teach, dramatize, evoke, reason, uplift, enable, engage, spell out. The hymn "Won't You Let Me Be Your Servant?" has the paradoxical message that if we offer to be servants, we must be open to being served.

47. In Hebrew Scriptures, the chosen nation of Israel, its peoples, prophets, and kings, are described as servants of God. They are in a covenantal relationship. The prophet Isaiah speaks of the nation and a Messiah as "suffering servants." Jesus spoke of himself as "the servant of all." See M. Miller and Miller, *Harper's Bible Dictionary*, 666.

48. Patel, *Interfaith Leadership*. See also his *Acts of Faith*, xxvii–xxviii, and his *Out of Many Faiths*.

49. Palmer, *Let Your Life Speak*, 74 (for the larger context, see *Let Your Life Speak*, "Leading from Within," 73–94).

If you are open to considering leadership, here are some resources. They include lists of desirable qualities, along with multiple examples of success and failure.[50] On many lists, the top quality is "learner," followed by being "a good listener" and "empathetic." Another big one is "adaptability."[51] One study of leaders from different generations found that while the style in which these leaders approached problem-solving mirrored the common way things were done in the era in which they grew up, these leaders all understood how to remain calm under stress because each one had been through a crucible experience, a transforming event that helped them with meaning-making.[52] Why is this important? Each of us, in a home, business, or social situation, has dealt with and will confront change.[53]

TRAVELER: READY TO "RE-FORM" YOUR IDENTITY AND BECOME A LISTENING VOICE?

You may wonder if there are any fine print requirements when you become involved with a spiritual home. Must you become a disciple, friend, or moral servant leader? Answer: no! But your true self comes to understand why spiritual communities function with covenants rather than contracts. It's based on the concept that the creative Power has given you a better deal than you can imagine. In religious language, you are loved, forgiven, and granted grace even when you break your side of the bargain. When you hear and accept that message, your goal is not to be perfect but do the best you can. That commits you to "re-form" your voice and vocation by living your unique righteous life.[54]

Here's the fine print. There's no soul protection vaccine. There is a cost to being a disciplined spiritual traveler. Most important, you will best

50. Heifetz, *Leadership without Easy Answers*.

51. Parks, *Leadership Can Be Taught*, 153–55, 251–52. See 289–90 on religious leadership. Listening is also critical with families and relatives as Ogletree, "When You Become," reminds us.

52. Bennis and Thomas, *Geeks and Geezers*, 4, 17–18, 104–5, 161–62.

53. Heifetz and Linsky, *Leadership on the Line*. Searcy and Thomas, *Activate*, 64–71, argue that when organizations recruit prospective leaders, they should be called "apprentices" rather than "experts."

54. Inspired while at a revival in 1926, Daniel Iverson wrote a text asking God for such a re-forming, by being "melted, molded, filled, used." See the hymn "Spirit of the Living God," #283, in United Church of Christ, *New Century Hymnal*.

project your spiritual voice if you have first been an active listener. Then, as a leader, your voice is heard more through deeds than words. How do I know that? My careers taught me that every adult has an agenda. Trusting souls share their beliefs, goals, strengths, and weaknesses. Devious individuals bluff or lie about their shortcomings and assert support for outcomes they will undermine. A majority fall in the middle, cautiously sharing their visions, abilities, and challenges; they are minimal risk-takers. As mentioned earlier, there are parallel choices to going on a new venture like the bike ride. Your voice will tell others if you are a reluctant pioneer or an exuberant explorer when it comes to your spiritual adventure.

Traveler, the good news is that you are never alone. As your voice becomes stronger, as others see you grow in your vocation day in, day out, your voice can join with others in words, in songs, in deeds done, to build healthy spiritual homes and healthy neighborhoods.

Chapter 3 Activities

ACTIVITY 3.1: GOLD, SILVER, BRONZE

Early in the chapter, I used the analogy of becoming an excellent athlete as a positive example of discipline. Or as one of the saints of the historic church, Ambrose (c. 340–397 CE), supposedly said—and I'm paraphrasing—"A spiritual home should be like a gymnasium" or, today, a fitness club. If you are called to model and promote love for others, you can't rest on your laurels or, more bluntly, your backside. Just as an athlete must train, so a religious or spiritual person must be committed to a regimen of learning and growing in one's faith. That is, one must be disciplined, a disciple.

What is your inner voice telling you to prepare to do in life? If your voice is saying you have several things to work toward or accomplish, how would you prioritize them? What are its demands?

- Gold: what is the highest priority you have now?

- Silver: what is the second highest priority you have?

- Bronze: what is something important you wish to accomplish, but not as important as the previous two?

ACTIVITY 3.2: BLENDING MY VOICE WITH THE VOICE OF MY SPIRITUAL HOME[55]

1. Where were you born and reared?

2. What do you want to share about your natal/first family?

3. What brought you to this community (town or city)?

4. Who or what influenced you to become a _____ (specific religious denomination, faith tradition, or practitioner of a

---

55. Based in part upon a practice used in the Learning Center, an adult study group in the Ames United Church of Christ, Ames, IA (2018). From time to time, persons joining the congregation are invited to share what is called their "faith journey." These questions are meant only as a guide.

(*Activity 3.2 continued*)

5. specific spiritual lifestyle, or to become someone without a spiritual tradition)?

6. What brought you to this specific congregation?

7. How would you describe your current faith/spiritual outlook?

8. What is the most rewarding thing about being a part of this community?

9. What brings you your greatest joy(s)?

10. What are your greatest disappointments?

11. What has been the greatest change/challenge in your lifetime and how would you describe your response to it?

12. What would be the biggest hope you have for your spiritual home and your biggest concern or challenge it faces?

ACTIVITY 3.3: YOUR FAVORITE SPIRITUAL LEADER

Who is the spiritual leader you most admire, whom you now follow or would consider following? Is it a familiar person? Moses, Jesus, Muhammad, the Buddha, Confucius, Swami Vivekananda or another Hindu guru, or someone else? How much do you know about that person? If it is not a well-known figure, how did you learn about that individual? What did he or she say or do that makes him or her so special? What is it that you can do in your daily life that would best honor that person? Or, if you prefer to state it differently, how would that person want you to live your life?

ACTIVITY 3.4: CONVERSATIONS WITH FRIENDS, BECOMING A SERVANT LEADER

Do you make friends easily? When you are with new friends or business acquaintances or holding a conversation at a spiritual

(*Activity 3.4 continued*)

community, is it difficult to know what to say? Here are some possible questions to use.[56] Are there other questions you prefer?

- What keeps you busy outside of work?

- What are you concerned about (current issue)?

- What's new since the last time we talked?

- Suggestion: if asked to talk about yourself, give a one-sentence answer.

- If you are in a group, say, "What are everyone's plans?"

- With teenagers or young adults, "How do you make sense of what's happening?"

- Your questions: _____

"Truly great leaders are skilled at building healthy relationships."[57]

Assuming research supports the statement above (and it does, for businesses and non-profit organizations as well as religious organizations), what skills do you think are most important in building healthy relationships? Use single words or short phrases. Which ones do you believe you have now or could develop?

- Patience: showing self-control

- Kindness: giving attention, appreciation, and encouragement

- Humility: being authentic and without pretense or arrogance

- Respectfulness: treating everyone as important people

- Selflessness: meeting the needs of others

- Forgiveness: giving up resentment when wrong

- Honesty: being free from deception

- Commitment: sticking with decisions made

56. Fine, "First Art," 13.

57. Hunter, *Servant*, 101–19.

FOR ADDITIONAL CONVERSATIONS

Your identity and the process of developing a distinctive voice were dominant themes of this chapter. The subtle question is as you re-form yourself, will you also seek to re-form others?

- A helpful start to answer this question and related ones is Parker J. Palmer, *Let Your Life Speak: Listening for the Voice of Vocation*. A Quaker, the author's style suggests times of silence and meditation.

- For those who are research-oriented and still wrestling with the relevance of religion or spirituality, consider Christian Smith with Melinda Lundquist Denton, *Soul Searching: The Religious and Spiritual Lives of American Teenagers*.

- Still bugged about discipline and perfection? You will appreciate *The Spirituality of Imperfection: Storytelling and the Search for Meaning*. Authors Ernest Kurtz and Katherine Ketcham reflect the principles of Alcoholics Anonymous.

- Eboo Patel, founder and president of Interfaith Youth Core, promotes community improvement projects with the deliberate strategy of forming groups of persons from different faith perspectives. Read *Interfaith Leadership: A Primer*.

- How to engage in productive reflection on big questions and bring about change in yourself?—Marilee Adams, *Change Your Questions, Change Your Life: Twelve Powerful Tools for Leadership, Coaching, and Life*. If in organizations, Timothy R. Clark, *EPIC Change: How to Lead Change in the Global Age*.

4

Community— "Con-Formed" by Comfort and Confrontation

The Lord is my shepherd: therefore, I lack nothing. He shall feed me in a green pasture; and lead me forth beside the waters of comfort. . . . Yea, though I walk through the valley of the shadow of death, I will fear no evil; for thou art with me; thy rod and thy staff comfort me.

—Psalm 23:1–2, 4–5, *Book of Common Prayer* (1662)

Then, when the prayer is finished, scatter in the land and seek God's bounty, and remember God frequently, happily you will prosper . . . . Say: "What is with God is better than diversion and merchandise. God is the best of providers."

—Qur'an, LXII, Congregation

Choose confrontation wisely, but when it is your time don't be afraid to stand up, speak up, and speak out against injustice.

—John Lewis (d. 2020), Congressman, civil rights leader

Once upon a time, a town had a Temperance Society—we might call that AA today. Would you believe it took out an ad in the local paper advertising that its next meeting would begin with a cocktail hour? Point: be watchful to see that your spiritual community maintains its integrity and credibility.

—retelling of a story from Halford E. Luccock, *Like A Mighty Army*, 81–83

YOUR COMMISSION AND COMMUNITY: TO COMFORT AND CONFRONT

- Invitation: To become a welcoming stranger on the Spiritual Express

- Why begin talking about a commission?—Your ticket for the Spiritual Express

- To what does comfort refer?

- What do sacred scriptures and stories say about comfort?

- What about spiritual practices of comfort for today and tomorrow?

- What is confrontation?

- What do sacred scriptures and stories say about confrontation?

- Are you willing to confront with love?

- What practices relate to ways of loving confrontation today?

- Traveler: What's your commission: are you becoming a welcoming stranger?

- Activities

- For Additional Conversations

In chapters 1 and 2, I used two stories—my conversation with a voice and the foiled bank robbery—to illustrate we are all spiritual; we search for life's meanings but find them in different ways. Chapter 3, with the metaphor of a bicycle event, suggests we have choices as disciplined travelers to become one or more of the following: disciples, friends, and moral servant leaders. Ultimately, our intended outcome is to develop our unique spiritual voices and vocations.

INVITATION: TO BECOME A WELCOMING STRANGER ON THE SPIRITUAL EXPRESS

Chapter 4 uses a second transportation metaphor: a train trip. Imagine being invited to go on a trip by train I'm calling the Spiritual Express. No, not a plush dome car viewing the wilds of Alaska, hobnobbing on the mysterious Orient Express, or hiding on the Twentieth-Century Limited in the Alfred Hitchcock thriller *North by Northwest* (1959). Picture instead one where singer Kenny Rogers met a dying gambler who taught him "when to hold 'em" and "when to fold 'em." I recall a hissing steam engine with bumpy cars I took from Texas to Chicago going to college, or later grimy diesel commuters in New York City. Whatever your train image, the passengers represent a diversity of ages, ethnicities, social classes, and political and religious persuasions.

As a passenger on that train, you have a choice to engage or not to engage in conversations with other passengers. Would you or they initiate the getting acquainted ritual? I urge you to become a welcoming stranger. Why? So when you visit a new spiritual community, you will feel more comfortable meeting other spiritual travelers.

Now, more on the express. Assume you and others have chosen to go to a common destination. If it is a spiritual location, what are the spiritual outcomes you and others expect to achieve? I assume it is not the dystopia of *The Hunger Games* (2012–2015). A positive answer—parallel to a natal or first home—could be that you are seeking a place that provides something you are missing: comfort, care, and vibrant adventures. Would you also want those at this destination to challenge you, thoughtfully, about critical life decisions you are making? Would you want them to help you to fulfill your worthy dreams? If this train is truly special—like Disney's 2004 *Polar Express*—its conductors would guide you to its amenities and caution you about its dangers. Who knows, in time, you might take on the conducting role.[1]

Turn your Spiritual Express itinerary into an adventure! Don't we all crave adventure?[2] The summer of 1959 was an adventure for me. Newly married, with one year of seminary under my belt, I served as a licensed minister in Danville, Illinois. One day the church custodian and I had a conversation. His friend was the janitor for a different congregation in town, which he referred to as "the seven-day adventure" church. I knew he meant the Seventh-Day Adventist church, but I thought, what a wonderful image for a vibrant spiritual community! Through the years, often in surprising locations and conditions, I've seen small and large groups who were, individually and corporately, having loving, caring, sharing adventures.

"Slow down," you say. "Why can't I be spiritual on my own, out in the garden on a Sunday morning? What's wrong with meditating solo on a mountaintop watching a sunrise or sunset?" If you are a millennial, Gen Z, or a None of the above, I could expect, "My time is limited. I can't get too involved," or "I am willing to be a believer but not a belonger."[3] Another option to check out is New Monasticism. Please note, I am not saying that you shouldn't or couldn't become a spiritual hermit. A famous group of "withdrawers," the Essenes, lived in isolation near the Dead Sea.[4] The Essenes were Jews wanting to reform Judaism. Followers of the Buddha, Muhammad, and Confucius sometimes preferred solitary lifestyles and became monks and nuns.[5] Consider these realities. We need to be

---

1. Rupp, *Globalization Challenged*, 32. The author notes that Confucians, Jews, and Muslims especially make clear that the community "has logical, temporal, and normative priority over the individual." In an earlier book, *Commitment and Community*, Rupp emphasizes ways that spiritual communities influence the wider cultures.

2. Attributed to Helen Keller (1880–1968):"Security is mostly a superstition. It does not exist in nature. Life is either a daring adventure or nothing."

3. Mercadante, *Belief without Borders*. The linkage of believing and belonging was described as a post-World War II phenomenon by Grace Davie in *Religion in Britain*. See also Oakes, *Nones Are Alright*, and Drescher, *Choosing Our Religion*.

4. Latourette, *History of Christianity*, ch. 7, "The Rise of Monasticism," 221–35.

5. Freedman and McClymond, *Rivers of Paradise*, 178–80, focus on Buddhist monastic life. Zavada, "Monasticism," states the term *monks* comes from the Greek word *monachos*, which means a solitary life. Johnston's *Encyclopedia of Monasticism* is a survey of monastic traditions around the world.

affirmed, accepted, and appreciated; we want to be a part of something successful.[6] Most of us learn best from others, be it teachers, a support group, coaches, trade masters, or artists. These mentors critique what we think we have learned, evaluate, and help us hone our skills. They boost our confidence, so that as individuals or in teams we can experience amazing results. Anthropologist Margaret Mead (1901–1978) is said to have observed: "Never doubt that a small group of thoughtful, committed citizens can change the world; indeed, it's the only thing that ever has." Religious and educational organizations have proven that for years.[7]

It follows that healthy spiritual homes, mirroring our biological homes, provide us with excellent odds of positively experiencing two fundamental facets of life: comfort—safety, shelter, encouragement, and validation—and confrontation—meaningful questions as we test boundaries, grapple with unexpected illnesses and grief, and weigh life-changing decisions. No wonder that after we complete adventures, we often want to journey home.

WHY BEGIN TALKING ABOUT A COMMISSION?— YOUR TICKET FOR THE SPIRITUAL EXPRESS

Back to the train. Buying a ticket indicates you're willing to make a commitment of time and money to do something—granted, in a train analogy, it could include a vacation, but here it is more serious—to enhance your spirituality. I'm going to call it a commission not only for you but for the community of which you become a part. While I'm citing the Christian tradition, other faith traditions have similar imperatives.[8] Jesus commissioned his followers to go out "two by two" to share their view

6. Wolf, *Treating the Self*, 55, adds that although we need to be with others and "like" others, we want an environment where we can express a diverse point of view that is not discouraged.

7. Donahue and Robinson, *Church of Small Groups*, recounts this strategy at Willow Creek Community Church (IL), one of the nation's first megachurches. The largest United Church of Christ congregation is Trinity Church, Chicago, which insists that every member join a committee to avoid "getting lost." Recall Daniel's comment about spiritual homes, *Apologizing*, 131, cited in ch. 1. The first international book club, the Chautauqua Literary and Scientific Circle, was successful in large part because its readers met in small circles of readers. See Talbot, *Chautauqua's Heart*.

8. Paris, *Virtues and Values*, 5, begins a discussion of why and how "the preservation and promotion of community is the paramount goal of African peoples in all spheres of life."

of God's good news, and recruit others to then spread the word.[9] What is meant by commission? Embedded in it is the word *mission*. In secular examples, a commission may be a group chosen to find solutions to a problem like the coronavirus or a sales staff being paid a commission on the percentage of sales. A spiritual community is often called to do a task at a specific destination.

Another Danville, Illinois, story. That summer of 1959, I was challenged to rethink what a spiritual commission meant. One day I received a phone call. The frantic voice on the other end pleaded, "Please come as soon as you can. Our mother just died of a pulmonary embolism!" The grieving husband and grown children were in deep shock. They shared details of this beloved woman's death, and we all cried. I offered what I hoped were words of comfort, followed by a prayer. The family, self-admittedly only Christmas and Easter church attenders, wanted to make initial funeral service and burial arrangements. As the husband escorted me to the door, he blurted, "I don't know much about church and know nothing about funerals, but I do know you need to be paid; what's your commission?" It was much more than a mistaken impression of how ministers are paid; it was a profound theological question. Every one of us, be it a disciple, minister, or community member, should ask himself/herself that question frequently. "What is my/our commission?" For religious believers, "What does God want me/us to do?" A worthy dreamer might think, "How should I use my talents for good now?"[10] The answer may come through sacred scriptures, words and examples from the founder, current authorities, practices developed by the historic body of believers, and personal prayer.

In case the term *commission* doesn't float your boat, put it another way. A popular term in sports or coach-speak today is *culture*. To be successful, everyone on the team needs to buy in to common objectives so a championship is won. That requires commitments by everyone to conditioning, roles taken and given up, studying, and practicing. The best

9. See the Great Commission (Mark 16:15; Matt 28:18–20) and another passage that describes a variety of specific ministries (Matt 25).

10. Rasnake, *Spiritual Gifts*, offers extensive examples for identifying and equipping oneself with spiritual gifts. He has a conversative Christian perspective. Nangle, *Engaged Spirituality*, includes descriptions of more generalized and politically oriented responses (gifts). Parachin, *Engaged Spirituality*, describes ten individuals and how their inspiring gifts reformed and transformed the lives of many others.

coaches are masters of knowing when to offer comfort and when to challenge so the culture's goal can be reached.

Imagine you are now boarding the express. Understandably, you may still wonder about where you are to sit and how to interact with other passengers. I know speaking with strangers, or even some relatives, isn't always easy. In 2017, a study found one in six Americans reported they no longer spoke with family or friends following the 2016 election. In 2019, researchers learned that nearly 20 percent of American respondents believed the US would be better off if significant numbers of the opposing party died. One-third of some survey respondents assume a civil war is coming.[11] Assume you are in a coach car but don't have a specific seat. Especially if you are uncomfortable with strangers, you may feel the Spiritual Express is a wheeled wilderness!

Recall chapter 2, where I described how it is common in spiritual travels that individuals facing a crisis need time alone, away, or in isolation—a wilderness—to find what they are about. Walter Brueggemann, in *Journey to the Common Good*, describes how the Hebrews in slavery to the pharoah of Egypt made their escape to the Sinai desert. Their exodus became a people's wilderness.[12] During that time, individually and communally, they sorted out who they were and what they valued and charted their future. I submit that today, individually, nationally, and internationally, we passengers on planet Earth need time to think alone. But we need time together, in tribes, agencies, and communities to face the future. As you travel, you will find opportunities when you need to sit with and recognize the needs and dreams of former strangers. Who knows? Your role may become that of the conductor in a club car or diner offering comfort and confrontation. Bless you when you provide both![13]

11. Ruger, "Science Gives Us Recipe."

12. Brueggemann, *Journey to Common Good*.

13. H. Gates, "How Black Churches," 14, alerts readers to the 2021 PBS documentary *The Black Church: This Is Our Story, This Is Our Song*. Pitts, "Small Wonder," describes how religious traditions are shrinking because of being too willing to let politics control their mission. See also Pitts, "Greed Is Only Greed." The columnist identifies us as living in an "era of famished decency" and calls on us to give each other a generosity of spirit, "emotional comfort food." Richard Rohr warns us to avoid emptiness, individual and community. (*Immortal Diamond*, 32, 63).

TO WHAT DOES COMFORT REFER?

It is easy to understand the concept of comfort. If you grew up in a loving home, you found it a safe and secure environment. It provided you with clothing, food, a warm bed, and lots of love. When you bruised a knee or cut a finger, someone there put on a patch and kissed the hurt away. When thunder boomed or a neighbor's dog growled, a parent's voice or presence reassured you. Through vacations, your family introduced you to new places and people. As you progressed through school, engaged in athletics, or stressed about jobs and career choices, your home encouraged you. These are examples of comfort to which we want to "con-form."

Yes, there is unhealthy comfort and, worse, misdirected care. Helicopter parents' hover about their children, stifling their independence. Snowplow parents make trips to college campuses, meet their child's professors, and sign up their offspring for classes. Tragically, some families not only destroy comfort but maim and kill their children. A drug-fueled parent puts a toddler on a chair in the middle of a busy street. A guardian sells a child to sex traffickers. An immoral patriarch models cruelty. For most of us, our homes were mainly comfortable, with minimal dysfunction.

Similarly, healthy spiritual homes offer comfort through deeds of caregiving.[14] For example, trusting teachers nurture faith formation, youth group mentors and summer camp counselors assist the passage through difficult teen experiences, and caring spiritual leaders guide couples experiencing pre-marriage jitters. Scriptural passages like Ps 23 bring peace to grieving families.[15]

Just as biological homes can fail at providing the proper kinds of comfort, so can faith communities. Sociologist Robert Wuthnow described a seductively flawed model in 1950s congregations, who "became comfortable, familiar, domestic, offering an image of God that was basically congruent with the domestic tranquility of the ideal home."[16] What

14. Wuthnow, *After Heaven*, 28, offers the example of millions of Jews who migrated to the United States between the 1870s and 1920s and were offered "homes" by benevolent societies and synagogues.

15. Westberg, *Good Grief*, is a long-standing popular resource for assisting those experiencing grief. Rabbi Steve Leder, *Beauty of What Remains*, 113–15, always recites Ps 23 at burials. His two emphases: first, we aren't in the valley forever, and second, we see shadow because of light, and that light eventually restores hope.

16. Wuthnow, *After Heaven*, as cited in Diana Bass, *Strength for the Journey*, 109. That "ideal" interpretation assumes that the family was structured "with divine

is wrong with that? Spiritual homes are different from civic clubs. Yes, they both urge us to serve others, but spiritual homes challenge us to have higher goals as they understand a divine being or are consistent with what their religious forebears prescribed.

WHAT DO SACRED SCRIPTURES AND STORIES SAY ABOUT COMFORT?

Most spiritual traditions agree that it is during times of distress that spiritual friends are needed the most.[17] A Buddhist prayer begins, "May [name of intended recipient] be well, happy, and peaceful," then repeats the phrase for his or her teachers, parents, relatives, friends—even the indifferent and unfriendly ones—and all beings. Thich Nhat Hanh writes that the *sangha*, or community, is the place for healing of the self and society. "If your society is in trouble, if your family is broken, if your [faith] is no longer capable of providing you with spiritual life, then you work to take refuge in the *sangha* so that you can restore your strength, your understanding, your compassion, your confidence."[18] An Islamic prayer reminds Muslims that they are sheltered by Allah and are safe, protected, warm, and have nothing to fear or regret. As such, all should be at peace. In the Hebrew Scriptures, many psalms (1, 22, 23, 42, and 43) mention *shalom*, or peace. An African American spiritual recalls the healing oil, "the balm of Gilead."[19] Likewise, the prophet Isaiah's words to the nation Israel wanting a messiah were, "Comfort, comfort my people" (Isa 40:1). Jeremiah, another prophet, bought a field while Jerusalem was under siege as a sign that the people who were previously taken into captivity would be returning (Jer 32). We may debate whether I am emphasizing comfort over care. I think not.

---

predictability: God, husband, wife, children, servants . . ." Is that the only acceptable model for families?

17. Stewart-Sicking, *Spiritual Friendship after Religion*, 61. Beadle and Haskins, *Acting on Faith*, have numerous stories of multifaith activism. Harvey, *Direct Path*, describes many situations in which friends suggested helpful spiritual practices.

18. Hanh, "What Is Sangha?"

19. McCann, *Great Psalms*, 1. The author analyzes twelve psalms with many examples of both comfort and confrontation. Jeremiah 8:22 bemoans Israel's disobedience which will not be comforted by the famous healing oil.

WHAT ABOUT SPIRITUAL PRACTICES OF COMFORT FOR TODAY AND TOMORROW?

What follows here are examples of what spiritual homes are doing today or could do in the future. Providing comfort during the COVID-19 pandemic became essential. Some faith communities offered comfort to countless families and friends grieving the too-soon deaths of loved ones and assisted those suffering economically due to lost jobs. Some spiritual homes focused on supporting stressed medical personnel. You might say, "Stop!" Given the scale of this or any other global tragedy, why not depend upon our governments or large corporations? It seems obvious that religious communities are no longer the major force for comfort. How can spiritual homes provide consolation to the relatives of the deceased pandemic victims?[20] What about the world's estimated 70-80 million refugees and 250 million migrants?[21] Even governments feel stretched thin. They can't do enough for survivors of disasters like tsunamis and tornadoes or for communities devastated by human evil, such as a mass shooting.

Diana Butler Bass, a journalist turned church historian, counters these observations. Over the span of two decades, she compiled inspiring stories of congregations from many settings—rural, small-town, and city, small and large, liberal and conservative—that thrived because of spiritual practices. Their practices brought comfort to others, including many not members of their spiritual homes.[22] Historically, hospitality is the practice of truly welcoming strangers; its purpose today "is not to change people, but to offer them a space where change can take place."[23] Another form of hospitality empowers interfaith programs to reduce prejudice,

---

20. Dr. Sabrina D. MisirHiralall provided me this account in May 2020 in a phone interview:"Usually, Hindu families keep a wake until sunrise until the body of the departed is cremated. However, due to the COVID-19 pandemic, that is not possible. Now, wakes are done all night through social media. We sing religious songs and listen to *kathas*, religious scriptural teaching, usually from a *pandit*, a Hindu priest."

21. Haass, *World*, 193–200, and Beadle and Haskins, *Acting on Faith*, 35–49. See this book's ch. 8 for further discussion.

22. Diana Bass, *Strength for the Journey*, details her own spiritual awakening. Later, after writing about Trinity Episcopal Church's resurrection and community service in Santa Barbara, she received a three-year research grant from the Lilly Endowment (IN) to study ten congregations' unique programs. Their stories are told by Diana Bass in *Christianity for the Rest*. For a thorough background of spiritual practices, see Dorothy Bass, *Practicing Our Faith*, and McLaren, *Finding Our Way Again*.

23. Nouwen, *Reaching Out*, 51.

acknowledging identity-based conflict while addressing social problems in concrete ways.[24]

Providing food is another form of hospitality. Members of the Church of the Epiphany in Washington, DC, have welcomed the homeless, not only in their food kitchen but also for worship services. They offer a place where the homeless produce a newsletter.[25] A rural community in Baxter, Iowa, expresses their hospitality by volunteering in the concession stands at local sporting events. In Ames, Iowa, where I live, three downtown congregations—First United Methodist Church, First Christian Church, and the Ames United Church of Christ—created a program called Food at First. Other congregations and businesses provide funding. Numerous volunteers, including students from Iowa State University, offer the needed assistance in preparing the food, serving, washing the dishes, and cleaning up.

If hospitality and food aren't your thing, consider looking for a spiritual community engaged in the practice of discernment by finding new uses for a church building that is vacant most of the week.[26] Houses of worship can donate—or rent at a minimal rate—their building to a childcare program such as MOPS—Mothers of Preschoolers—or a daycare center. They can offer meeting spaces to support groups that minister to persons addicted to drugs or alcohol.[27] Knowing older persons will be a larger percentage of the population, anticipate there will be isolated "elder orphans" in urban and rural areas who will need assistance going to medical appointments or picking up groceries and prescriptions.

An inherited third spiritual practice providing comfort is beauty.[28] Can you or others volunteer to take those who need transportation to see local or regional geological wonders? Could your spiritual home arrange trips to art shows or museum events? Those may not meet your definition of beautiful, but let beauty be in the eyes of receiving beholders! Spiritual

24. Patel, *Interfaith Leadership.*

25. Diana Bass described this in Ames, IA, in 2008, when she was the theologian-in-residence.

26. Diana Bass, *Christianity for the Rest*, 89–102.

27. *The Black Church: This is Our Story: This is Our Song* is a PBS documentary (2021) written, produced, and directed by Henry Louis Gates Jr. that provides many examples. Baskette gives moving illustrations of multiple comfort activities at a rejuvenated urban church in *Real Good Church*, the Congregational church in Somerville, MA.

28. Diana Bass, *Christianity for the Rest*, 201–18.

homes should be known for providing "beautiful" caring, comforting programs in their communities.[29]

WHAT IS CONFRONTATION?

The word *confront* literally means "face to face." Richard Colligan reminded me the Hawaiian greeting *aloha* actually means "sharing breaths." It also means "to speak out boldly." Confrontation can be positive as well as negative. Think back to growing up in your family, perhaps when you were a two-year old constantly saying no. Did your parents always let you get away with that? Were you or your siblings always adorable kids who were never reprimanded or held accountable? Can you recall a dumb choice you made regarding friends, romantic prospects, friends and boundaries, a career option, that was rightly challenged by someone in your family? Uncomfortable, but constructive.[30] When World War I ended, and some predicted there would never be conflagrations like it again, poet William Butler Yeats observed, "The best lack all conviction while the worst are full of passionate intensity."[31] Sound familiar? We need to speak boldly.

Granted, confrontations often conjure negative images—parents divorcing, relatives disputing a will, neighbors debating a president's performance, strangers haggling over who caused a collision, and, yes, parents and children disagreeing.[32] Sometimes, it comes out of the blue— an illness or job loss. Other confrontations are positive. A career opportunity. An offer to join a band or club. A benefactor's gift invites a move to a new community. We confront ourselves in the mirror about minor choices; it's no big deal. Granted, confrontations can be shipwrecks or

29. Wuthnow, *All in Sync.* A different kind of comfort, aiding women in prison, comes from Texas, where a couple at Faith UCC in Bryan began visiting a facility for five thousand inmates, many who had been "mules," assisting in drug deliveries. Texas A & M provided job training in several areas. The congregation was able to assist in arranging family visits and in one case, its pastor (me!) officiated at a wedding ceremony of an inmate who eventually became a landscaper.

30. Warren, *Liturgy of the Ordinary,* 83, describes a neighbor who appreciated all the support she—Warren, the author and pastor—and her husband had provided. But the neighbor admitted that he often gave them unconventional comments to "destabilize" their usual, comfortable routines. Imaginative confrontations!

31. William Butler Yeats, "The Second Coming" (1919), lines 7–8, as cited in Platt, *Respectfully Quoted,* 90.

32. In M. Robinson's *Home,* a son and father, a retired minister, have brutal confrontations about racism.

crucibles with results that make us feel like we've given up Wheaties, breakfast of champions, for Defeaties, breakfast of losers.[33] Either way, confrontations can require us to make life-changing choices, providing us with unanticipated dreams or nightmares. See **activity 4.1**.

Let's end with a confrontation story that begins negatively but ends positively. At a memorial service for a friend, the friend's adult son Doug began by describing how, as a teenager, he had lost a tournament tennis match and stormed home in a foul mood. He grumbled to his mother, "I've lost several matches in a row. I'm really in a slump." She, in her day a state tennis singles high school champion, observed, "You are such a poor player, you can't have a slump." Result: the son said it cured him of self-pity.[34] Let's be clear: love flowed in the mother's comment. With her faith in a God of love and truth, she felt her son needed the hard truth at that moment.

Family dynamics and spiritual/religious community business are like rivers; the currents become turbulent at times. Values, rules, and norms found in bylaws, budgets, educational curricula, and strategic plans will become boulders that direct or redirect the current. Beginning as trickles in quiet pools, rumors and confrontations can become floods, depending on how they are communicated in messages, newsletters, worship bulletins, committee activities, and parking lot conversations. A sage preacher once advised me that it's always better to try to solve a confrontation with a conversation or dialogue rather than in the typical monologue of a sermon.[35] Simply put, dialogue and good relationships, built on love, are the building blocks of home and community.[36]

---

33. Parks, *Big Questions*, 43–44, 47, describes how Richard R. Niebuhr, her favorite professor, used the metaphor of a shipwreck for confrontations humans experience. Niebuhr believed when people find their "shore," they will end by experiencing gladness and amazement. Bennis and Thomas, *Geeks and Geezers*, 87–120, use the metaphor of a crucible. A crucible is a life-transforming event, like fire melting metal, that can be positive or negative. Leaders, they found, were those who successfully met the crisis of their crucibles.

34. The family has given me permission to tell the story. An aunt of mine told me a story about parental false praise. The mother of a high school marching band member told her child, "Congratulations, you were the only one who kept in step."

35. The sage pastor was a Presbyterian minister in Bryan, TX. Churches and higher education institutions are similar in the context we are discussing. See Nash et al., *How to Talk*, 8, 28–29, and appendices. A similar work by college chaplains is Franklin and Zartman's *Belovedness*, with excellent guidelines for conversations. If you are interested in historical examples of spiritual conversations, see Jung, *Lost Discipline of Conversation*.

36. Griffith and Griffith, *Encountering the Sacred*, as cited in Chickering et al.,

WHAT DO SACRED SCRIPTURES AND STORIES SAY ABOUT CONFRONTATION?

Numerous religious traditions confirm confrontation is essential for spiritual living. Prince Siddhartha Gautama led a sheltered comfortable life, but about the time he was thirty years old, he encountered four persons in conditions he had never experienced before—a corpse, one suffering with illness, an elderly one, and an ascetic. He became the founder of Buddhism. Confucius, like the Buddha, had experiences that moved him to speak truth to power, especially advising subjects how to speak out against their immoral rulers.[37] For him, compassion and empathy were more important than money or status. Muhammad, Islam's founder, had a particular fear of poets. He viewed their confronting words as potent weapons that could inspire or condemn.[38] For Jesus's first followers, his teachings lifted their daily lives while humbling those in power. In the Hebrew Scriptures, Amos, a shepherd from the Southern Kingdom of Judah, confronts the high priest of the Northern Kingdom of Israel, telling him that God wants justice and care for the poor instead of magnificent worship services (Amos 1–3). The book of Esther tells of a king's wife who reveals her Jewish heritage to prevent the slaughter of her people. Using a parable, the prophet Nathan confronts King David regarding his adultery with Bathsheba (2 Sam 12: 1–15).

In theistic traditions, prophets were "God's truth-tellers."[39] Their hard truth messages were unpopular with royalty, religious authorities, and often the public. Prophets urged change, knowing the consequences of inaction would be devastating. They and their non-theistic counterparts want life to improve. Roman Catholic orders such as the Benedictines make clear that service to others outside the order is expected but acknowledge that learning how to live near their brothers is difficult but essential.[40] Over time, religious and spiritual traditions have developed

---

Encouraging Authenticity, 184.

37. Prothero, *God Is Not One*, 126–27.

38. Freedman and McClymond, *Rivers of Paradise*, 549–50.

39. Holloway, *Little History of Religion*, 53–58. He states prophets are not "foretellers," but "forth-tellers," sharing the message they have received from God.

40. Norris, *Dakota*. The author's visits to an abbey and conversations with the monks include examples of difficulties of close-quarter living.

ways to challenge their disciples' levels of commitment to speak out and live out their beliefs.[41] See **activity 4.2.**

ARE YOU WILLING TO CONFRONT WITH LOVE?

We know from experience that disagreements in families, like the political world, can become toxic. How do we counter this? It isn't easy. Too often, fueled by social media and partisan television stations, we want to believe only what we hear from our tribe. One recommendation: St. John Greer Ervine (1883–1971), an Irish novelist, suggested that each of us "should periodically be compelled to listen to opinions which are infuriating . . . . To hear nothing but what is pleasing to one is to make a pillow of the mind."[42] Whom have you or would you confront, and how? A reporter of the January 6, 2021, insurrection in Washington, DC, observed that some invaders of the US Senate chambers offered prayers, thanking the divine for support of the incursion.[43] Would you have comfronted them? In early 2018, the administration of United States President Donald J. Trump wanted to discourage Latin American immigrants from coming to the US. In June, Attorney General Jeff Sessions cited the plan of separating families at the border. To justify the policy against mounting criticism, he cited the Christian Scripture Romans 13, which begins, "Let every person be subject to the governing authorities; for there is no authority except from God, and those authorities that exist have been instituted by God."[44] A few days later, First Lady Melania Trump boarded Air Force One, wearing a jacket with the message "I really don't care, do U?" A wide range of responses followed, from support for the government's actions to legal challenges, protesting legislative actions, and demonstrations against "kids in cages." My granddaughter's action was to

41. See, e.g., "Keisaku." See also "Land of the Disappearing Buddha" from the television series *The Long Search.*

42. Ervine quote, title page of Sewell Stokes' 1928 book of interviews, *Pilloried!* Wilkerson, *Caste,* 13–14, uses the analogy of the choice we have filling out a medical history form, asking if it is better for our health to share or ignore past family illnesses or addictions. While painful, it is best to be complete and accurate about past behaviors. A controversy in state legislatures in 2020–2021 is elimination of a curriculum unit on slavery, 1619, to avoid discussion of systemic racism.

43. Belitsos, "Religious Beliefs."

44. Romans 13:1–7, reflects Paul's theology that all worldly authorities are instituted by God. That said, it does not mean they are all good.

design and sell a T-shirt of the Statue of Liberty with the words "I care, do you?"[45]

Yes, these situations open cans of theological and ethical worms. Where is God?[46] What authorities do I recognize, religious or civil? In America specifically, what about church-state relations? For Christians, what would Jesus do?[47] Don't the immigrants have a responsibility for their actions? Why should I care about this world if my citizenship is in the next life?[48]

Put yourself back on the Spiritual Express. What if your seatmate pushed you to be more specific about confronting injustice? Consider these roles and strategies, including some that avoid controversy through inaction, neutrality, and silence; which one would you choose?[49]

♦ Spiritual monk or nun: As far as worldly affairs are concerned, I am AWOL (absent without leave). The physical world is transient and as much as possible, I don't want to be involved in it. I must retreat.

♦ Temporary tourist: My stance is that the secular affairs of this world are not my priority, I'm just a visitor. However, in small ways, I will

45. Soboroff, *Separated*, details the development of the policy, its implementation, and status in 2019. As of Oct. 2019, 4,210 children had been separated from their parents. In 2020, federal officials acknowledged over 500 children were still not united with their families.

46. Diana Bass, *Grounded*, 10–11. Bass argues, with others, that global cultures respond quite differently, depending upon their beliefs about God's presence.

47. Diana Bass, *Grounded*, 14–15, reminds readers that H. Richard Niebuhr, in his classic work *Christ and Culture*, argues that theologians have variously described Jesus Christ as being against the world, of the world, above the world, in tension with the world, and in a perpetual struggle to transform the world.

48. Hauerwas and Willimon, *Resident Aliens*, urge readers to be less concerned about the world and more about being faithful disciples, citing Phil 3:20, which speaks of disciples' ultimate home being "a colony in heaven" or "citizenship in heaven." For a discussion on authority, see Michalson, "Authority." For a discussion about public involvement, see Palmer, *Company of Strangers*.

49. "Inaction/Neutrality/Silence," Abrahamic Initiative on the Middle East (http://aimeproject.org/inaction_neutrality_silence.htm): "All that is necessary for the triumph of evil is that good men (and women) do nothing."—Edmund Burke; "Neutrality helps the oppressor, never the victim."—Elie Wiesel; "Not to take sides is to effectively weigh in on the side of the stronger."—William Sloan Coffin; "Once you see it, you can't unsee it. And once you've seen it, keeping quiet, saying nothing, becomes as political an act as speaking out. Either way, you're accountable."—Suzanna Arundhati Roy.

be involved in improving my spiritual community as it witnesses to the world.

+ Religious ambassador: I will be a representative of my faith, interacting with the world's foreign cultures.

+ Conductor on Spiritual Express: I'm good at being neutral. I'll be like a judge or referee, helping each side get a fair chance to explain its views.

+ Reluctant pioneer: I believe that both spiritual realms and political realms should be improved. Pilgrim-like, I will cautiously but deliberately try to change both.

+ Revolutionary: Both religious and secular worlds must be radically improved. In this earthly life, I feel called to resist evil, to the point of likely sacrificing my life for the causes of justice and peace.[50]

WHAT PRACTICES RELATE TO WAYS OF LOVING CONFRONTATION TODAY?

Face it. Ministers and religious organizations don't like conflict. My wife, years ago, was an instructor in a church-related school of nursing and told me ministers submitted only positive recommendation letters for prospective students. Ultimately, the admissions committee of the nursing school deemed these letters useless. A reason pastors in Protestant churches avoid controversy is fear of being fired. Legend has it that a minister in a tobacco-producing state preached an anti-smoking sermon. Speaking for church leadership, a deacon warned him, "That's not preaching; now you're meddling."

That said, what are constructive, loving ways to be what some call a social critic? Here's an article about responding to extreme views in families.[51] In a discussion, could you refer to or use any of these sources or examples to reflect your religious or spiritual perspective?

---

50. The writer of those words was a professor at Union Seminary, New York, James Cone, *Black Theology of Liberation*, 10–20. Cone contends that the Christian faith is based on racism and is highly oppressive. In a reflection twenty years after the book first appeared, he adds that his theology of liberation should also be applied to sexism and economic classism.

51. Miller-Idriss and Corke, "Parents Can Learn."

- Art: Picasso, *Guernica* (1937)—painting of the Spanish Civil War

- Music: Simon & Garfunkel, "The Sound of Silence"

- Films/Documentaries/Photos: *The Miracle Worker* (1962), the story of the education of Helen Keller

- Moral Conversations: See Robert Nash et al., *How to Talk.*

- Social Media: Countering false misinformation and disinformation

- Free Press: Woodward and Bernstein, Watergate (1972)

- Education/Schooling: Elizabeth Peabody began the American kindergarten movement in 1860. She often had meals with advocates and critics.

- Storytelling: Family stories; Mother Goose tales used for political commentary (1700–1800s)

- Non-Violent Demonstrations: Mahatma Gandhi; Martin L. King Jr.

Some of the above possibilities are one-time or short-term confrontations. As a spiritual traveler, what are some practices that could enhance your life for the long haul? Diana Butler Bass describes three practices that address how spiritual homes can positively and productively confront some issues: diversity, justice, and reflection.[52] I'll add another practice: humor.

The Black Lives Matter (BLM) movement of the 2010s and 2020s underscores diversity issues in race and immigration. Books such as *Dying of Whiteness*[53] address issues that reveal protest marches will only begin to bring change. Bass shares an account of an upper-middle-class congregation in Cincinnati, Ohio, that cited archbishop Desmond Tutu's *ubuntu* theology, sometimes translated as "I cannot be without you,"[54] to confront political, social, and theological diversity in their community.

---

52. Diana Bass, *Christianity for the Rest*, "Diversity," 143–56; "Justice, "157–70, and "Reflection,"185–199. Eck, *New Religious America*, 69, would prefer the term *pluralism* because it calls for active engagement with others that is more than tolerance of the other; it truly respects differences. On numerous strategies for diversity, see Nascoste.

53. Metzl, *Dying of Whiteness*, interviewed persons in Tennessee, Missouri, and Kansas. He concluded many were undermining their own health and children's education because of racial and class bias.

54. Diana Bass, *Christianity for the Rest*, 151–52. Bass here describes the Episcopal Church of the Redeemer in Cincinnati's struggles and strategies for confronting diverse points of view.

The second practice, justice, helps congregations build upon biblical principles including reconciliation.

Reflection also encompasses deep studies of Scriptures, a willingness to have open discussions, and what I personally would recommend, sharing one's values and the community's values. A concrete example of this occurred in my community, Ames, Iowa, in 2005. Upset that a political party implied that they were the sole proprietors of "family values," an ecumenical group developed a values statement that certainly had a different slant on some values. See **appendix 4A**. Bass describes a church in Scottsdale, Arizona, that developed a somewhat similar statement, the Phoenix Affirmations.[55]

My experience is that humor is a wonderful "weapon" that can be used effectively along with these three practices. Whether in novels, short stories, poetry, cartoons, letters to the editor, jokes, or even scriptural stories, the ridiculous excesses, blatant injustices, and stupidity of human behavior that too often result in tragedy can be pointedly and effectively addressed utilizing humor.[56]

As positive, open, and accepting as you may be, you will not always be welcomed, accepted, or praised. In fact, multiple sacred scriptures make clear that you will be misunderstood, unappreciated, opposed, reviled, and hated. Be honest. You don't expect to get through life without criticism, do you? Consider the great organist and composer, J. S. Bach. One of his bosses (evaluators) claimed that Bach's playing was so intense that, if continued for two years, the town would need a new organ and half the congregation would be deaf. More recently, the Netflix series *The Crown* has Prime Minister Margaret Thatcher responding to Queen Elizabeth's concern that her policies were making enemies, with the Charles Mackay poem "No Enemies." The poet asserts that if one has no enemies, "small is the work that you have done." Thatcher agreed.

---

55. Diana Bass, *Christianity for the Rest*, 194–95: "[They are] a set of twelve beliefs that articulate what members call progressive Christianity. Based in scripture, the twelve points elaborate the theme of loving God, loving neighbor, and loving the self .... [They are] more than a creedal statement or a pledge. Members of the congregation are working to turn them into a movement to challenge both the religious right and . . . secular left." In 2006 members intended to walk three thousand miles to the Lincoln Memorial as a "call for a new Protestant Reformation."

56. Martin, *Between Heaven and Mirth*.

TRAVELER: WHAT'S YOUR COMMISSION: ARE YOU BECOMING A WELCOMING STRANGER?

Has this chapter helped you clarify what you might be looking for in a spiritual home, especially in terms of being comforting and confronting? Do you now have a different image of a spiritual home? I'll make several observations as you decide your commission, should you move forward to finding a spiritual home that is both comforting and discomforting.

The first observation concerns the truth. You must be true to yourself, as William Shakespeare told us. Every healthy spiritual tradition speaks of a core value being a search for the truth. I join Barbara Brown Taylor in saying that your own truths will be enriched when you learn the truths of other faith perspectives.[57] You and your spiritual home are commissioned to search for the truth, and you must be open to the truths others bring to the table.[58] I literally mean tables. Eating with others in a group is essential. See **appendix 4B** on how to hold moral conversations. Another option: discuss the meaning of the song "Everyone is Welcome."[59] Allegedly, a true story from an Iowa church's Christmas pageant told of an eleven-year-old innkeeper's unscripted response to Mary and Joseph's plea for housing, "There is no room in the inn, but would you like to come in for a drink?" Now, that's quite a welcome!

If the concept of comfort still seems abstract to you, consider the story of a restaurant dishwasher who told a minister friend he had wished for years to be invited to become part of a congregation. When he was, he became one of its most active members. Did you have a friend in high school or a buddy in college or a stranger who said to you, "I'll walk you home" or "I'll take you home"? Comfort can be an invitation when things are on the line.

Next, confrontation. History—or more specifically, historical interpretations, with January 6, 2021, as an example—and current events make it difficult for spiritual beings who want to make a positive difference to be isolationists. Healthy spiritual homes, like their biological

57. Taylor, *Holy Envy*.

58. Nash et al., *How to Talk*, 91–92, have four criteria for pragmatic religious truth: "A belief should help the believer, not harm others, should not be imposed on others, and should not harm the believer." Page 181 has a humorous list of how different philosophies determine what is "truth."

59. There are at least two versions: in a film, *The Lion Guard* (2017), or Shirley Erena Murray's "A Place at the Table" (1996, https://hymnary.org/text/for_everyone_born_a_place_at_the_table).

counterparts, will have shortcomings. For the love of God and neighbor they are called to confront injustice, but too often, they succumb to temptations to become self-righteous about their actions or want too much credit for changes accomplished. In simple language, as ethicist Larry Rasmussen phrases it, "Life is a mess . . . . Just as our bodies do poorly without food, bodies politic [and spiritual] do poorly without governance . . . to be communities, they must be ordered, cared for, led."[60]

Let me add another warning. If you have a preconceived vision of what a perfect spiritual community or home will be and attempt to impose it on others, the community will fail. What will help you and the community to meet your call or commission is to be clear about the reasons for your actions. That's where "con-formation" comes in. Your spiritual home members need, for example, to have consensus on what civil rights activist Rep. John Lewis described as "good trouble." To begin or enhance spiritual practices for yourself, in concert with others on the spiritual express, will be an adventure. May there be many other adventures that come your way, as both a comfort and a challenge! Become a welcoming stranger.

60. Rasmussen, "Shaping Communities," 120.

Chapter 4 Activities

ACTIVITY 4.1: COMFORT AND CONFRONTATION

Do you agree with the imperative that both individual believers and spiritual homes should "comfort the afflicted" and "afflict the comfortable"? You may feel that you are not gifted toward one or both, or that the time or circumstances aren't right. Hebrew prophets were notorious for giving reasons to God why they shouldn't be asked to witness through comforting and confronting. Discuss with a spiritual friend or in your spiritual home about specific persons and agencies in your area that need assistance and issues that need addressing. The emphasis in this activity is upon a physical presence. Granted, in a time of social distancing, it may mean actions taken through social media, making financial contributions, or decisions to support or no longer support certain advertisers, businesses, or organizations.

Comfort: If you need comfort, to whom would you turn? Is there someone you know who needs comfort now? Contemplate what you should do.

Confrontation: Visualize a situation, personal, professional, perhaps political, where confrontation is needed. Give thought to how you, perhaps with others, would be able to confront it in a constructive way.

ACTIVITY 4.2: SPEAK UP! SPEAK OUT! AND ACT: STAND UP FOR YOUR VALUES!

For background, read Walter Brueggemann, *Interrupting Silence: God's Command to Speak Out*. Want a new world? Listen to Bryan Sirchio's song "Dream God's Dream" (www.sirchio.com).

What issue(s) matter the most to you? Whom might you call or write about this issue? Will you take this issue on alone? Should your spiritual home?

Should your spiritual home create a list of its beliefs and values to share with local, regional, state legislatures and boards and commissions? See appendix 4A for such a statement. Granted, it

(*Activity 4.2 continued*)

reflects a Christian perspective but can be used as a template for your statement.

Want to call or write about an issue? Make a list of phone numbers below. If you want to write a letter to a newspaper, they typically want no more than two hundred to three hundred words, or one page double-spaced.

Willing to make a phone call? Write in the numbers of your legislators here:

US Congress: _____

US Senate: _____

White House: 202–456–1111

State Legislature: _____

FOR ADDITIONAL CONVERSATIONS

So what? If you still aren't convinced that you would benefit from involvement with a healthy spiritual home or community, you might read these:

- Called a "guidebook for the soul," this pioneering work anticipated the world we inhabit, with its complexity, confusions, and need for commitment. Laurent A. Parks Daloz et al. in *Common Fire: Leading Lives of Commitment in a Complex World* relate significant ways to connect from home to the wider community.

- The emphasis upon personal liberty and freedom of choice seems to drown out what responsibilities we have for neighbors. The most recent version of Walter Brueggemann's *Journey to the Common Good* gives biblical and theological rationale for communities that have a wider view of the world.

- To those with mixed-faith marriages or contemplating a partnership with someone of no or little formal religious background, Stina Kielsmeier-Cook's *Blessed Are the Nones: Mixed-Faith Marriage and My Search for Spiritual Community* is a first-person account of a young family coming to grips with it. The author, a conservative, finds support from a surprising community.

- A key benefit of spiritual homes is comfort. A rabbi struggling with his own father's death, Steve Leder, who has counseled others who are fearful and need comfort, offers inspiring stories and suggestions in *The Beauty of What Remains: How Our Greatest Fear Becomes Our Greatest Gift*.

- Can we truly relate to others who have different opinions? Are there such things as groups who solve problems even when there is dissent? Yes, say two college chaplains, James Franklin and Becky Zartman, with other contributors, in *Belovedness: Finding God (and Self) on Campus*.

Part II

Qualities of a Spiritual Home: YESS to Life!

A VITAL SPIRITUAL LIFE IS A TRANSFORMED LIFE

Part II is for you, traveler, if you want to find ways to enhance your current spiritual community or locate a new spiritual home. Part I focused on how you were formed, ideally sustained with love, informed about life's values and choices, and as a young adult, accepted, or rejected attempts to "re-form" yourself. Its pages assumed that you knew there have been forces, secular and sacred, benign or aggressive, that wanted to "conform" you. Chapter 4 ended part I by asserting that as social and spiritual beings, most humans want to be associated with a spiritual community that forms us. Assuming it is healthy, that spiritual home will want you to retain the right to discern which of its beliefs and practices you accept.

The chapters of part II describe four attributes of a healthy spiritual home. Each contributes uniquely to your spiritual growth or transformation. The root *trans* means "across." The stem *form* is linked to Greek words for change. Together, they signal changes in external form or inner nature. I associate *trans* with crossing international borders or, today, boundaries such as gender changes.

My belief is that a spiritual life that makes a difference is one that has been transformed. One of the metaphors used in these four chapters is architecture or, more specifically, the process of buying a house and transforming it into a home. Another metaphor is how water transforms. The Mississippi River begins as a trickle from a Minnesota lake, becomes a stream, the stream a river, that empties into the ocean. A spiritual home of integrity can transform you and transform others through joy, truth, trust, and love.

5

Yearning— "Trans-Formed" by Joy

Worship is a unique art form combining music, theology, performance, history, Scripture, leadership, technology, architecture, art, and drama.

—GREG SCHEER, *THE ART OF WORSHIP*, 87

Rituals are important among Brahmin forms of the Hindu tradition . . . practices such as yoga in the Buddhist and Hindu traditions, methods of stilling the self in Eastern Orthodox mysticism, meditations which can help to increase compassion and love, and so on. Such practices can be combined with rituals of worship, where meditation is directed toward union with God.

—NINIAN SMART, *THE WORLD'S RELIGIONS*, 13–14

People tattoo their bodies with KISS faces, name their children after our songs, and have KISS conventions. This is Planet Kiss; we just live on it. The stage is holy ground; and what we do is electric church.

—GENE SIMMONS, MEMBER OF THE BAND KISS

Music washes away from the soul the dust of everyday life.

—BERTHOLD AUERBACH (1812–1882)

Note: I respect all religious traditions and have tried to incorporate some elements from them in this book. But I realize that my references to them are not complete and may sometimes be inaccurate. I trust readers will understand the spirit in which I have included them. My deepest appreciation to colleagues and dear friends of diverse traditions who have given me greater insights and understandings into Abrahamic religions and non-theistic traditions. Several of them have read drafts of this chapter.

That said, based on survey data, the largest number of Nones, SBNR, and other readers are those who have some familiarity with Roman Catholic, Orthodox, or Protestant traditions. I will give somewhat more attention to trends in worship practices of those faiths than the other two categories of meditation and connection. My experiences and education reflect my years in a Protestant Christian affiliation.

YESS: YOUR EXPLORATION THROUGH SCRIPTURES AND SONGS

- Invitation: To become part of a community of yearning, "trans-formed" by joy

- Why do I yearn? What do I get out of it?

- Why is worship such a big deal?

- What's happening with worship?

- What are the key "plays" in worship services?

- What's happening with worship?

- What should I get out of meditation (spiritual practices)?

- What are the benefits of spiritual practices?

- What are the trends in meditation (spiritual practices)?

- What if all I want is to be in connection with others?

- What are trends in connecting?

- Traveler: Ready to become a prisoner of choice and joy?

- Activities

- For Additional Conversations

INVITATION: TO BECOME PART OF A COMMUNITY OF YEARNING, "TRANS-FORMED" BY JOY

What can pull you out of a funk? It could be a laugh, a happy surprise, a child's achievement, or, on a big scale, moving into a better home, getting away to a cabin, or taking an ocean cruise. As much as we love our families, hasn't the pandemic, with prohibitions on dining out and attending our houses of worship, convinced us we enjoy being with others? Whether it is life's triumphs or tragedies, we feel better sharing. Joy transforms us. From that, we develop a spirit of generosity, more thankful for gifts received, more open to sharing of ourselves as well as our money. Welcome to discussing three ways to meet the human DNA of yearning. In case you're concerned that this chapter has the Right Reverends' Seal of Approval, I have deliberately written it for lay people, not academics or professional clergy.

WHY DO I YEARN? WHAT DO I GET OUT OF IT?

My answers are not based on specific psychological or sociological research, much less theological justifications.[1] To be clear, yearning is more than wishing for a knickknack or a mansion from the genie. It is a desire to be united with something greater, whether that is God, a transcendent power, the Great Spirit, an ultimate mystery. I believe humans yearn because of the seriousness of surviving day-to-day uncertainties. We crave companionship with others, celebrating face-to-face our triumphs, sharing our tragedies, finding solutions to struggles. In times past, more out of fear than hope, our ancestors believed they had to call on a higher being. They tried everything from shouting and singing to dancing and

1. Long, *Beyond the Worship Wars*, 15–41, offers multiple answers to why people worship, from awe to mystery, from needing a sense of belonging to providing welcome to strangers. See Westerberg, *Te Deum*, 28–29, on joy; but he reminds us that if God is all-powerful, attendees can never be casual about what to expect. These and other writers warn about worship losing its integrity if it simply responds to market surveys to please potential attendees.

offering animal and human sacrifice to please their gods. I've visited the Mayan ruins in Copan, Honduras, and seen the stone where priests placed still-beating hearts. Yes, joyful people gave thanks when wars were won, dangers avoided, crops harvested, children born. Music and art describe other secular and sacred reasons to have joy.[2] You may argue that the questions we're going to discuss—Why worship? Why meditate and practice? Why connect?—have outcomes other than joy, such as praise, fear, awe, thanksgiving, comfort, blessing, or duty. I'd agree, but joy and a growing sense of giving of yourself to others is the grandest gift you receive.

If you concede that most yearning focuses on what people traditionally call God, you will probably agree with James Baldwin's point that "if the concept of God has any validity or any use, it can only be to make us larger, freer, and more loving."[3] In other words, God or that unfathomable mystery wants us to be joy-full! To be clear, joy is different than happiness. Joy is from the heart, the soul, an internal change for the better, while happiness is a tangible, temporary pleasure.[4] A major outcome of joy is generosity of spirit. Think beyond giving money, although that shouldn't be denied. I once heard a minister give a stewardship message that became known as "the drive-by sermon." During the previous week, he reported, he had driven by the homes of members. His conclusion— proportionately, their pledges didn't reflect their house values! Generosity includes everything from wanting to hum, sing, and smile to offering kindnesses, feeling better, and embracing others with hugs of love and appreciation.[5]

2. M. Miller and Miller, *Harper's Bible Dictionary*, 354. See Raman, *Deus Ubiquitus*, 145–74, for multiple examples of joy expressed in the music of world religions. Two classic examples hymns are Isaac Watts's "Joy to the World" and Ludwig van Beethoven's tune, HYMN TO JOY, for "Joyful, Joyful, We Adore You." For other examples, see www.hymnary.org.

3. Baldwin, *Collected Essays*, 314. Multiple times, Young quotes Baldwin's description of God as an enormous power of love and control that cannot be overcome (Young, *James Baldwin's Understanding*, 32, 101, 136, 194, 197). Brueggemann describes Hebrew psalms and Christian hymns as expressions of "glad obedience" (Brueggemann, *Glad Obedience*). Later, I will explain what is meant by my term "prisoner by choice."

4. Lama and Tutu, *Book of Joy*; Lewis, *Surprised by Joy*; and Heath, *Glorify*, 24–36.

5. Putnam et al., *American Grace*, as cited in Patel, *Out of Many Faiths*, 15.

Two Metaphors

Ready, traveler? Before we make our first stop at a potential house or home of spiritual practices, may I suggest two metaphors to help you answer the question of what you get from yearning. First metaphor: home. As Scott Sanders reminds us, there is an immense difference between house and home: "A house is a garment, easily put off or on . . . a home is skin . . . change homes and you will be disoriented; change homes and you bleed."[6] Beyond buying a house or apartment for shelter, often the largest financial investment we make is making it a joy-filled home. To be the receptacle of our deepest, most joyous memories, we want it to be safe and solid, as worry-free as possible. Its architecture, from foundations to framing to roof, has integrity, heart, passion, and joy.[7] What meanings and values do that home's residents express? How do they share their joys and sorrows—in their silences and sounds, in their prohibitions and practices? Our dream is a home, sweet home.

Second metaphor: water. As noted in the introduction to part II, many people gravitate to water for relaxation and contemplation. What form of water helps you experience the joys of life: a babbling brook, a quiet lake, running rapids, or an ocean wave? Is swimming, fishing, boating, or floating a form of personal or family "worth-ship" for you?

With either metaphor, does that environment help you to determine what is meaningful to you? Does that setting, your home or that spot in nature, make it easier to clarify your dreams? Do you have a favorite story that captures a family trait or value? I've heard many such stories. Relished through generations, they become a virtual religious or spiritual ritual because they answer some of life's most pressing questions.

Yearning comes in three sizes, each size related to milestones.

We yearn for joy because it gives us a positive response to life's challenges. This chapter describe three different ways we yearn. You can focus on

6. Sanders, *Staying Put*, 35.

7. Cherry, *Worship Architect*. I am sensitive to traditions that hold worship is for their belief in the one true God; anything else is idolatry. This book's purpose is to be descriptive, not prescriptive. I join with Raman's dedication in *Deus Ubiquitus* "to [those] believers who pray and worship as well as to unbelievers who reject the idea of the Ultimate Unfathomable Mystery many call God."

one, but they are interdependent. The first is worship, which for many readers is the most familiar form. Worship relates to the big questions of life and death. The second is spiritual practices, which I cluster under meditation. By their repetition, we gain knowledge and skills in our yearning. The third way brings comfort, security, and joy through connections and associations.

Odds are that your favorite family stories occurred at or are retold at what I call milestone events: births, youth-to-adult passages, marriages, and services of remembrance. Even when we do private prayers or meditations, we often have our personal milestones in mind. Spiritual communities share their best stories at these times because we attribute successes and failures to the mysteries of life. Three milestones are especially joyful: birth, transitioning from youth to adulthood, and marriage. While end-of-life services focus on grief and loss, they too celebrate life.

Isn't the chief purpose of milestone events to transform participants, whether traditional worship services, meditative exercises, or rituals of connection? Done well, their spiritual nourishment engages and enriches us. I'm not denying that you may have a singular spontaneous event that redirects your life. But for sustained spiritual formation, we need regular infusions of significant words, rituals, music, food, and art that are well-crafted. Simple? No. I challenge you to design a milestone service. Go to **activity 5.1.** Enjoy its humorous story! My belief is that in-depth spiritual growth will not occur through incidental or casual commitment.

WHY IS WORSHIP SUCH A BIG DEAL?

Many people conclude it isn't. Older surveys suggest three out of four Americans have had a negative or ho-hum experience with a religious tradition. More recent studies indicate 80 percent of Nones and Spiritual but Not Religious (SBNR) people are turned off by traditional religious services, with an estimated 2.7 million Americans dropping out of worship attendance each year. Further, an estimated 30 to likely 40 percent of Americans have never been inside of a house of worship.[8] Granted, even

8. If you're a stranger to religious ceremonies, see vols. 1 and 2 of Magida and Matlins's *How to Be a Perfect Stranger*. In the 1990s, it was alleged that one of four entering students a military academy had never been in a house of worship. Current studies cited in this book suggest that the percentage of never-attenders is in the 30 percent range. McLaren, *Faith after Doubt*, xv, includes estimated yearly declines in attendance. For church membership data, see J. Jones, "U.S. Church Membership."

though there has been a significant attendance drop from the 1960s until now, an estimated 20 percent of Americans (roughly 60 million) say they attend a religious service once a week. A Gallup poll indicates, for the first time, less than 50 percent of respondents say they are members of a religious faith.[9]

What is worship?

Let's begin with a perspective on why and how historic faith traditions developed worship services. Some ancestors experienced a creator of the cosmos, distant as the stars but close as breath; lived with saints who also sinned; became favored people who too often were fugitives from responsibility; and tolerated preachers helping the poor while promoting their own prosperity, power, and privilege. Worship reflected their stories and became holy traditions and inherited truths which are claimed to be relevant today. One biblical scholar calls their narratives "the isness of the wasness."[10]

The word *worship* has an Old English lineage which we could translate as "worth-ship."[11] Mark Chaves asserts, "Worship is the most central and public activity engaged in by American religious congregations."[12] But what is it?[13] Let's assume most people hearing the word *worship* picture a service in a church, synagogue, or mosque. But some, like the Amish, believe our daily life is how we worship God. Still others think of a specific practice, like a choral anthem or a prayer as worship. For

9. Grant, "Great Decline." A point to consider, looking at church history, is that high attendance has been the blip; the percentage of a community that belongs to a congregation historically is low, with most congregations having no more than seventy-five members.

10. Napier, *Song of the Vineyard*, 2. People debate whether the garden of Eden story, for example, occurred. In terms of literary style, it is a myth, a story involving a god and humans. Napier posits that the important point is that the myth conveys a truth or truths, "What IS true?" rather than "WAS it an historical event?"

11. Duck, *Worship for Whole People*, 3–5. The Old English word *weorth-scipe* is literally *weorth* (worth) and *scipe* (ship). Duck notes that another important word is *liturgy*, which comes from the Greek word *leitourgia*, based on the words for people (*laós*) and work (*érgon*). A liturgy in ancient Greece was a work produced for the public.

12. Chaves, *How Do We Worship*, 1.

13. See John Witvliet, "On Three Meanings of the Term Worship," as cited in Scheer, *Art of Worship*.

this discussion, we'll stick with the first description.[14] If you're interested, read Ruth Duck's description of five *r* purposes of worship: "While it is appropriate for every person, congregation, and denomination to emphasize one element—ritual, revelation, response, relationship, or rehearsal—more than others in their understanding of worship, a wholesome theology of worship includes all these dimensions."[15] Augustine (c. 300 CE), a famous saint in the Christian tradition, captured worship's purpose this way: "Our hearts are restless until they find their rest in [God]."[16]

Pentecostals and charismatic congregations have free-flowing, Spirit-filled services, while Quakers prefer silence and quiet discussions.[17] Place, while important, isn't everything. Some, like the Amish, worship at home; others attend cathedrals.[18] Emergent congregations enjoy informal settings in coffee shops, bars, or strip malls.[19]

Theologian Walter Brueggemann posits that these services and music especially reflect "glad obedience."[20] I prefer the term yearning, a thankfulness for God's love and grace, not considered a prescription to earn one's way into heaven, but a joy, a commitment to live more righteously, including serving neighbors and strangers. While they have similar worship purposes, the diversities within the three so-called Abrahamic traditions are immense.[21] Within each, there are factions based on ethnic,

14. White, *Introduction to Christian Worship*, 17–47. This classic text will give you a thorough history of the evolution of Western worship, its purposes, structures, and elements such as rituals and sacraments.

15. Duck, *Worship for Whole People*, 16.

16. Modernized from "For Thou madest us for Thyself, and our heart is restless until it repose in Thee" (Augustine, *Confession*, 1).

17. Norris, *Amazing Grace*, 16–20, offers insights about the benefits of silence and has a salient quote on silence from a monk: "Silence reminds me to take my soul with me wherever I go."

18. Diana Bass, *Christianity after Religion*, 209.

19. Tickle, *Emergence Christianity*, "Worshipping with Heart, Mind, Soul, and Strength," 167–77.

20. Brueggemann, *Glad Obedience*, uses that phrase from Ps 105 as his title. Ps 2 describes singing as "joyful trembling," which the author likens to how subjects feel before earthly kings and a merciful divine ruler.

21. Judaism has three principal branches: Orthodox, Conservative, and Reform. Islam has two major bodies: Shia and Sunni. The Christian tradition developed two branches: the Eastern Orthodox tradition has many geographical siblings (Russian, Greek, etc.); the Western Church's largest unit, Roman Catholic, was divided in the 1500s by the Protestant Reformation, which now has unnumbered denominations

racial, geographical, and political differences, far too many to cover in this book.[22] As intriguing as it may be to explore unusual sects, past or present, space prohibits me from offering even the CliffsNotes version of a world religions course. If you are interested in further exploration of a faith or spiritual tradition's worship perspective, I recommend checking the notes for resources.[23] There are many texts on world religions and the world's growing religious pluralism.[24]

Before we go on, let me explain who I picture as some readers of this chapter: those who have little experience with worship services. That's not a put-down. I'm assuming you want to learn more about worship. I'm comparing you, if you are a first-time worship goer, to a first-time attendee at a baseball game. I'm trying to tell you what the rules are. It may be frustrating for both of us, because in no way can this be comprehensive. Quick examples: while a service has music in many forms, I can't describe with any depth the relationship of congregational hymns, seasons, and biblical texts.[25] The significance of silence and symbols in paintings, carvings, and banners is complex. I'll just say that the arts and music "create a visual, auditory, kinesthetic, and sometimes . . . a tactile worship experience."[26] Since music is important in different ways, I do include a section toward the end about music's role in worship. During the

and divisions stoked by differences based on doctrines—word-centered vs. feeling-centered, i.e., the presence of the Spirit—and practices—the number of sacraments and when and how to celebrate them.

22. Duck, *Worship for Whole People*, "Diverse Worship," 35–56. A sample overview of some of today's traditions: African American Christian worship (38–41), Korean and Korean American Worship (41–44), Latina-Latino Worship (44–46), White Worship (47–51). See her hymn "Diverse in Culture, Nation, Race" (55–56).

23. See Magida and Matlins, *How to be a Perfect Stranger*, especially when you are invited to attend a service at an unfamiliar faith tradition. Academic descriptions of the major faith traditions are described in Davies, *Westminster Dictionary of Worship*, and Willis, *Religion Book*.

24. See Niles, *Doing Theology with Humility*; Taylor, *Holy Envy*; Hanh and Pagels, *Living Buddha*; Esack, *On Being a Muslim*; and Palmer, *Hidden Wholeness*.

25. Horn, *Christian Year*, 16. The second most important date for early Christians was Pentecost, the founding of the church (Acts 20:16). The third great early festival was Epiphany (Jan. 6), which commemorated the incarnation, i.e., God in human form, both the birth and baptism of Jesus. Lectionary readings in mainline faith traditions are on a three-year cycle (Year A, Year B, Year C).

26. Wuthnow, *All in Sync*, 176. He believes the architecture, vestments, and banners are part of the tactile experience; they blend historical memories with current experiences.

COVID-19 surges, researchers discovered that singing, by congregations and choirs, can spread the virus. The Center for Congregational Song, an ecumenical group, provides resources regarding music as services are resumed.[27]

What is worship supposed to accomplish?

What or who is life's ultimate mystery, and how do we relate to it? Who's invited to come and who's in charge? The answer is both God and humans. Based on the common assumption that houses of worship are always trying to get more people to come, we also assume that clergy are organizing the service to attract people to be spectators. Søren Kierkegaard disagreed, arguing that God is the audience, and people are the actors.[28]

Worship is filled with paradox. A big one is that God is thought of as the Beginning and the End—in Greek, the Alpha and Omega. While these paradoxes do not occur in every service, each is always possible. Worshipers remember the past but try to redeem the present; embrace the inherited while inviting in new generations; sense wonder while contemplating senseless sufferings; expect rational leadership while remaining open to mystical experiences; emphasize speaking yet sing; pray, individually and communally, for blessings received and wrongs to be forgiven. As another author puts it, worship is "messy," because it is a "living organism" constantly subject to change.[29]

What should attendees gain from a worship service? Some say it will boost your physical and mental health.[30] Tom Long describes nine goals of a service:

- ◆ make room for the experience of mystery
- ◆ make concerted efforts to show hospitality to the stranger
- ◆ make visible the sense of drama inherent in scriptural stories

27. For resources and updates, go to https://thehymnsociety.org/covid-19/.

28. Kierkegaard, as cited in "Be a Part." The Hebrew prophet Amos had a similar perspective (c. 750 BCE) because he contended God wanted justice more than worship (Amos 5:21–24).

29. Saliers, *Worship and Spirituality*, 4–5. The list of paradoxes or dichotomies developed above were suggested in his discussion of remembrance. See also Glick, *With All Thy Mind*, ix.

30. Andersen, "How to Boost," and Norton, "Early Findings."

- emphasize congregational music that is both excellent and eclectic in style and genre

- creatively adapt the space and environment

- forge a strong connection between worship and local outreach projects

- maintain a relatively stable order of service, including a significant repertoire of elements and responses members know by heart

- move to a joyous festival experience toward the end of the service

- recruit leaders who have confidence and enthusiasm[31]

Why are the services organized the way(s) they are?

These goals sound great in theory, but how should a service be organized in practice? What are the essential elements of worship? The text of the hymn "God Is Here!" paints a poetic summary of those elements.[32] It can be "exasperating" to understand the many dimensions of worship— not my word but that of James White. Especially if you are a newcomer or tourist attending a worship service, many resources are available to help.[33]

If you have never or infrequently attended a house of worship, might I suggest that if you are willing to go, take a copy of **activity 5.2** along with you to help frame questions you could ask. Believe me, there are many variations! I'm describing a familiar model here.[34]

Coming from a conservative musical heritage and a position as a music leader, Greg Scheer identifies three general types of worship service structures in churches: liturgical, thematic, and experiential. Mainline church services are liturgical, tied to the traditions of their Reformation pasts, plus a new interest in rediscovering what the early church (100–200

31. Long, *Beyond the Worship Wars*, 13. Long was a seminary professor of preaching and worship for much of his career. Note: I have made some modifications in his terminology.

32. Fred Pratt Green, "God Is Here!," #70, in United Church of Christ, *New Century Hymnal*. See www.hymnary.org for additional information.

33. Theologians believe worship reflects theological doctrines, such as the belief in the Trinity, i.e., God as Father, Son, and Holy Spirit. See White, *Introduction to Worship*, and Cherry, *Worship Architect*.

34. Wild Goose Worship Group, *Wee Worship Book*. The wild goose is an ancient symbol for the Holy Spirit. The Iona Community of Scotland created this service.

CE) practiced. The four major liturgical elements are gathering, word, responses to the word, and dismissal.[35] Non-denominational churches and charismatic congregations tend to use a thematic structure. They are sermon-dominated, with the "worship wallpaper" leading to the sermon and eventually the altar call. Typically, megachurches—those with thousands of members—use the experiential structure, as do neo-Pentecostal churches and praise and worship congregations.[36]

WHAT ARE THE KEY "PLAYS" IN WORSHIP SERVICES?

Return to the four parts of a worship service: gathering, word (Scripture), responses to the word, and dismissal. You'll notice liturgical services use many rituals. Some services offer familiarity, and others are more freely structured. Our well-being desires some things to be familiar, especially when our lives are in periods of uncertainty and chaos, but we also need rituals that give us the tools to break boredom and old patterns.[37]

Gathering

♦ Worship usually begins with an acknowledgment of awe and deep respect.[38]

35. An Evangelical Lutheran Church in America worship book states it succinctly: "From the earliest days of the Church, Christian worship has been marked by a pattern of gathering, word, meal, and sending. These basic elements—revealed in the New Testament, the writings of the early Church, . . . confessions, and ecumenical documents—constitute the center of the Church's worship" (ELCA, *With One Voice*, 5). Cherry uses a supporting analogy: like a home, a "house" of worship's four pillars are gathering, word read and preached, responses to the word, and sending (Cherry, *Worship Architect*, xiv–xvii). See also Dawn, *Reaching Out*.

36. Sheer, *Art of Worship*, 88–101.

37. The paradox of the need for both inherited and revised rituals is emphasized in Driver, *Liberating Rites*.

38. Glick, *With All Thy Mind*, 62–63: "The most frequently used Hebrew word translated as 'worship' in English is *shachah* (shaw-KHAW). Its root meaning conveys the idea of prostration to royalty or a deity. . . . The second most common word translated in Scripture as worship, 'service,' is found in both the Hebrew Scriptures and Christian Scriptures, 'Serve the Lord with gladness'" (Ps 100:2).

◆ The opening music is often instrumental or organ preludes, congregational hymns.[39]

◆ Some liturgies—order of service or, in Greek, *liturgi*, "the work of the people"—follow with a contrast to human unworthiness, i.e., prayers of confession and forgiveness.[40]

Stories (Scriptures) Read and Interpreted

◆ Sacred texts are read and interpreted. Depending on the tradition, interpreters may be limited by gender or education. Non-deist traditions have significant writings for their disciples to learn. The Muslim faith bases its teaching on the *Qur'an*, the Arab word for "recitation;" English pronunciation Koran), which is believed to be a divine revelation from Allah to Muhammad.

◆ Choral responses or chants often precede or follow the readings. In some traditions, congregants stand for the reading of the Gospel lesson.

Responses to the Scripture Reading or Word

◆ Congregational singing, choral anthems, and instrumental music are powerful ways to express feelings about the words heard and the meaning learned. See **appendix 5A**. This can be a call to discipleship, appreciation of children, a prophetic insight regarding a social justice issue, or a time to address an unexpected loss.[41]

39. An oft-cited admonition from Christian Scripture is: "Let the word of Christ dwell in you richly; teach and admonish one another in all wisdom, and with gratitude in your hearts sing psalms, hymns, and spiritual songs to God" (Col 3:16). A gospel song could be "Learning on the Everlasting Arms." Evangelicals might favor "How Great Thou Art," while "Holy, Holy, Holy" would be an example of a mainline congregation's hymn choice. Unitarians and spiritualists could sing "Morning Has Broken." For background on these hymns, go to www.hymnary.org.

40. Buechner, *Room Called Remember*, 27: "Like Moses we come here as we are . . . because wherever it is that we truly belong, whatever it is that is truly home for us, we know in our hearts that we have somehow lost it and gotten lost . . . . We come here to find what we have lost . . . . We come here to confess our sins."

41. Possible hymns for the circumstances mentioned: for discipleship, "O Master, Let Me Walk with You;" for children, "Jesus Loves Me"; for justice, "Be Thou My Vision"; for an end-of-life service, "Our God, Our Help in Ages Past."

+ Prayers: In some traditions, only the clergy offer or lead the prayers in worship, while in others, any person present can share joys and concerns. In Islam, adherents are called to prayer (*salat*) five times a day.[42] Make no mistake about the importance of both individual and corporate prayer. They should both be done; they link the individual to the community.[43] The diversity of prayer practices and observances is also extensive.[44] Some may be prescribed prayers; others are spontaneous, focused on joys and concerns. In Christian traditions, the most famous of recited prayers is the Lord's Prayer.[45]

+ Offering: In gratitude for the diverse and abundant gifts received from God, including time, talent, and treasure, worshippers respond with an offering. Traditionally, attendees place money in offering plates or velvet bags; they are brought to the altar and dedicated to God. Some churches do not take an offering during the service. A growing trend in many congregations is to encourage donating online.

+ Sacraments: Another form of offering that worshipers in the Christian tradition experience is the sacraments. The Latin root word *sacer* signifies the sacred or holy, what Augustine referred to as visible signs of God's invisible grace—God's gifts, which humans don't earn.[46] Some theologians argue that only practices associated with Jesus and described in the Bible can be sacraments, i.e., baptism and communion.[47]

---

42. Willis, *Religion Book*, 280.

43. John Calvin: "Whoever refuses to pray in the holy assembly of the godly knows not what it is to pray individually . . . . Again, he who neglects to pray alone and in private . . . in public assemblies will contrive only windy prayers" (Calvin, *Institutes of the Christian Religion*, 3.20.29, as cited by Gillis, *Let Us Pray*). See also Heschel, *Man's Quest for God*, 45: "Those who cherish genuine prayer yet feel driven away from the houses of worship because of the sterility of public worship today, seem to believe that private prayer is the only way. Yet, the truth is that private prayer will not survive unless it is inspired by public prayer."

44. Diana Bass, *Christianity after Religion*, 54–57.

45. It is considered a prayer Jesus of Nazareth taught his disciples (Matt 6:5–15; Luke 11:1–13). Borg, *Speaking Christian*, 223–30, has a provocative analysis of what this prayer includes and does not include. He recommends another book, Crossan, *Greatest Prayer*, for additional interpretation.

46. Migliore, *Faith Seeking Understanding*, 211–12, 224–26.

47. "The baptized devoted themselves to the apostles' teaching and fellowship, to the breaking of bread and the prayers" (Acts 2:42). Regarding baptism, church history is riddled with debates whether it should be limited to adult believers or available

Sending or Dismissal

◆ The conclusion of the service emphasizes that disciples are to be "lights" to the world through their actions, especially their service.[48]

◆ The worship leader may give a commissioning or benediction.[49]

◆ In traditional services, an organist or instrumentalist plays a postlude (from Latin, *ludere*, to play after).

Music and Worship

Music is a central focus in many religious traditions.[50] Music can be unifying or dividing, inspiring or insipid, hilarious to horrific.[51] Music unites people in times of celebrations and calamities, in creeds shared and dreams dared. Spiritual songs are so potent because we sing what we believe; it's also been said that music more often helps us remember how we felt than what actually occurred.

---

for children. Traditions that don't practice infant baptism have dedication services for babies and toddlers. See Marty, *Baptism*. Jesus was baptized by immersion; it was considered symbolic of cleansing, dying to an old way, receiving a new way. In time, for children, sprinkling with drops of water became common. Communion is also known as the Lord's Supper or the Eucharist. See Duck, *Worship for Whole People*, for more information on these two sacraments in Christian worship. The Roman Catholic (RC) and Eastern Orthodox (EO) traditions have five other sacraments: penance/reconciliation (RC) or repentance and confession (EO), matrimony, anointing of the sick (RC) or unction (EO), confirmation (RC) or chrismation (EO), and orders/ordination. Some spiritual communities refer to these as rites while some Protestant groups do not believe in any sacraments.

48. Symbolically, candles are lit as disciples gather; they are extinguished at service's end as disciples take the light into the world. In some traditions, evangelizing, i.e., converting non-believers, is promoted. In mainline congregations, the focus is more on social justice actions.

49. The word *benediction* has Latin root words meaning "to speak well," and *benedictio* is "blessing." Recall ch. 4 for discussion on commission.

50. Raman, *Deus Ubiquitus*, 145–74. The breadth and depth of his chapter on music is amazing. From chants to choral examples, the author provides an enriching explosion of examples on the significance of spiritual music.

51. Drescher, *Choosing Our Religion*, 106–9 reports that music is incredibly important to Nones. One None interviewee stated the music in the movie *Love Story* was "the way, the truth, and the life for me and my generation." It mirrors Ludwig van Beethoven's (1770-1826) sentiment, "music is the mediator between the spiritual and the sensual life."

Some traditions, past more than present, believe singing or musical instruments are distractions to be banned. More recently, some say worship and religious drama are too commercialized or consumer-centered—long on sentiment and short on substance. The result: "worship wars,"[52] with one compromise being that the congregation provides both a "traditional" service and a "contemporary" service.[53] Another strategy—I view it positively—is to have spiritual homes appoint worship, music, and arts teams or committees of lay members and professionals (ministers and musicians) to plan the service.[54]

WHAT'S HAPPENING WITH WORSHIP?

In *Grounded*, Diana Butler Bass reported religious traditions were experiencing what she named "spiritual awakening" and "spiritual revolution," often finding God in nature.[55] A legitimate question would be, was that spirituality reflected in increased worship attendance? The answer is probably not. Bass reports some congregations began planting gardens and becoming more sensitive to environmental issues. Yet, ironically, many were rejecting what she called the theology associated with many churches, a God "up there" (my term). One factor that makes it difficult to connect spirituality with worship attendance is that the 2020 pandemic closed houses of worship as a preventative measure. There were immediate protests, debates, and defiant actions.[56] An innovative

52. Long, *Beyond the Worship Wars*. See also Woods and Walrath, *Message in the Music*.

53. Vanderwell, *Church of All Ages*, believes all generations should worship together. The Calvin Institute of Christian Worship at Calvin College, Grand Rapids, with John D. Witvliet as director, is committed to expanding the use of global hymns and new hymns that reach across generations. Hawn, *New Songs of Celebration*, chronicles in detail the changing styles of music and religious songs in recent years.

54. De Waal Malefyt and Vanderwall, *Designing Worship Together*.

55. Diana Bass, *Grounded*, in which she followed a similar theme from her earlier work, *Christianity after Religion*. For historical explanations and examples of spirituality, see Come, *Human Spirit and Holy Spirit*. For descriptions of another trend among mainline denominations in the US and Canada, see Andrus, "Contemporary Worship," and "Emerging Worship Initiative."

56. Boston, "Inside Information," 10–11, summarizes the legal aspects, such as although the First Amendment's free exercise clause is cited, i.e., government can't control religious behaviors, government health regulations can forbid certain practices when dangerous health conditions exist.

response emerged: the use of social media and platforms like YouTube and Zoom.[57] Now, with vaccinations and returning of in-person worship services, there are mixed responses. Pastors have informed me that their congregations are receiving similar messages from members as well as new attendees: some prefer the new format, others the traditional. Some congregations report steep declines in attendance, while others cite increases, thanks to their streaming of services. As discussed in the connections section, people need that sense of touch and socialization to satisfy "skin hunger," but in convenient formats. Conclusion: online offerings will continue, in some shape or another.

Responding to the Zoom situation, one congregation in a Midwestern college town found its worship attendance tripled as it evolved electronically. From early YouTube broadcasts focused on the minister preaching, to piecing together various choir members singing, to adding video clips of children's messages, streaming allowed this spiritual home to reach friends and former university student attendees—and new viewers in a variety of states and countries.[58]

A relatively new or planted church in Chicago reflects this movement. It is known proudly by its mainly younger members (in their twenties to thirties) as the Queer Bar Storyteller Church. According to Pastor Vince Amlin, the congregation appeals to those who find God in their worlds in non-traditional ways; they crave services that speak to them in their language and locations. The theme of a service is set; two members offer short, five-minute, related stories—sounds a bit like NPR's *The Moth Radio Hour*—followed by pop music. Examples of artists included Madonna and the Eagles.[59] In a similar story, the Olive Branch Community in Rochester, Minnesota, emphasizes "longing" music, for those, including LGBTQ people, hurt by past church experiences.

---

57. The Ecumenical Consultation on Protocols for Worship, Fellowship, and Sacraments has created a thirty-six-page document, "Resuming Care-Filled Worship and Sacramental Life during a Pandemic."

58. Linda Westgate, Northminster Presbyterian Church, Ames, IA. Phone interview July 15, 2021.

59. Rev. Vince Amlin, phone conversation, July 15, 2021. One theme was "why people get tattoos"; another was "going to camp." After each story, the assertion was made that "this is the word of God for the people of God," i.e., that God is still speaking today. Then the pop songs are played and discussed.

WHAT SHOULD I GET OUT OF MEDITATION (SPIRITUAL PRACTICES)?

Yearning is part of the human DNA, so I've asserted, but do you agree that it takes various shapes? If you are among those who don't want to try worship, explore the form of yearning known as meditation. It includes some theistic traditions but others which are not. You may say that your beliefs focus on your "center of value."[60] Its practices wrestle with aspects of desire, rejection, and love. They assert we humans are not whole and want to be connected to something we don't have. We have deep longings, with feelings of tenderness, anxiousness, and triumph. Some of its adherents believe confrontation with mystery will end with personal dreams fulfilled, an ultimate better life achieved. The truth or truths we discover on that journey come from the diverse ways people before us have searched and shared. Through gumption and glimpses of grace, our episodes of yearning can be awe-fully inspiring.[61] If you are inclined toward this outlook on life but want a different name for it, consider sociologist of religion Peter Berger's description: "signals of transcendence."[62]

WHAT ARE THE BENEFITS OF SPIRITUAL PRACTICES?

Yearning is more than wishful, positive thinking. Yearning includes the dimension of anxiousness, the feeling something is missing, the recognition that something specific needs to be done. It's been said that worship emphasizes what adherents profess or say they believe. As we cope with the struggles of daily life, our true spirituality is shown in what disciplines and

---

60. "To deny the reality of a supernatural being called God is one thing; to live without confidence in some center of value and without loyalty is another" (H. Richard Niebuhr, *Radical Monotheism*, 25). Ariarajah, *Not Without My Neighbour*, 38, emphasizes the communal nature of worship, which he asserts is more about thanksgiving than seeking or questing. He adds that storytelling is central to worship.

61. Taylor, *Holy Envy*, provides a reflection of her years of teaching a world religions course. Various chapters describe meditative practices and interviews with adherents of different spiritual practices.

62. Heim, "Peter Berger's Rumors," discusses the deceased sociologist's view found in Berger's *A Rumor of Angels*, that humans have the propensity and capacity to learn, to play, to find hope in the face of death, to discern right and wrong, and to laugh, which he said were signals of transcendence.

practices we do.[63] **Activity 5.3** encourages you to begin practices; **appendix 5B** lists approximately one hundred of them. Let me offer a sampling of four types of practices. Some practices will be communal, others individual. Some are done infrequently, others daily. Don't assume practices must be exotic, laborious, or painful. Many relate to ordinary circumstances with family, friends, food, and Fido (pets).[64] Non-theistic traditions such as Buddhism, Confucianism, and Taoism could be emphasized here, but theistic religions have a legacy with spiritual practices, too.[65]

Meditation

A meditation involves an incident, idea, or phrase that strikes a person, who then thinks about it; it may not involve any divinity. A similar practice is contemplation, which is more open-ended, with the focus typically on experiencing rather than understanding.[66] That said, Buddhist meditation seems to be becoming quite popular. The simplest form is following one's breathing patterns. A second form is *vipassana* or mindfulness meditation, which focuses on feelings, thoughts, or sensations. A third form, *metta* or loving-kindness, is for oneself first, then extends as unconditional love for others. These are just a few of many meditation or centering practices.[67]

Prayer

Prayer is the "soul of religion," its core.[68] The many facets of prayer, including its importance as a means to learn, are beautifully and

63. Diana Bass, *Christianity for the Rest*, describes ten practices in detail: hospitality, discernment, healing, contemplation, testimony, diversity, justice, worship, reflection, and beauty.

64. Drescher, *Choosing Our Religion*, 116–52; Warren, *Liturgies of the Ordinary*.

65. McLaren, *Finding Our Way Again*. A helpful summary is found at spiritual-practice.ca/what/what-2/the-common-christian-practices/. Samples of personal disciplines or practices include meditation, prayer, fasting, study, forgiveness, dying well, and solitude; communal disciplines are keeping the holy seasons, testimony, and worship; missional disciplines include service, justice, and hospitality.

66 Willis, *Religion Book*, 393–94.

67. Prothero, *God Is Not One*, 177–79; Harvey, *Direct Path*, 110–35.

68. Fosdick, *Meaning of Prayer*. An Eastern Orthodox priest described prayer as something always occurring somewhere in the world, likening it to a river. Using that

profoundly described in an essay by Rabbi Abraham Joshua Heschel, where it is viewed as "the essence of spiritual living"; "prayer is like a beam thrown from a flashlight . . . in this light we who grope, stumble, and climb discover where we stand, what surrounds us, and the course which one should choose."[69] Prayer, for Heschel, is not an informal conversation with God but communication with God or gods, allowing us to listen, speak, or petition. That said, public prayers need to respect both believers and those who don't believe prayer has value.[70]

Well-Being

The focus here is on the body. It includes practices that improve one's physical health through yoga, rest, closing one's eyes, dancing, fasting, following dietetic restrictions, kneeling, or genuflecting. Some practices include decorating the body with coloring or wearing special beads and clothes. Conversely, in some cultures and religions, the body is "improved" by self-flagellation. In various societies, either sexual abstinence or sexual activity are recommended practices. See chapter 7 to discuss other dimensions of well-being.

Hospitality

Preparing and sharing food is essential, and in some religions, providing meals for the holy is considered necessary. Hosting strangers, making pilgrimages, honoring family ancestors, and involvement with other disciples are a few examples. Beyond food, hospitality also includes the setting, accessibility, comfortable furniture, and appropriate temperature.[71]

With thanks to "Coach" Dennis Eastin, consider the Buddhist practice of Tonglen—in Tibetan, "giving and receiving"—which he learned from Pema Chödrön. You may wish to look at Chödrön's "Tonglen Meditation" video, listed in the bibliography. Eastin states that this practice can enhance a worship experience, showing the connection of all humans to each other, helping persons find the sacred in life. It is a yearning to address suffering in the world and overcome fear. Its benefits include

image, Christopher Grundy wrote the song "Stepping In."

69. Heschel, *Man's Quest for God*, 45.

70. Avalos, "Imagine."

71. Pavlovitz, *Bigger Table*, 55–102.

alleviating suffering, increasing gratefulness, enhancing compassion, building kindness for oneself, reducing fears and anxieties, improving relationships with other, and growing one's spirituality.

Music and Meditation

For many, music less often comes to mind as a part of meditative practices. V. V. Raman, a physicist-philosopher, offers some excellent examples for us. Confucius believed that "Music is the Harmony of Heaven and Earth . . . when music and rites are fully realized, Heaven and Earth function in perfect order." In the dharmic tradition, sound is sacred; the chants of the Sama Veda are the musical mode of reciting Vedic hymns. The chant of the peace-generating *om* is especially calming. Prayers may be sung as chants. Greek culture also was filled with poetry and hymns as meditative devices.[72]

WHAT ARE THE TRENDS IN MEDITATION (SPIRITUAL PRACTICE)?

Granted, meditation is no longer used only to gain spiritual enlightenment; however, meditation is common among many groups. Unsurprisingly, Buddhists and Hindus meditate the most.[73] Consider these 2021 statistics: over 14 percent of US adults have tried meditation; since 2012, the number of people practicing meditation has tripled; general wellness is the number one reason given for meditating; and it is estimated, worldwide, that between 200 and 500 million people meditate.[74] If you are interested, there are many apps and websites for practices sponsored by specific religious traditions.

What of spiritual practices in a theistic tradition? A Hindu temple in Minneapolis opened in 2020. Its members built what is claimed to be the largest temple in the United States. It will contain various chapels for different gods. A typical service involves readings, observing holidays, and bringing gifts of food and clothing for the statutes. Milestone services are especially festive, lasting several days, in some cases. In weekly services,

72. Raman, *Deus Ubiquitus*, 145–51; quote from 147.
73. Masci and Hackett, "Meditation Is Common."
74. Good Body, "Twenty-Four Meditation Statistics."

leaders share stories about the adventures of the gods and their advice for living that benefit individuals and the wider society.[75]

WHAT IF ALL I WANT IS TO BE IN CONNECTION WITH OTHERS?

You may be a spiritual traveler who feels neither the worship nor meditation categories fit you. Yet you yearn to belong to a community that provides moral support and ways to explore living your spiritual life.[76] All of us can be lonely, but surprisingly, perhaps, research studies indicate loneliness is experienced more by Gen Z and millennials than older persons. Or it could be that you may have an even bigger picture. This one is expressed by my friend, V. V. Raman:

> As conscious beings . . . we have two dimensions: one is our individual survival, and the other is our collective existence. The latter dimension prompts a need and yearning for connection with others. This connection starts with love and affiliation, tying us to our parents and siblings. It gradually evolves and includes one's community, nation, and humanity. Then there is the yearning to connect with all of nature and the Universe at large. This happens when, at a spiritually sophisticated stage, we become aware of our individual selves as fragments of the Cosmic Whole. Religion is essentially a collective expression of this awareness and the related longing for the cosmic connection. Every religious rite and ritual, hymn and prayer, meditation and music, is a mode by which this longing is fulfilled.[77]

Milestones

Recall our opening discussion about milestone services. Some clergy call them "womb to tomb" services or "hatch-match-attach-dispatch"

75. Like all traditions, the Hindu temple in Minneapolis is not representative of all that may or may not occur in Hindu services. Magida and Matlins, *How to Be a Perfect Stranger* 1, 157–71. A second volume is also available. Each section provides a brief understanding of the tradition's beliefs and describes the elements of a typical service.

76. As noted earlier, some churches are using an instrument, Spiritual Locations, to help individuals find their niche. See **activity 2.4**. Other churches use small groups; see Searcy and Thomas, *Activate*.

77. Raman, July 20, 2021; written statement given to author and used with permission.

ceremonies. Heads up: they vary tremendously from tradition to tradition but fit this connection category. No doubt you know that civil authorities and others perform similar services from time to time. Make it known to your family, friends, and coworkers that you look forward to celebrating wedding anniversaries, retirements, returning or leaving members of the military, and student graduations.

Celebrations and Festivals

To remember key events in their traditions' history, Hinduism, Islam, Judaism, and Christianity have major festivals and services that reflect special seasons of the year. For example, most religions have celebrations during winter months celebrating hope for new beginnings, what anthropologists view as "world renewal ceremonies.[78]

Often, festivals and seasons involve special foods. Although not new, there appears to be a growing trend of persons and communities of different faiths invite others to sacred gatherings: Jewish with seder services, Muslims with iftar dinners, Sikhs with langar, Hindus with many festivals, including Diwali. A similar connection activity in Christian churches is called the Dinner Church Movement. In 2008, Rev. Emily M. D. Scott and Rachel Kroh founded St. Lydia's Dinner Church.[79] The concept was to make a sacred meal the primary liturgical celebration. One outcome is to join established and new congregations in mutual services.[80]

Holidays

The United States is a country with a civil religion. The Pledge of Allegiance contains a reference to God. Holidays such as Thanksgiving and the Fourth of July have proclamations calling for divine blessings. Political leaders finish their addresses with "God bless America." Branches

78. Gradwohl, Iowa State University, handout prepared for Green Hills Community in 2021.

79. https://www.dinnerchurchmovement.org.

80. Rev. Dr. Jo Hudson, senior pastor, New Church, Chiesa Nuova UCC, Dallas, TX, phone conversation, December 10, 2020. Prior to the pandemic, a common practice for the congregation was to host light meals during the seasons of Advent and Lent. A separate practice was the Pastor and wife would host "Pop-up Dinner" for FaceBook friends, a random gathering.

of Christianity, specifically the Roman Catholic Church and mainline Protestant denominations, have congregational song books that include hymns appropriate for the major holidays and seasons.[81] The US Congress has chaplains; clergy are asked to deliver prayers at public meetings (legislators and city councils now debate if only the locally recognized faith leaders or broader groups are invited to lead such opening prayers). One form of association is to participate in communal holiday events, or world renewal ceremonies, as described earlier.

Music

The purpose of patriotic music is to unite citizens.[82] It can be a great connector in other ways. I have witnessed over one hundred tuba players offering a holiday concert. Friends describe an international concert in which the program consisted of selections of sacred music from different traditions within that country. Music is the unifying force behind many programs for children from disadvantaged homes; support for these programs has come from spiritual and religious communities.[83]

What are your own favorite songs? See **activity 5.4.** St. Augustine had it right: singing a hymn is equivalent to praying twice.[84] Music can be a miracle. In hospitals or long-term care facilities, persons silent with severe medical conditions still begin singing when they hear familiar hymns. Certain praise songs and hymns glorify the source of our power and motivate us to care for those less fortunate in numerous ways.[85] Music, as art, has perennial themes but texts and tunes are always evolving.[86] According to a professional musician, Richard Bruxvoort Colligan, many

---

81. Horn, *Christian Year*, 16. Also, Olsen, *Wisdom of the Seasons.*

82. Meacham and McGraw, *Songs of America.* A number of songs come from religious traditions. For example, ch. 3, "Mine Eyes Have seen the Glory"; ch. 6, "We Shall Overcome"; and finale, "Lift Every Voice."

83. https://www.ed.ac.uk/impact/people/music-beyond-borders;   https://exilophone.com/.

84. Wren, *Praying Twice*, 1. Wren, as others do, attributes the quote to Augustine (354–430 CE; Wren, *Praying Twice*, 2).

85. See Routley, *Panorama of Christian Hymnody*; Dowley, *Christian Music*; Westermeyer, *Te Deum.*

86. See Brueggemann, *Glad Obedience*; Cook, *What a Friend*; Sirchio, *Six Marks*; McLean, *New Harmonies.*

songs today have "longing" messages similar to expressions in the Hebrew psalms.

WHAT ARE TRENDS IN CONNECTING?

Why are ministers in metropolitan areas finding their religious and spiritual communities so intent on connecting? Most are in a mode of entrenchment, still weighing the impact of COVID-19. They feel a need to be with others. At the same time, the world's speed and noise have generated requests to slow down and have more occasions for silence in worship. A coming trend is spiritual communities partnering with regional voluntary associations that focus on assisting fellow citizens, for example, with health and housing issues.[87]

TRAVELER: READY TO BECOME A PRISONER BY CHOICE AND JOY?

Your journey has taken you to a place you might consider a possible spiritual home; you've now learned that one mark is a joyful, vibrant yearning service, built on integrity, beset with beauty. With practices and voices, you and your community of friends (remember ch. 3) will be commissioned to go out joyfully to serve others. If you chose to design a milestone service (**activity 5.1**), were joy and generosity of spirit outcomes?

A reality you will face is that there will be differences of opinion about worship services or community offerings for meditation and contemplation. What shouldn't be disputed is that disciples are called to yearn (worship), to share big questions, and move to meet dreams. The worship and meditation goals of spiritual homes must be bigger and better than any one person, one community, or one religion. Spiritual homes, large and small, in various climates, have used and will continue to observe rituals, music, and art to pay homage to that which they believe is of ultimate worth.[88] Talk to worshipers and yearners. Typically, they feel

87. A national example is the Industrial Areas Foundations (IAF). The IAF currently works with thousands of religious congregations, non-profits, civic organizations, and unions, in more than sixty-five cities across the United States and in Canada, Australia, the United Kingdom, and Germany, to address policy issues for citizens in need. In my area, the affiliated organization is AMOS, a Mid-Iowa Organizing Strategy.

88. Mercadante, *Belief without Borders*, 251. This journalist/minister learned in her interviews with SBNRs that their hope was for a "re-sacralization" of the world, which

abundantly blessed and thankful for the intangible gifts received, and in turn, they become more generous in terms of time and commitment to appreciating and helping others. See **activity 5.5.**

The image of a "prisoner by choice" for yearning and worship may seem strange. It begins with a Christian scriptural account of the disciple Paul, who was often jailed, stating he had made the decision to be in prison based on his call and mission (Eph 5:1). You may think of other spiritual sages, some for political or for ethical reasons, who accepted their imprisonment.

A somewhat different motivation is the realization that we are or can be sociologically, psychologically, or accidentally manipulated, then entrapped by others or our own desires. The sixteenth-century German reformer Martin Luther described it in this way: we humans are like mules; we will be ridden either by the devil or Jesus Christ. We have a choice.

Here is a stanza of a hymn text I have written. Its message is that, through engaged spirituality, we can experience the joy of escaping our self-made prisons:

> We are caught in our own prisons,
> First in cells of status quo.
> Sad our few and timid visions,
> Walls of wanting cause us woe.
> Let us now make our confession
> From our squalid jails of greed.
> Grant us justice with compassion,
> Freely serving those in need.[89]

---

included an appreciation of traditional liturgies. The question is whether houses of worship are trying too hard to offer practical, non-demanding, friendly congregations, downplaying the awe, respect, and humility that should be felt in the presence of God.

89. Kniker, "Prisoners by Choice," in "Songs of Disciples," n.p.

Chapter 5 Activities

ACTIVITY 5.1: DESIGNING A MILESTONE EVENT

Suppose a family member or friend asked you to help them plan a milestone service—1) a baptism or dedication service; 2) a youth-to-adult passage ceremony; 3) a wedding; 4) end-of-life service. Your decisions: Who will be involved in the service and what roles will they play? Is special clothing required or suggested? Who will attend? Where it will be held? What music, if allowed? Are food and drink a part of the service or after the event?

Why so much effort? Regardless of whether it is a religious or non-religious service, these milestone events celebrate a significant change in multiple relationships. After they occur, we remember them with stories, often humorous, because we have been *altered* by these major events.[90] These milestones are often the foundations of family traditions.

Some advice. I suggest your milestone event should include the five senses: sound, sight, touch, taste, and smell.[91] Why? Because our human wholeness and well-being respond to all the senses. We have feelings; we are moved by love, music, art, and food. We know that spirit is real, for athletic teams, for community bonding. Voices within us urge us to probe, perform, imagine, dream, and achieve. Does the event's structure allow for flexibility? Granted, just as sports fans, rock band followers, or hobby enthusiasts want familiarity, regular

90. A story about a wedding: following the rehearsal, the evening before the marriage service, a nervous bride whispered to the minister she already had forgotten all her instructions. To calm her, the clergy tells her she has only three things to remember: her father will escort her down the *aisle;* the vows, repeated in short phrases, will be at the *altar;* and following the announcement that she and her partner are now husband and wife, those attending will sing a *hymn* of celebration. Keep repeating those three words, said the officiant: aisle, altar, hymn. Unfortunately, the groom became extremely upset, because he thought she said repeatedly, "I'll alter him."

91. Ariarajah, *Not without My Neighbour*, 46, captures this beautifully in describing a Hindu service, at the time of the *puja* (giving a gift to a deity; the word means "offering a flower"), smelling the aroma from the burning camphor and incense; viewing the sculptures and paintings clothed and garlanded and the raised *arathi* (lamp); hearing the chanting mantra, the ringing of bells, and the thumping drums; receiving the *prasad* (a mixture of milk, water, and fruit), and prostrating oneself on the floor.

(*Activity 5.1 continued*)

"yearners" also expect occasional novelty along with familiar rituals. Unconsciously, frequent and infrequent worship attendees want polished performances based on movies and television standards. Your service needs to blend familiar and new words, transform ancient rituals into new settings, and translate past testimonies into stirring contemporary stories. Go for it!

ACTIVITY 5.2: ANSWERING A STRANGER'S QUESTIONS

If you are a visitor, a stranger, or a newcomer who is making your first visit to a spiritual home, you will probably have some questions. At one time or another, all of us are strangers before God. Hopefully you can find someone there to answer them. These questions relate to a visit at a mainline Protestant worship service but can be easily modified to use for any spiritual community you are visiting.

1. Does this congregation truly welcome strangers?
2. Why do most people come to this house of worship/fellowship?
3. What are some other reasons for coming?
4. What's the point of a worship service?
5. Is the after-service time just for members?
6. Why do you have a printed bulletin?
7. What do you have to believe to be a member here?
8. Who is the minister/leader? (Do the leaders have special clothing, like robes?)
9. Why greet other people during the service?
10. Why does the minister have an assistant for worship?
11. What's this business of "eating the body" and "drinking the blood" all about?
12. What is the other sacrament you have?

(Activity 5.2 continued)

13. Should I bring my children to this house of worship?

14. Is your music "traditional" or "contemporary"?

15. Am I expected to give money? Or other forms of support (like time)?

16. Will I be hassled by people because I came to the service?

17. When do you stand, sit, kneel, and why?

18. Why should I return?

ACTIVITY 5.3: YOUR SPIRITUAL PRACTICES[92]

To deepen your spirituality, as the book suggests, you need to exercise, spiritually. The guideline is that it is something done repeatedly, although a once-in-a-lifetime pilgrimage could be on your spiritual bucket list.

If the examples from the four spiritual practices of meditation, prayer, yoga, or hospitality described in the text don't get you excited, look at the list of one hundred in **appendix 5B**.

Recall also that these don't have to be ancient practices but ones that could relate to your family, friends, food, or Fido (pets).

Indicate here what a FIRST practice is: when you began it _____, how often you did it for three months _____ (___ times a _____), and the benefit(s) derived:

_____

_____.

Has it ended? _____ If so, when? _____

****

Indicate here a SECOND practice: you began it _____, how often you did it for three months _____ (___ times a _____), and the benefit(s) derived:

92. Consult these and other sources from this chapter (see also ch. 7): McLaren, *Finding Our Way Again;* Diana Bass, *Christianity for the Rest*; Diana Bass, *Practicing Congregation*; Dorothy Bass, *Practicing Our Faith*; Harvey, *Direct Path*; Warren, *Liturgy of the Ordinary*.

(*Activity 5.3 continued*)

_____.

Has it ended? If so, when? _____

ACTIVITY 5.4: YOUR SPECIAL SONG(S)

Almost all of us have a song that has a special meaning. It may or may not have what you consider a spiritual meaning—at least you didn't think so. But consider it again.

I have created a survey about music where you can list several of your favorite songs that are meaningful to you. The survey takes about ten minutes and is simple to fill out. You may leave some of the categories blank. Your responses are anonymous, and no personally identifiable information will be collected or shared with anyone else.

Instructions: To access the survey, please type the following URL into your web browser to participate: https://www.surveymonkey.com/r/spiritualmusic.

Survey Results: If you are interested, you can then learn what songs others have indicated are their favorites. Updated survey results are presented at the following site (please type this link into your web browser to view survey results): https://www.surveymonkey.com/stories/SM-7SFXSDSJ/.

ACTIVITY 5.5: UNIVERSAL REFLECTIONS: A PRAYER FOR ALL RELIGIONS[93]

In striving to recognize the primacy of Fire and Light,
  I feel kinship with my Zoroastrian sisters and brothers.
In striving to respect the Ten Commandments,
  I feel kinship with my Jewish sisters and brothers.
In striving to be kind to neighbor and the needy,
  I feel kinship with my Christian sisters and brothers.

93. Created by V. V. Raman. Composed at the Cape of Good Hope, South Africa. Inspired by the Parliament of the World's Religions at Cape Town, Dec. 1999. Used with permission of the author.

(Activity 5.5 continued)

In striving to be compassionate to creatures great and small,
  I feel kinship with my Buddhist and Jaina sisters and brothers.
In striving to surrender myself completely to the Divine,
  I feel kinship with my Muslim sisters and brothers.

In the recognition that religious wisdom flows from the Masters,
  I feel kinship with my Sikh sisters and brothers.
In the recognition that serving fellow humans should be the goal of all religions,
  I feel kinship with my Bahai sisters and brothers.

In my reverence for plants and trees, for lakes and mountains,
  I feel kinship with my Native American sisters and brothers.
In my respect for those who see the world only as natural phenomena arising from physical laws,
  I feel kinship with my religious naturalist sisters and brothers.
In feeling that all these and more are all paths to the same Unfathomable Mystery,
  I feel kinship with my Hindu sisters and brothers.

In my love and laughter, joy and pain,
  I feel kinship with all my fellow humans.
In my need for nourishment and instinct to live on,
  I feel kinship with all beings of the planet.
In my spiritual ecstasy with this wondrous world,
  I feel kinship with the Cosmic Whole.

FOR ADDITIONAL CONVERSATIONS

Truly hundreds, if not thousands, of resources are available to you regarding spiritual yearning. Listed below are a few that focus on areas discussed in this chapter.

◆ To be vital, worship needs to be vibrant. Discussing worship for Christians, Ruth Duck has examples from African American, Asian, Euro-American, and Hispanic cultures. *Worship for the Whole People of God: Vital Worship for the Twenty-First Century* describes multiple patterns of worship as well as resources for music and art.

◆ Congregational singing and other forms of music are thoroughly integrated with the history of religious traditions, as this author so ably posits. Brian Wren, a poet, pastor, and hymn composer can speak authoritatively about global music. *Praying Twice: The Music and Words of Congregational Song* offers a fountain of resources.

◆ For those who are attracted to Eastern religions and non-traditional spiritual approaches, I highly recommend Varadaraja Raman's *Deus Ubiquitus*. An editorial board member of several science and religion journals, this philosopher-physicist has an amazing array of experiences and examples that deserve contemplation.

◆ The autobiography of C.S. Lewis, *Surprised by Joy,* is the story of a youth who overcomes the death of his mother by reluctantly becoming involved in a faith tradition.

◆ Researchers of religion/spirituality have noted a trend of interest and participation in historical spiritual practices, especially Buddhist. Although focused on Christian practices, Brian Mclaren's *Finding Our Way Again: The Return of the Ancient Practices* illustrates some that touch other traditions.

◆ Mentioned in the text, Tish Harrison Warren's *Liturgy of the Ordinary: Sacred Practices in Everyday Life* is a joy for those who feel their lives are too busy to get involved with in-depth, time-away-from-home activities.

6

Education—
"Trans-Formed" by Truth

The essence of education is that it be religious.

—ALFRED NORTH WHITEHEAD, *THE AIMS OF EDUCATION AND OTHER ESSAYS*, 25

My heart has become capable of every form:
It is a pasture for gazelles,
And a monastery for Christian monks,
And a temple for idols.
And the pilgrim's Ka-ba,
And the tablets of the Torah,
And the Book of the Qur'an.
I follow the religion of Love:
Whatever way Love's camel takes,
That is my religion and my faith.

—IBN ARABI, SUFI MASTER

The greatest obstacle to discovery is not ignorance—it is the illusion of knowledge.

—DANIEL J. BOORSTIN, LIBRARIAN OF UNITED STATES CONGRESS, *THE DISCOVERERS* (1983)

The nation that expects to be ignorant and free expects what never was and never will be.

—THOMAS JEFFERSON, LETTER TO CHARLES YANCY (1816)

YESS: YOUR EDUCATION OF SELF FOR SOCIETY

- Invitation: To become part of a community of learning, "trans-formed" by truth

- Truth in a time of transition

- What is education? Religious education? Spiritual formation?

- What are the outcomes of spiritual learning?

- Why lifelong learning?

- What is (are) your learning style(s)?

- Whom would you choose as a teacher, a mentor?

- What is there to learn—and how?

- What are the best places and spaces to learn?

- Traveler: ready to become a questioning truth-teller?

- Activities

- For Additional Conversations

INVITATION: TO BECOME PART OF A COMMUNITY "TRANS-FORMED" BY TRUTH

The previous chapter offered you the first of four qualities of a healthy spiritual home: joy. The second component is truth. To understand the power of truth, I suggest you continue to use the metaphor of transforming a purchased house into a home. Prior to the sale, you would want to know how well it had been maintained. You would not want it to collapse!

My son and daughter-in-law purchased a two-hundred-year-old colonial farmhouse with a barn. Not fixer-uppers, they appreciated the previous owners' preservations and renovations, including a gourmet kitchen, updated bathrooms, and a large floor above the stable. For them, in time, it became their twins' learning and play areas. It fit. Other modifications followed. A house becomes a home when it embraces and reflects the truths of a family.[1] Visiting a transformed home is a precious experience.

Likewise, your spiritual home should fit you. It will reflect your authenticity, your true self. Remember, our truths change over time.[2] If this story isn't true, it should be: an arrogant PhD graduate in family studies, single, published his dissertation with the title *Ten Commandments for Raising Children*. After marriage and parenthood, succeeding edition titles were: *Ten Rules . . .*, *Ten Guidelines . . .*, *Ten Suggestions . . .*, and the final edition, *Ten Things I've Observed about Children*.

Antoine de Saint-Exupéry, author of the children's classic *The Little Prince*, advised, "If you want to build a ship, don't drum up people to collect wood and assign them tasks and work, but rather teach them to

---

1. The word *truth* comes from the German word *troth*, which means a person is faithful and be trusted in a relationship. You may recall worship services of the past included the word *betrothed*. Nash et al., *How to Talk*, 91–92, 181, discuss differences between "pragmatic truths" and religious truths.

2. Tournier, *Meaning of Persons*, 22–23, acknowledges that objective scientific evidence is demonstrably true, but life's experience and therapy reveal the shadings they have in everyday life. Søren Kierkegaard advises: "There are two ways to be fooled. One is to believe what isn't true. The other is to refuse to accept what is true."

long for the endless immensity of the sea." Then, they will find a way to build a ship.[3] Chapter 6 is not asking you to build the *Good Ship Spiritual Education* or serve on its crew. My hope is for you to feel and see breathtaking examples of the vistas learning offers when we engage in searching for truth, while acknowledging at times we live with mystery and uncertainty. While I'll suggest specific teaching styles, curriculum content, and a variety of learning locations, my emphasis is on the quest and zest for learning that transforms lives.[4] Few trips are straight-line excursions. Detours happen. All of us receive tempting itineraries to elsewhere. Myth-like, some call us to return to familiar locales; others entice us to be part of new worlds, with few, if any, familiar boundaries.[5]

TRUTH IN A TIME OF TRANSITION

Every generation believes it is experiencing unique circumstances. Allegedly, Adam and Eve's first conversation began with "we're in a time of transition." At this writing, many nations, political parties, and families are in conflict; unfortunately, so also are spiritual and religious traditions. Bracketed by forces that are pro- and anti-intellectual, pro- and anti-science, pro- and anti-immigrant, and pro- and anti-common good, which spiritualities are valid? How and with whom can we navigate the currents of hate and oceans of prejudice? In matters of race, economics, communications, and education, how do we best approach learning what is opinion and what is factful?

A fair starting question is "Are there eternal truths?" The stance of some faith traditions is there is only one truth, one ultimate mystery, countered by others who believe that while there is one truth, there are many ways to get there. Can we save that theological debate for another time? My immediate concern is the down-to-earth issue of "alternate

---

3. Thanks to the Rev. Dirk Ficca for this metaphor from "Problems That Solve Us," 1.

4. In the Christian tradition, the purpose of transformation is to discern the will of God for one's life. See various translations of Rom 12:2.

5. Hoge et al., *Vanishing Boundaries*, describe a world losing traditional social and religious boundaries. Mercadante, *Belief without Borders*, and Drescher, *Choosing Our Religion*, speak of younger generations suspicious of borders and boundaries, economics, and methods of communication. Brueggemann, *Virus as a Summons*, uses the analogy of microscopic boundary changers; see also Brueggemann's second edition of *Journey to Common Good*.

facts." If we assume all facts are relative and all assertions are true, there is no point in having conversations about truth.[6] If we are not committed to finding what can be verified but hold that every assertion is valid, learning loses.[7] Worse, power wins. Most world religions hold that the divine gift of the mind indicates humans are to use our brains. If we reject scientific, historical, and visual evidence, then nothing and no one can be trusted; civil discourse is hardly possible. You might as well throw your relationships, schooling, career, health, and spiritual well-being into the trash can. Misinformation, whether ignorant or unintelligent, and disinformation, deliberately deceptive actions, must be confronted. Gaslighting—psychologically abusing people so they question their beliefs and actions—needs to be confronted. Conversely, truth demands we admit when we can't alter the situation and admit mistakes. A modern parable likens that to buying bad sushi at a gas station, then gulping it down even after we know how awful it is.[8]

I would not have written this prior to the fallout from the 2020 United States presidential election, over the big lie that Biden did not win the election. Like a virus, falsehoods have spread to matters regarding climate crises, pandemics, global economies, immigration, and wealth inequalities. Social, religious, and political communications have stripped the world of moral boundaries. Transformative education resists the claim that truth is gone. The late Thayer S. Warshaw, the pioneer of teaching secondary school Bible as literature courses, laughingly recalled pupil answers to pretest questions that asked students to complete famous lines such as "The truth shall make you ____." One student, obviously guessing, scribbled, "The truth shall make you shudder."[9] Over centuries, religious and spiritual communities have used an amazing array of curriculum materials and instructional methods to teach what they believe

6. Suza, "Too Little, Too Late," asserts "alternate facts" carry the virus of disinformation. She offers helpful ways to restart conversations. Political scientist Hannah Arendt concluded that when only lies are told people begin to refuse to believe anything is true. When that happens, they cannot discern the truth and tyrants can tell them anything. See Arendt, "Interview."

7. Research from the Deepest Beliefs Lab at the University of North Carolina suggests that people change their points of view more based on personal stories than information they are given (Gray, "Personal Stories").

8. Lear, "GOP Should Cut." Refusing to admit we've been fooled or believe untruths ultimately has bad results.

9. The missing word is "free" (John 8:31–32). Warshaw, a high school teacher in Newton, MA, was a pioneer in the field of teaching the Bible as/in literature.

is true, even when it makes people shudder.[10] What makes education or learning worthwhile? If you find the truth, it will "trans-form" you. An outcome from truth should be the courage to do what is right.

WHAT IS EDUCATION? RELIGIOUS EDUCATION? SPIRITUAL FORMATION?

Education

What is the difference between education and learning? The Latin root of education, *educare*, means "to bring up, rear, to train" or "to draw out." Historically, it meant a broad sweep of experiences. However, it is now synonymous with schooling, a highly structured system "to develop knowledge, skill, mind, and character." In traveling terms, you are on a course of study or *curriculum*, which is the Latin word some translate as "racetrack." The word *learn* means "to gain knowledge, skills," with the implication that it is built on student interest. Unlike top-down education, the architect and explorer of the learning journey is the student.

While education has been and is used in the same breath as schooling, I think that is wrong. I'll concede that education and schooling today imply a structured, orderly system. When public education began in the 1800s in the United States, it was referred to as the common school movement, intended to teach the community's shared values. The strategy was to have common curriculum and teaching methods, especially for immigrant children to be taught the predominant values and culture of their new land.[11] Over the next two centuries, schools were asked to solve myriad societal problems as well, ranging from home economics to driver's training after World War II, to scientific knowledge—after Sputnik. The reality: schools can't do it all; they are imperfect panaceas.[12]

Diane Moore offers three purposes for today's secular K-12 schools. Schools help students become: 1) active citizens who promote the ideals

10. Cully, *Education for Spiritual Growth*, 29–31, includes examples from Buddhist monks, Hindu monasticism, the Jewish Qumran (Essenes) community, a Sufi mystic community, and Christianity, Moravian, and Anabaptist traditions.

11. Cremin, *Republic and the School*, 81; Kniker, "Reflections." Common and later public schools reflected values of the Protestant majority. In my research I found within a decade after every major American war, public schools were asked to also emphasize values, in addition to the 3 r's of reading, 'riting, and 'rithmetic.

12. Perkinson, *Imperfect Panacea*, discusses how schools since the Civil War have been charged with curing America's social ills and have usually failed.

of democracy; 2) thoughtful and informed agents for improving society; and 3) persons with fulfilling lives.[13] She states these three are interrelated and interdependent. I cite Moore because she is an advocate for one of my special interests, teaching about religion in public schools.[14]

Religious Education

Congregational educational programs and schools from the 1800s to early 1900s offered a different vision—to teach immigrant children to retain the old country's culture and its specific faith. Even with similar courses to public schools, like English and science, their structured educational curriculum focused on its relation to their faith perspective. Regardless of theological orientation, those schools, their supporting congregations, and students' parents asked the question, "Will our children have faith?" Today, with declining student attendance in many traditions, the question is reversed: "Will our faith have children?"[15] To be clear, the influence of religious education institutions has been profound in the United States.[16] It needs to be better known and appreciated.

13. Moore, *Overcoming Religious Illiteracy*, 9–25. With Moore, I support teaching the ideals of democracy because they wrestle with such issues of diversity, equality, and freedom of expression. We both advocate teaching about religion objectively in public schools, which was my reason for founding *Religion & Education*.

14. The US Supreme Court agreed. In Abington v. Schempp 374 U.S. 203 (1963), a dictum, or opinion, by Justice Tom Clark virtually prescribed that Bible as literature, the role of religion in history, and world religions should be taught because "one's education is not complete without a study of religion." Warshaw, cited earlier, with faculty at the University of Indiana, authored handbooks for teaching the Bible as/in literature by secondary school English instructors.

15. Westerhoff, *Will Our Children*. The Theologian-in-Residence program at the Ames, IA, United Church of Christ featured Rev. Dr. David Csinos in 2018. His theme was "Will Our Faith Have Children?" See Csinos and Bray, *Faith Forward*. See also Root, *Unpacking Scripture*, which includes meaning-making questions for youth. Evans, *Inspired* and *Faith Unraveled*, reveals a baby boomer challenging her evangelical roots.

16. A general source is the two-volume reference work edited by Carper and Hunt, *Praeger Handbook of Religions*. R. Lynn and Wright, *Big Little School*, is a history of the Sunday School movement. See also Schmidt, *History of Religious Education*, for trends; and Westerhoff, *Colloquy on Christian Education*, for essays from scholars of many faiths.

Spiritual Formation

The term *formation* has come into use because it assumes humans innately possess spirituality but need to find shapes and images to express it. Spirituality is not something that needs to be drummed into the student.[17] Children and adolescents, sociologists remind us, while they may be driven by raging hormones, they are not aliens from outer space. Like adults, they ask questions, and we need to listen to their spiritual questions.[18] Ultimately, the purposes of spirituality and formational discipleship for natal and spiritual homes involve every generation.[19] David M. Csinos and Ivy Beckwith offer this perspective:

> If both spirituality and religion matter to spiritual formation, then those of us who minister with children need to pay special attention to encouraging children to embrace that innate interest in God and helping them see real connections between their spirituality and the rituals and relationships of a faith community or tradition.[20]

If you accept spirituality and religion as distinct destinations, can you agree that both are passionately committed to spiritual formation but do it differently? They both frame questions to assist seekers in finding confessional—not necessarily religious—meanings to "the Mysteries of Life."[21] While public schools and higher education institutions can focus on big questions and the construction of worthy dreams built on beliefs about truth, they do not become advocates for faith-based theologies.[22] However, my observation is that most present houses of worship

17. See Westerhoff and Csinos in n15. See also Csinos and Bray, *Faith Forward*.

18. C. Smith and Lundquist, *Soul Searching*, 264–66; Borgo, *Spiritual Conversations with Children*, 24–33.

19. Csinos and Beckwith, *Children's Ministry*, 39–51 and 52–62. See especially p. 45.

20. Csinos and Beckwith, *Children's Ministry*, 45. On p. 44, the authors state that "religion is about community . . . . Religions are only religions when they involve multiple people who affirm ways of understanding and expressing their spiritual lives." Later, the authors make clear that there are many ways of instruction for spiritual goals.

21. Cully, *Education for Spiritual Growth*. Considering its year of publication, 1984, Cully has many still relevant illustrations of faith practices other than her Christian tradition. See Raman, "Three Kinds of Mysteries," in **appendix 1A**.

22. Based on conversations with ministers, curriculum editors, and Christian educators, I found consensus that church education materials now emphasize spiritual

are structured toward traditional educational methods and passing on inherited knowledge. They focus on beliefs and minimize development of skills, practices, and dispositions. Agree or not?

Let's get back to spiritual learning for travelers, which shouldn't be competitive or require grades. Confucius (551–479 BCE), a philosopher/educator, offered a "total education" plan to reform moral and political life in China.[23] Clearly, he expected adults to master, then model and teach values-related behaviors to their children.

WHAT ARE THE OUTCOMES OF SPIRITUAL LEARNING?

Here is my philosophy of spiritual learning—or education, if you prefer. Do you agree or disagree with it? In individual terms, it assumes a healthy spiritual home will transform my life by helping me base my actions on what is true, just, and beneficial. Changes occur all through life; therefore, learning over my lifespan is necessary for reaching the following personal outcomes:

- ◆ to become aware of my personal strengths and needs, ultimately preparing me for my roles in service and support to others in the community and broader cultures. This includes answering my big questions and setting worthy dreams.

- ◆ to model my actions living in relation to others based on love of self and neighbor.[24]

- ◆ to study the teachings and history of the spiritual community I become a part of, not blindly accepting all its practices but learning enough to discern, with humility and courage, the truth of its

---

formation rather than Bible-oriented themes. On denominational websites, there are "streams" of material to help children and adults with such themes as "Living Big, Living Great." These foreshadow the questions emerging adults ask in Parks, *Big Questions*.

23. Eliade, *From Gautama Buddha*, 24. The goal of Confucius's teachings is to improve civic society, but his ideas on morality apply to one's business relations and family life as well. His expectation was that such qualities as intelligence, respect, and good manners would lead to a responsive government. Many consider his teachings a philosophy, not a religion.

24. Harvey, *Direct Path*.

mission and relevance for today, committing myself to meaningful practices.[25]

Are these just "words, words, words," to quote Eliza Doolittle's song in *My Fair Lady*. What's the point of spending time, like a tourist, on what some see as just "required electives"?[26] Should your spiritual being—or faith, if you call it that—have visible behaviors that others notice? Someone once quipped: assuming you profess to be a Christian (or any other spiritual tradition); if it became illegal to be of that tradition, would there be enough evidence to arrest you?[27] If your spiritual activities don't make a noticeable difference, why make the trip? **Activity 6.1** gives you an opportunity to answer that question. I'm open to debate, but my belief is that to be truly spiritual, you will have knowledge, skills, and dispositions that are faithfully supported by practices.

What are the outcomes you are hoping for on your spiritual path? And for your loved ones? Would you choose a small community that equips you to try out a variety of spiritual practices, even strenuous ones? Or would you prefer a spiritual home with an informal curriculum that meets in a bar, restaurant, strip mall, or former warehouse? The options are endless. Factor in the use of print and digital resources, paid teachers as well as volunteer mentors, and attending non-Sunday daytime classes or evening meetings.[28]

Ask yourself: as I make my spiritual journey, how important is it to be accepted fully in a genuine, joyous spiritual home, true to itself as I am true to myself? Is this, possibly my new community, asking relevant questions, or are they like a family still chewing over stale or brittle bones from past arguments? Is my desired community exploring affective

25. Parker, *To Know*, 18, calls them "communities of truth," committed to "mutual encouragement and mutual testing, keeping me both hopeful and honest about the love that seeks me, the love I seek to be."

26. That's an inside joke. I was on a university curriculum committee that received a catalog proposal from the Engineering College that recommended some elective courses be made required.

27. Moore, *Overcoming Religious Illiteracy*, 27–52, cites examples, as does Nord, *Religion and American Education*, 199–200, who offers disappointing results of biblical literacy tests of collegiate students.

28. In the US, approximately 70 percent of Americans have grown up with some religious education, but that percentage is shrinking. Taylor, *Holy Envy*, provides excellent examples of how to teach about major world religions. For an account of a Christian learning about other faiths, especially Hinduism, see Thangaraj, *Relating to People*. Eliade, *From Gautama Buddha*, provides general background material.

dimensions—values, emotions—of life? Is my or our community of truth *acting* meaningfully for the common good?[29]

Put another way, we think of education as an amount of stuff to be learned from others, whether religious education teachers, professors, mentors, masters, or gurus. Parker Palmer, a Quaker, views education differently. If he organized your trip, you would have a guide on the side rather than a sage on the stage, someone focused on the ongoing process of asking deep questions rather than seeking specific outcomes.[30] If David Csinos organized your trip or cruise, he would assume you are already spiritual. He would highlight where you are now and draw spiritual inferences from what you are currently experiencing. With him, your trips are likely to be much less structured, prompted largely by learning style and interest.[31] To be fair, I'm painting these approaches in broad strokes that don't do them full justice, but I hope the point is clear. There are many routes to becoming a spiritually mature person. At its heart, spiritual "trans-formation" is self-directed learning.

WHY LIFELONG LEARNING?

Please note that the quotation in this paragraph could apply to any spiritual tradition, although written by Christian theologian Reinhold Niebuhr (1892–1971):

> Nothing that is worth doing is completed in our lifetime; therefore, we must be saved by hope. Nothing true or beautiful or good makes complete sense in any immediate context of history; therefore, we must be saved by faith. Nothing we do, however virtuous, can be accomplished alone; therefore, we are saved by love. No virtuous act is quite as virtuous from the standpoint of our friend or foe as it is from our standpoint. Therefore, we must be saved by the final form of love which is forgiveness.[32]

Do you agree that hope, faith, love, and forgiveness are transformative elements of spiritual growth? Do you also agree it takes many

29. Schickler, "Finding Common Ground"; Brueggemann, *Journey to Common Good*; Sandel, *Tyranny of Merit*.

30. Palmer, *To Know*.

31. Csinos, *Children's Ministry*, 48–79.

32. Niebuhr, *Irony of American History*, 510. Look at Deut 4:9, which encourages adults to remember their stories and interpret them to their children and future generations.

experiences before we fully understand what they mean? A characteristic of good leaders is that they continue to learn. Do you agree that truths are difficult to comprehend, and each generation must learn how to apply truths in their unique settings? What must spiritual travelers learn? Parker Palmer believes the fundamentals include sacred texts, the practice of prayer and contemplation, and the gathered life of the community itself.[33]

You and I are hardly the first travelers on the way to an uncertain spiritual future. Odds are that we will not be the creators of new beliefs or practices; we will build on previous generations' efforts and become models and mentors to the next generation. Our ancestors developed a variety of instructional vehicles to make their trips; we'll accept some and discard others. An excellent summary of the long-term perspectives of Judaism, Islam, Christianity, Hindu, Buddhist, and Sufi can be found in the chapters of Iris Cully's book.[34] Another source would be textbooks for world religions courses.[35]

WHAT IS (ARE) YOUR LEARNING STYLE(S)?

Since you have the responsibility to learn for yourself, how do you learn best? To illustrate the point: David Csinos, mentioned earlier, is a proponent of spiritual formation.[36] Csinos holds that every person is innately spiritual. With youngsters—and, I submit, novice travelers—he and colleagues use four learning styles as ways of knowing God: words, emotions, symbols, and action. Which style do you prefer? The word-centered approach is intellectually based, focusing on reading scriptures and devotions, analyzing sermons, and valuing precision and clarity of thought. You may prefer the emotion-centered approach, which emphasizes feelings and often incorporates music, drama, and dance. Or would you favor a symbol-centered learning style, which at times exhibits a mystical approach involving prayers and silent meditations? Csinos states practitioners of this approach are most likely to be uncomfortable

33. Parker, *To Know*, 17; for context, see his ch. 2, "Education as Spiritual Formation," 17–32.

34. Cully, *Education for Spiritual Growth*, "Learning from One Another," 66–79.

35. Mahn, "Taking Religion to Heart." High school textbooks include Neusner, *World Religions in America*, and Biallas, *World Religions: Story Approach.* Boyett, *Twelve Major World Religions*, emphasizes their beliefs and practices.

36. Csinos, *Children's Ministry*, 55–66, 159–63, and Csinos and Bray, *Faith Forward*, 2. Use these or other sources that match your learning style.

with organized religion. Finally, some travelers favor what is the least common approach, which is action-centered. These pilgrims emphasize social justice involvement. To learn more about these approaches, see the citations on David Csinos or the bibliography.

Karen Tye has an alternate way of describing learning styles.[37] I relate to two of them. Traveler, how many apply to you? Three are quite familiar: visual—including demonstrations and maps rather than written directions; print—including written instructions; and aural—including viewing of media and observations. Less familiar are interactive—lots of questions, discussions, verbal reports; haptic—touching, handling objects; olfactory—smell, use of fragrances; and kinesthetic—movement and actions.

Today's world is using old formats while exploring many new educational designs, from traditional books—approximately four thousand are published per day—to journaling groups, to tech-savvy board and video games.[38] However, this consumer culture produces split-personality behaviors. We're impatient yet passive, wanting complex knowledge quickly, cheaply, but without much effort on our part. If you are spiritual but not religious, consider this: whatever learning style(s) you favor, as you attempt to understand a past theological belief or experience an ancient practice, you can't sever it from its roots. Opening yourself to the truth of past rituals and then recasting them for your world can be mind blowing.[39]

A blended style of learning is infused in the Godly Play curriculum.[40] It is tactile. While teachers are prepared to retell biblical stories in their own words, they use aids, including sand tables and small objects of people, animals, and structures that are central to the story. Children are then encouraged to retell the story in their own words. A somewhat similar movement begun in England is called Messy Church.[41] Family-

37. Tye, *Basics of Christian Education*, 83–85.

38. Drescher, *Choosing Our Religion*, 57, 148, 149.

39. Mercadante, *Belief without Borders*, 244, 251.

40. Berryman, *Teaching Godly Play*. You can learn more by watching founder Berryman's "Introduction to the Godly Play Foundation" on YouTube or visiting his website at https://www.godlyplayfoundation.org. This approach is based on Montessori principles. I feel confident you can find a network of other congregations using this approach.

41. A Google search can direct you to videos of congregations in England. There is a website for congregations in the United States, www.messychurchusa.org.

oriented, it might be a Friday evening program beginning with a simple meal, followed by small groups with different topics based on a common scriptural story. Some groups are for children, some for adults exploring textual analysis, and one is always "messy," such as finger painting.

WHOM WOULD YOU CHOOSE AS A TEACHER, A MENTOR?

Although I had other career plans, the year in Honduras convinced me I should teach. As I often told students in my teacher education classes, one of the most exciting examples of helping people gain insights is what I call the "magic chair" technique. You, a passionate teacher, can travel with students sitting in their chairs to anywhere in time and space, reliving historic moments, holding meetings of the mind with past, present, and future luminaries. When you do that well, you are giving students passports to the past and the future.

Traveler, as much as I may emphasize self-learning, you and I know that some teachers have changed our lives. Our most influential instructor may be a parent, grandparent, or relative who was a great storyteller. A technique that some libraries are promoting is dialogic storytelling, with the teller periodically asking listeners about what they are hearing, seeing, or feeling. Sharon Daloz Parks shared with me what she believes a spiritual teacher models for us and instills in us: celebration, curiosity, creativity, commitment, courage, and hospitality.[42] I would add confrontation. Teaching is not so much filling up a bucket as building a fire.[43] Let's be clear. Paradoxically, the best teachers don't make it easy for us; they have high standards and demand our best.[44] A lesson taught by a Sufi to a friend was "I think of my body like a musical instrument my soul is always trying to play. If the instrument isn't constantly tuned, how can the

42. Sharon Daloz Parks, phone conversation, Oct. 5, 2020.

43. Attributed to William Butler Yeats: "Education is not the filling of a pail but the lighting of a fire." A personal story about an aunt of mine: at age ninety, she wanted to quit teaching a Lutheran Sunday school class near Austin, Texas. Congregation members begged her to continue because they, their children, and grandchildren had learned so much from her! What she taught that endeared her to students was the inner love and light she projected, her respect for all, and, yes, her demanding discipleship.

44. For Christian texts about teaching, see 1 Cor 12:4–11 and Eph 4:11–12. For secular books filled with examples of remarkable teachers see Peterson, *Great Teachers*, and Highet, *Art of Teaching*.

divine music . . . be created?" In nineteenth-century America, President James Garfield described a college education as "Mark Hopkins on one end of a log and the student at the other." In that quaint time, a college president like Hopkins taught the keystone senior course of moral philosophy and took time to work with individual students.[45] Can you think of a teacher you've had whom you would like to be your Mark Hopkins?

Here are some descriptions I've created of teaching models. Which style teacher would you prefer as a student? Which style would you use if you became a teacher?[46]

♦ Would you want a skilled teacher—someone who is the perfect model, the holder of the set of skills you desire? If you are learning a specific ability—how to play a musical instrument, prepare food, build a cabinet, try different forms of prayer—doesn't it make sense to learn from someone who has mastered those skills? In addition to having expertise and experience, the teacher should be able to share stories of others who exhibit the special knowledge and behaviors you want to learn.

♦ Another choice is to find a "gold star" teacher who uses verbal and non-verbal cues along with tangible rewards to signal required and punishable behaviors. This works better for children than adults. It doesn't automatically encourage independent learning.

♦ A "wise owl" teacher employs a lot of who and why questions.[47] Paul Tillich, the late theologian, has suggested that teachers help children more if they respond to the learners' questions rather than providing answers to expected questions.[48] Done properly, questioning promotes what is called productive reflection.

♦ Why not consider a teacher who acts like a travel agent? The instructor takes a class to a foreign—for students—country or back

45. Hopkins was president of Williams College (MA) from 1836 to 1872; Garfield had been a student. See Rudolph, *American College and University*, 346.

46. I developed these models for Kniker, *You and Values Education*, 20–22.

47. Aristotle, a Greek philosopher (384–322 BCE), was known for prolonged walks with students, during which he kept asking probing questions. The term for that mobile teaching style is peripatetic. A modern version is called Online Collaborative Learning (OCL), described as "a new theory of learning that focuses on collaborative learning, knowledge building, and internet use to reshape formal, non-formal, and informal education for the Knowledge Age" (Harasim, *Learning Theory*, 81).

48. Tillich, *Theology of Culture*, 201–13.

in time. Learners become more than tourists in a variety of destinations. An enthusiastic teacher encourages students to take their own odysseys. Another strategy for the agent is to assign the student travelers to work in teams from different countries and see the fun when the tourists share their diverse experiences.

♦ Two more: how about selecting an instructor who mimics a detective? She or he uses an exciting scenario to probe an unresolved issue from the past or present. Your teacher might instead be like an investment adviser, listening to clients' dreams and helping them determine if they can find unique ways to pay for their trip. Periodically, the instructor/adviser would review the performance of assets and chart changes—great for any classes with numbers and statistics.

Perhaps none of these images matches your profile of a teacher with whom you want to study. Watch some film or TV dramas about classroom teachers. Or discuss with family and friends what you would expect of a spiritual guide.[49]

Having thought this through, you may conclude that as a traveler, you don't want to hire a teacher, and you couldn't become one. Then consider locating a mentor. Mentors have different roles than teachers. They aren't hired; they are volunteers. A mentor commits to being with the person mentored—the traveler or protégé. Mentors in spiritual communities, often in youth-to-adult contexts, are there to support, challenge, guide, and inspire the youth. They are stewards for the dreams to come.[50]

An adage is that if you become a teacher, you learn more than your students. Teaching and mentoring are spiritual practices, I believe. I think there should be another beatitude, "Blessed are teachers, for they shall be _____." You fill in the blank!

WHAT IS THERE TO LEARN—AND HOW?

Regarding spiritual formation, recall Parker Palmer said three things were involved for him: learning sacred texts—cognitive knowledge;

49. Some of my favorites are Robin Williams in *The Dead Poets Society* (1989), Sidney Poitier in *Blackboard Jungle* (1955), Michelle Pfeiffer in *Dangerous Minds* (1995), Richard Dreyfuss in *Mr. Holland's Opus* (1995), and Hilary Swank in *Freedom Writers* (2007).

50. Parks, *Big Questions*, 177–79.

developing practices—learning correctly and gaining skills by repetition; and being part of a community—participating in "belonging" activities.[51] Let's add some dimension to those ideas as you consider exploring one or more spiritual approaches. As many have said, if you know only one tradition, you really don't know even that one.[52] Another frequent quip is the paradox that Americans claim to be religious but are abysmally ignorant about their own, much less other, religious traditions.[53]

A Sufi saying is "Praise Allah, but first tie your camel to a post." That Middle Eastern advice referencing destructive desert winds reminds us that spirituality has concrete aspects as well as abstract principles. Spirituality, like religion, needs to be practical. Yes, it is founded on beliefs and stories one scholar calls "chains of memories."[54] Be sensitive, however, to how a community you visit or belong to is faithful, in its recollections and reflections, to its beliefs, stories, and literature. Unfortunately, survey data and interviewees consistently find youth and adults are weak in articulating their spiritual beliefs and faithfully demonstrating their practices.[55]

Sacred Texts

There are many sacred texts. See **appendix 6A**. Some questions to ask about them are: How are they viewed by believers of that faith tradition?[56] Are they divine words of truth, without error? Are they stories of supernatural wisdom interpreted by fallible humans? A guidebook to moral living? The world's best literature? In some traditions, sacred texts supersede all secular knowledge. In other traditions, they are part of multiple paths to truth. If you are going to shop around for spiritual homes, ask

51. Parker, *To Know*, 17. My interpretations of his categories in more traditional educational terms follow dashes.

52. The quotation is frequently attributed to Max Müller, a German philologist and comparative religionist, cited by Prothero, *God Is Not One*, 16.

53. See Wachlin and Johns, *Bible Literacy Report*, 31. on knowledge of world religions.

54. Hervieu-Léger, *Religion as Chain*.

55. Hervieu-Léger, *Religion as Chain*, 267. Jackson, *Politics of Storytelling*, cautions that there are many motives behind stories.

56. Bracke and Tye, *Teaching the Bible*, discuss the complexity of teaching sacred texts. Theirs is in a tradition of progressive Protestant theology. A somewhat similar but more conservative book is Root, *Unpacking Scripture*.

what are the sacred and special texts they follow. Which of their founders' scriptural beliefs must you observe or can you reject?

It should go without saying that leaders in most religious traditions bemoan the level of illiteracy about their sacred writings. This ironic quip reflects that reality: "I just misspelled 'Armageddon' on my exam. So what? It's not the end of the world!" Below are several resources on literacy projects about world religions and their texts.[57]

A related question: what has been the impact of those sacred texts over time? In some traditions, they become doctrines and dogmas, prescribed beliefs that dictate daily life behaviors, as well as broader social and political policies. Beyond the sacred texts, adherents pass on memories of beloved leaders and sainted members. These memorable stories are told through lectures, testimonies, memorization of texts, scholarly books, singing, and art. Today, these narratives are elaborated in everything from stained glass windows to printed curriculum sets to online cartoons and social media. Ask long-standing members in your potential spiritual home, are these accounts set in stone or open to interpretation? How open is the "truth" to debate? See **activity 6.2** for a sample of commonsense beliefs. Would you follow them—"religiously"?

Practices

To be effective, spiritual practices should be deliberately chosen, doable, and durable. To be effective, they must be done regularly and engrained in our muscle memory, if they are to become transformative. Some nontheist spiritual traditions focus on practices such as meditation and contemplation rather than physical exercises. Let's acknowledge, however, that beliefs and practices are interactive, a system we could call "spiritual plumbing." If you are interested in examples of communities committed to spiritual practices, look up references to the New Monasticism movement. See chapter 5 for a discussion of practices. Andrew Harvey's *The Direct Path* describes in detail numerous practices from non-theistic traditions that have become part of the journeys of theistic faith traditions' practitioners.[58] Another trend has been for members of Abrahamic faith

---

57. Prothero, *Religious Literacy;* Nord, *Religion and American Education;* Ackerman and Warshaw, *Bible as/in Literature,* a high school text.

58. Harvey, *Direct Path;* Bender, *Heaven's Kitchen,* 6–7, discusses diverse ways to describe and observe practices.

traditions to reshape practices and rituals of the past in modern clothing, some in everyday wear.[59] Don't forget, music and the arts are integral forms of practices, too!

Communities

Sooner or later, your choice of a spiritual community and the length of time you remain in it depend on how you and yours are welcomed, how supportive its members are, its authenticity of actions matching beliefs, and ultimately, how well it has sustained you in your spiritual growth. If it is like a healthy home, it will mold you, through information, conformation, and reformation. It can transform you into a better person. In time, you will also be able to transform others.

How and why, you ask. Look at some sociological realities. All of us are wired to belong to a tribe. We want to, we need to be with others who are like us—in dress, in appearance, in what we affirm, in what we hold to be true. We need networks of belonging. Predictably, they will be "communities of particularity."[60] I prefer to call them communities of truth. That truth, in my view, is linked significantly to the stories they tell, as well as the stories they refuse to share or ignore. The social fabric of healthy spiritual communities is expressed not only through their formal yearning services and social support, but their homelike environments with events that express the warmth of a fireplace and homemade food. Learning occurs at the kitchen table, as well as in the sanctuary and in seminar rooms.

WHAT ARE THE BEST PLACES AND SPACES TO LEARN?

The reality is that learning can occur anywhere. The scope of what any individual knows is mind blowing. An African proverb captures that sentiment: "When someone dies, a library burns."[61] The question here is,

---

59. See Warren, *Liturgy of the Ordinary*; Diana Bass, *Practicing Congregation*; Dorothy Bass, *Practicing Our Faith*; C. Smith, *Religion*, table on p. 27.

60. Parks, *Big Questions*, 125–27, 285–87. Elsewhere, Parks describes these communities offering mentoring as well as practices of hearth and table, or hospitality and food.

61. Madou Hampâté Bâ (1901–1991), a Malian writer and ethnologist, is credited for

beginning with learning at home, are there unique places and spaces that benefit spiritual learning?

Home

Even before the 2020 coronavirus, intuitively we knew home is or should be the primary place for spiritual formation. Nostalgically, we recall rituals such as table graces. Old-timers will remember Norman Rockwell's picture of a family Thanksgiving grace. For some, mealtime included readings from devotional booklets; for others, bedtime stories and songs with moral sayings. A second home, Luther Smith of Emory University reminded me, could be families from one's spiritual home. Those parents guided his spiritual growth by modeling, conversations, and, shall we say, oversight. Finally, home includes multiple generations. Frequently, grandparents' homes are a favorite vacation spot.

Social Media and Peers

Agreed, isn't it, although we may be at home physically, we can be a world away? Younger generations can immediately think of the "places" where they spend much of their time: on their smartphones or tablets with stories, tweets, and other emerging forms of social media.[62] Today, social media molds us more than we like to admit, reinforcing what we want to know but occasionally opening us to diverse points of view.[63] There are increasing debates about regulation of social media but little action regarding censuring disinformation. What impact will the internet have on attendance at religious services, considering the experience of Zoom services? It sounds quaint but relevant to mention the future of books. The death of books is, as was a report of Mark Twain's death, greatly

---

saying before UNESCO in 1960: "En Afrique, quand un vieillard meurt, c'est une bibliothèque qui brûle." Translation: "In Africa, when an old man dies, it's a library burning."

62. eMarketer estimates American adults spend over twelve hours a day with all media. The average time for social media in Europe, Latin America, and the United States by an adult is two to four hours

63. See Gergen, *Saturated Self*; Metev, "How Much Time."

exaggerated.[64] It used to be that ministers were the only ones with regular access to scholarly biblical and theological books. No more.[65]

The House Church Movement

Another place for organized spiritual formation is in someone's home. This was popular during the first centuries of the Christian movement. It has had a resurgence among Christians in China, and likewise when the Iranian government suppressed religious communities, including Islamic mosques.[66] While a group that meets in a private home may be a group not affiliated with a particular tradition, some may be. These groups may represent a group of neighbors who wish to form a spiritual community but don't have funds for renting or building a house of worship. If you become part of a home church, its structure could range from scriptural readings, singing, and simple sharing of food to a worship service. Individual members lead the meetings.

Spiritual and Religious Education

Sooner or later, in most religious traditions, homes become too small for attendees. Many local houses of worship rent or own educational facilities. Specific rooms and age-appropriate curricula are available for every age group, including adults. Features vary from a library to a bookstore. This option may be too formal, too restrictive, or too time-consuming for you. Indeed, as mentioned several other places in the book, spiritual groups often prefer locations like bars, restaurants, or strip malls. And they prefer to rent rather than buy. For some congregations, especially those working closely with higher education institutions, there are issues finding meeting spaces for those who have a non-Christian identity.[67]

64. The two countries who are the largest publishers of books annually are China and the US. In recent years China has published over 400,000 titles annually, while the United States has published over 300,000.

65. Phyllis Tickle, in a conversation at the Theologian-in-Residence Program, Ames, IA, 2014, remarked in this age of the Spirit, any individual or study group has as much access to theological books and papers as did seminarians fifty years ago.

66. Zdero, *Nexus.* Lenz, *God Land*, as cited in Felicetti, Review, offers a similar portrayal to Wuthnow, *Left Behind*, regarding farm decline and yet faith in renewal that rural Midwesterners have.

67. Seligmann, "Making Space for All."

Interest Groups and Work Projects

If so, how about groups on a special topic or volunteering for a cause? Just as you meet with friends for coffee, bridge, or sports chatter, why not join a group discussing spiritual books? Want to be more physically active? Serve meals at a food kitchen. Form a faith-sharing group.[68] Interviewers of younger generations conclude such generations do become involved when they believe meaningful actions will result.[69] On a less active level, volunteer at a senior retirement community, or join a group nature hike. If you need to gain a new perspective, try visiting the headquarters of a feminist organization, learning about funeral practices at a mortuary, or doing a hands-on project, such as building a house with a multifaith crew.[70]

Distance Learning

Willing to be bolder? Beverly Sills, the late opera star, offered this sage advice: "There are no shortcuts to any place worth going." Time and money become important factors, but you might take part in a formal learning program that lasts from one week to almost all summer. Various colleges offer such programs. Longer-term opportunities include the Chautauqua Institution in New York, which began in 1874 and continues today as a nine-week summer program.[71] There are also travel programs for el-

68. Dorothy Bass, *Practicing Our Faith*, 71–72, includes a description of small groups discussing faith questions, sometimes called "Strengthening Our Yes and Our No."

69. Drescher, *Choosing Our Religion*; Oakes, *Nones Are Alright*; Denton and Flory, *Back-Pocket God*; and Mercadante, *Belief without Borders* offer many stories.

70. Beadle and Haskins, *Acting on Faith*, describe many projects involving interfaith groups, as does Patel, *Interfaith Leadership*.

71. Originally begun as a training program for Sunday school teachers, the Chautauqua Institution became a respite for adults and families. In more recent years, it has become a haven for families. Preschool classes, girls' and boys' clubs, sailing and swimming keep children and youth active during the day. Parents can take courses, attend lectures, and do independent reading during the same time. At night, there are concerts, plays, and other events such as a movie theater. I consider Irwin, *Three Taps of Gavel*, to have the best description of its "heart."

ders.[72] If that is too much, check out some local spiritual homes that have designed their own introduction to faith programs.[73]

Camps

Two versions of camp come to mind. The first is a family or grandparents' weekend at a campsite. Get to know each other in new ways! The second camp is more intense, for teenagers to adults, lasting from a minimum of four to eight weeks. Call it spiritual basic training. Mornings at the camp would be spent with outstanding teachers and mentors learning the beliefs and practices of a tradition. Afternoons allow for rest, but times are made available for involvement with service projects. Not unlike sports or language camps, some may consider this camp's intensity non-recreational; ; I consider it "RE-creation."

Some closing thoughts on spaces. Being in any of the places I've described doesn't guarantee you have the right ambiance to develop your spirituality, just as the way a seminar room is organized, lighted, and decorated can encourage you either to participate or withdraw. Have you been in a packed classroom or retreat center and felt pressured to not speak or participate in an unfamiliar ritual? You may not feel ready to discuss any of the book you have been reading, much less a chapter or a specific page. You should always feel free to inform the teacher or mentor that you need space.[74]

TRAVELER: READY TO BECOME A QUESTIONING TRUTH-TELLER?

First, common to major religions is the expectation that converts will become *disciples*—OK, I prefer travelers—who want to deepen their spirituality. What does that mean if you want an engaged, interactive, transformative spirituality? Outcomes still begin with Parker Palmer's

72. Elderhostel programs, founded in 1975, invited participants to visit sites around the world and learn more about them. Rebranded as Road Scholars in 2010, they offer programs in all 50 states and 150 countries: https://www.roadscholar.org.

73. Diana Bass, *Christianity for the Rest*, 225–26, describes the requirement of Phinney Ridge Lutheran Church in Seattle, WA, that before a person can join the church, s/he engage in a year of worship, study, theological, reflection, prayer, and service.

74. Parker, *To Know*, ch. 5, "To Teach Is to Create a Space . . .," 69–87.

trinity: familiarity with sacred and special texts, engagement in spiritual practices, and active participation with a community that is obedient to pursuing the truth and acting on it. Watch out, here comes a subjective outcome: I believe if you are humble but confident that you have found the truth, there will be a glow about you. Yes, you, traveler, should have basic cognitive knowledge about the historic beliefs and practices of your spiritual ancestors, discern those which are relevant today, and be willing, with your gifts and circumstances, to provide caregiving and address injustices—a tall order. See **activity 6.3**. Like some Hebrew prophets and wise ones of other traditions, you may feel you are not competent or too shy to tell others about what is making you tick spiritually. You may feel you need more knowledge. And like the prophets, you question God.

Chapter 3 asserted you don't need to be perfect but rather committed to living a righteous life. In colonial American history, some religious communities instituted public laws to control moral behavior. It didn't work. Many "saints" were delinquents.[75] Whatever your spiritual quest, my hope is you will learn how to connect or reconnect with your own source of meaning to come to understand what is the truth that is appropriate in your life.

My grandfather, a minister, retired after fifty years of service, still preaching occasionally. From all accounts, he was a commanding truth-teller, what Germans call Herr Pastor. My feeling is that his long ministry related to another quality, his lifelong learning. Late on a Saturday evening, he told his wife, my grandmother, that he wanted to do some more reading before retiring. He was to preach again the following morning. When she awoke, she found that he had died in the library; he had an open book on his chest. In the chaos that followed, no one remembered which book it had been. Later, one daughter wanted to know. What was the title? What did he feel he still needed or wished to learn? What questions did he have that night? Lifelong learner, what is it you still feel you must know and be able to do skillfully and passionately? "Trans-formed" by truth, because you have been given a mind, you will always have questions and, hopefully, the courage to find answers.

75. Oberholzer, *Delinquent Saints*.

Chapter 6 Activities

ACTIVITY 6.1: A TRAVELER'S KNOWLEDGE, SKILLS, AND ATTITUDES

Do the following activity alone or as part of a group. The first column is you now; the second column is the traveler you would want to become. In the boxes labeled *knowledge*, give several examples of the knowledge you expect to have in time. Do the same for the boxes under skills and the boxes of attitudes/dispositions.

Trivia: As prior chapters, especially chapter 3 explained, many faith traditions use the word *disciple* for their travelers. Interestingly, disciple appears 269 times in the New Testament; the word *Christian* appears only three times.[76]

Note: You may feel you don't know enough now to fill in these boxes. As you learn about one or more spiritual homes, you can fill them in later.

A word or brief phrase to describe where you are *now* as a spiritual traveler.	A word or brief phrase to motivate you to become a more involved spiritual traveler.
Religious, spiritual knowledge I have now:	Knowledge to be gained:
Spiritual skills or practices I do:	Skills and practices I wish to do:
Spiritual attitudes/dispositions I possess:	Attitudes/dispositions I should embrace:
The word or phrase that describes my *current* spirituality:	The *new* word or phrase I hope will describe my spirituality:

76. A. Robinson, "Follow Me," 23.

ACTIVITY 6.2: THIS I BELIEVE . . . OR DON'T[77]
General

- Everyone has an agenda. Learn it, and you better understand the person.

- The grass may be greener on the other side of the fence, but it is just as hard to mow.

- The premises of civility are: 1) truth, however painful, is better than assertion without proof, and 2) no individual or group has all the truth.

- Accepting diversity as a positive makes it easier to turn strangers into friends.

- Proclaiming that "all people in a group are ___" is *all* wrong.

Religion and Spirituality

- The church, or any religious institution, should be a hospital for sinners rather than a museum for saints.

- Spiritual communities and families are like rivers; each has a current. At times, it is best to go with the flow; at others, the stream needs to be diverted.

- True prophets are often reluctant tellers of hard truths and needed changes, while false prophets are enthusiastic bearers of pleasant truths that support the powers of the status quo.

Political Observations

- Leaders without shame and prudence become dictators without fear.

- Demagogues appeal to our highest dreams and our worst nightmares.

- The closer churches and clergy get to power, the further their distance from courage and compassion.

- Blessings and curses are opposite sides of the same coin.

77. This list of statements was developed by Charles R. Kniker, 2018.

(*Activity 6.2 continued*)

On Age

+ Youth bring hope with little experience, while adults, too often, bring experience with too little hope.

+ Wise elders offer calm amid clouds of chaos.

Other

+ Learning has many parents, but the best are ambition, curiosity, and interest. Schooling, too often, is based not on these, but on fear, conformity, and obedience.

+ Sports and literature are popular because they include both suspense and certainty.

ACTIVITY 6.3: ADVICE TO A YOUNGER TRAVELER (YOU NOW TO YOURSELF)

From where you are on life's journey today, what advice would you give yourself if you are just beginning as a spiritual traveler?

1. The person, living or dead, whom I most admire now who would guide you on your spiritual formation. What more would you like to know about this person, and how might you go about finding your answers?

2. What are your key beliefs about life now? How certain are they? What would you tell your younger traveler about their usefulness for everyday living?

3. If your younger self won the "lottery of learning" and was given the opportunity to go anywhere to study with a teacher/mentor of any faith tradition, where would you advise yourself going? Would you do it now?

4. If your younger self is currently attending or considering a spiritual home and asked you to be a teacher or mentor there, what would you say?

FOR ADDITIONAL CONVERSATIONS

Teachers aren't supposed to have favorite students. With books, it is hard not to have personal preferences. These selections, I admit, reflect pages that have helped me. I've included some because they attempt to relate to numerous traditions.

- Cited often, this beautifully written, honest assessment of her years of teaching a college world religions course is a classic. Barbara Brown Taylor, *Holy Envy: Finding God in the Faith of Others.*

- Because of the importance of seeking truth not only for self and our like-minded classmates and spiritual partners, consider Michael S. Katz et al., *Justice and Caring: The Search for Common Ground in Education.*

- Numerous well-known educators, theologians, and psychologists challenge readers to once again be concerned about public discourse. Parker J. Palmer et al., *Caring for the Commonweal: Education for Religious and Public Life.*

- Teaching with imagination—priceless! Maria Harris, *Teaching and Religious Imagination: An Essay in the Theology of Teaching.* Another classic!

- Who hasn't heard that small groups are essential? Here are insights to do them well. Nelson Searcy and Kerrick Thomas, *Activate: An Entirely New Approach to Small Groups.*

- The chapter subjects are amazing, teaching for . . . mystery, belief, relationship, commitment, and more! Richard Robert Osmer, *Teaching for Faith: A Guide for Teachers of Adult Classes.*

- The beauty and power of stories is unquestioned. Michael Jackson, *The Politics of Storytelling,* analyzes the many purposes behind stories.

7

Soulcare— "Trans-Formed" by Trust

Now I lay me down to sleep; I pray the Lord my soul to keep. If I should die before I wake, I pray the Lord my soul to take.

—*NEW ENGLAND PRIMER*, 1871 EDITION

Question: What must I do to inherit eternal life? Teacher: What is written in the Law? Answer: You shall love the Lord your God with all your heart, and with all your soul, and with all your strength, and with all your mind; and your neighbor as yourself. Teacher: Do this and you will live.

—LEV 19:17–18; DEUT 6:4–5; LUKE 10: 25–28

The head [*ori*] is the greatest Orisa.

Note: In the Western Africa Yoruba religion, each person has at least two souls. Stephen Prothero explains one soul is *emi*, associated with breath, and a second, *ori*, is associated with destiny.[1] Here, *ori* is the center that chooses one's life direction. Orisa is the word for God, perhaps a reincarnated being.

There are many adults who for various reasons have escaped this essential discipline of their spirit. True, in terms of physical and intellectual development they have continued to grow. Their bodies and minds have moved through all the intervening stages to maturity, but they have remained essentially babies in what they expect of life.

—HOWARD THURMAN, *DISCIPLINES OF THE SPIRIT*, 41

---

1. Prothero, *God Is Not One*, 206.

YESS: YOUR EVERYDAY SOULCARE AND SUPPORT

◆ Invitation: to become part of a community of burning, "trans-formed" by trust

◆ What is the soul, and what is soulcare?

◆ What does soulcare mean in our lives today? Try self-care and caregiving!

◆ Are your beliefs open to doubt, imagination, curiosity?

◆ What are circles of caring?

◆ Traveler: ready to become a chef of soulcare?

◆ Activities

◆ For Additional Conversations

Let's recap. I recommend you use the analogy of transforming a house into a home to finding a healthy spiritual community. In chapters 5 and 6, we covered two steps. First you check out the foundation, the walls, the roof. In a spiritual home, you find its *worth-ship* as a community of yearning, how it signals its belief in a "trans-forming" power. Second, in a house, you check if everything is in good repair—essentially, that furnishings are up to date. In a spiritual home, you would want to see that it is a community of learning, with a commitment to lifelong education, because spirituality is dynamic, not static.

If a house becomes your home, you should determine whether it will support your physical well-being. Will your family feel comfortable in its rooms? Does the kitchen have comfortable table space, sufficient food storage, an oven encouraging baking? Will it have places providing warm welcomes to neighbors and special guests? A fireplace or nook suggesting holiday tastes and smells?

INVITATION: TO BE PART OF A COMMUNITY OF BURNING, "TRANS-FORMED" BY TRUST

In a spiritual home, the community will burn with passion. If you prefer, call it a community of caring or compassion, welcoming to all. Care about what? I use the term soulcare, a warming tonic of equal doses of self-nurturing and support of loved ones, neighbors, relatives, and, yes, strangers. Such soulcare is based on trust, which becomes a catalyst for hope.

Picture a hearth, a fireside, which is the heart of a family's home.[2] One of my fondest memories is of a seminary professor and his wife inviting students to their home. To end the Christmas season, as each one put a dried tree branch in the fire, we named a favorite holiday song. We then joined in singing it. In that warmth, with hot cider and cookies, we shared our concerns and dreams. The glowing embers sparked the fire in our souls. That night was transformative, because we felt trust from the

---

2. Parks, *Big Questions*, 212–13. She mentions hearth in several articles. The authors in Daloz et al., *Common Fire*, use the image of a campfire as a powerful metaphor for joining in caring for others.

professor and his wife—as friends more than mentors, in a setting that was preparing us for ministry. When you trust people, you believe what they say, what they promise to do, and how supportive they will be, of you and others. As Richard Rohr cautions, don't be naïve. "The real spiritual journey is work. You can make a naïve assertion that you trust in Jesus, but until it is tested a good, oh, 200 times, I doubt very much that it's true."[3] Bingo! If we don't truly trust individuals, we won't do what they ask us to do. Example: getting or rejecting COVID vaccinations. Trust has long-term as well as immediate benefits. When you trust, your hope for the future increases.

WHAT IS THE SOUL, AND WHAT IS SOULCARE?

Odds are that you have heard the word *soul*, but like most of us, you're not confident you can define it. In 2020, part of presidential candidate Joe Biden's message was that Biden wanted to restore the soul of the nation.[4] One hundred years ago, a British observer commented, "America has the soul of a church."[5] You also are familiar with the word *care*. Probably, you've used it in the romantic sense of "I care for you" and in the medical sense of "She needs care." Why put them together? My answer is, first, that our spiritual homes uniquely nourish and nurture our own souls and, second, call us to care for others. After you read more about soulcare, consider how you have received it in your life. See **activity 7.1**.

Two stories will make soulcare clearer. First, in her last years, my mother-in-law was a resident in an assisted living wing of a Beatrice, Nebraska, hospital. On multiple visits, my wife and I would hear the plaintive and persistent wails of another resident—every ten to fifteen seconds. "Somebody, help me!" While the staff was attentive to this resident whose short-term memory loss blotted out how frequently she had received care, the heart-wrenching cries raised the questions: Is there a better response to her needs? Is it medicine or empathy she needs? Second, a story told to me

---

3. As quoted in AZ Quotes, https://www.azquotes.com/quote/1162889. Substitute the founder or force you most trust.

4. Meacham, *Soul of America*, 7–8, describes ancient Western interpretations of the word *soul*. Throughout the book, he cites musical as well as oratorical uses of it, prior to candidate Joe Biden's adoption of the word.

5. Chesterton, *What I Saw*, 47. Chesterton said, after he visited in the 1920s, the United States is "the only nation in the world founded on a creed" (*What I Saw*, 41). The remark can be interpreted both positively and negatively.

by a niece. Years ago, she traveled to Italy with her father, my brother, the medical doctor to whom this book is dedicated. While touring in Venice, a man near them collapsed. Her dad immediately responded, checking vital signs, then told her to cradle the man's head in her lap. After the stranger was no longer in danger and help was on the way, they left quickly and quietly. My brother wanted no recognition, no compensation. Why are souls motivated to help others? Have you ever been in a situation, not necessarily medical, where you needed help? Were you too embarrassed or afraid to ask for assistance but silently screamed? Have you been in a situation where you recognized someone needed care, and you gave it?

What is the soul? Let's look at some major concepts[6] without getting bogged down in deep theological terminology. We humans, like animals, have a physical body, and our bodies must breathe. We witness that miracle from birth to the final gasp of a person at death.[7] In the Hebrew language, the word for soul, *nephesh*, has several meanings but assumes the physical body and the wind or breath (*rûaḥ*) are one. Greek philosophers and later theologians hold that there are three parts to a human: the physical body; the breath, which they called the soul; and the spirit, which focused on intellectual processes (1 Thess 5:23).

Consider the following views of what the soul is:

- ◆ The late psychiatrist and author of a series of Road Less Traveled books, M. Scott Peck, surmised that the soul is "a God-created, God-nurtured, unique, developable, immortal human spirit."[8]

- ◆ "The soul is the life force of a unique individual. There is always one soul per person, which never departs until that person dies."[9]

- ◆ "The soul identifies our unique essence, our capacity for centered decisions, our capacity for taking initiatives."[10]

6. Gehman, *Dictionary of the Bible*, 901–2, provides a summary of various beliefs about souls. Boyd, *Reclaiming the Soul*, xxi, has a chart comparing soul and self; Means with Nelson, *Trauma and Evil*, 89–91, describe differences between the self and soul.

7. The text of a famous hymn, "When Peace, Like a River," or better known as "It Is Well with My Soul," was written by Horatio G. Safford, grieving the loss of four daughters in the sinking of the SS Ville du Havre.

8. Peck, *Road Less Traveled*, 97. He adds that each adjective he used had important characteristics and consequences.

9. Boyd, *Reclaiming the Soul*, 77. He believes the soul overlaps considerably with spirit, but there are "oozy and indistinct differences."

10. James B. Ashbrook, *Minding the Soul*, 178, as cited and further defined in Means with Nelson, *Trauma and Evil*, 89–91; also 218–19.

"Time out!" you might be shouting about now. Let's get down to a street-level view of soul. What about soul music, captured in the documentary *Summer of Soul* or the movie *Soul*?[11] As simply as I can put it, soul is your essence. It's what makes you who you are.

Before you assume I'm promoting only the view of Judaism, Christianity, and Islam, the Abrahamic tribes, I suggest you read Robert Coles's discussion about children's "secular soul searching."[12] More recently, the term *soul searching* has been used to describe survey results of what American teens and emerging adults are doing. Researchers conclude that most people focus more on what they struggle to believe than on how it affects their actions.[13]

Personally, I am moved by the words of Rabbi Abraham Joshua Heschel:

> The human being is uniquely graced with the ability to search the soul and reflect. For what purpose am I alive? Does my life have a meaning, a reason? Is there a need for my existence? Will anything on earth be impaired by my disappearance? Would my absence create a vacuum in the world? . . . Is it incumbent upon me to fulfill a purpose in this life? Do I exist that I might build or restore?[14]

Heschel summarizes it this way: our souls wrestle with what life means, what elsewhere is called engaged spirituality. Why exist? What is life's purpose? No one can be a proxy for you or me. No one can answer for all of us or claim all generations, all religions, all spiritual traditions have identical answers to these questions. In various traditions, the soul may be linked to or separate from heart, mind, and body. Most make the connection that compassion, neighborliness, hospitality, and empathy, taken together, comprise the soul. A second voice, Father Richard Rohr, has another perspective I can accept. Our True Self reflects the best in

---

11. The documentary *Summer of Soul* captures the 1969 Harlem Cultural Festival, which occurred over six consecutive Sundays. The film, *Soul*, released in 2020 by Pixer/Disney, portrays an account of a middle school musician who tries to reunite his body and soul after his accidental death.

12. Coles, *Spiritual Life of Children*, 277–302.

13. C. Smith with Lundquist, *Soul Searching*; C. Smith with Snell, *Souls in Transition*. The focus of both books follows interview statements over several years for the National Study of Youth and Religion (NSYR). Ironically, the concept of *soul* is never fully described in either of these two books.

14. Heschel, *Moral Grandeur*, 54.

us—the "one who shares our own deepest subjectivity"—God."[15] When recognized and acted upon, it builds a hotly burning fire of soulcare.[16]

Soulcare is a term I thought I had made up. Turns out I'm wrong: German theologians were debating about *Seelsorge*—caring for souls— hundreds of years ago. For them, it was related to balancing the priorities of clergy—how much time should be given to *Seelsorge* versus rituals such as confession and parish administration. More recently, for example, some hospital chaplains want to change a description of their work—pastoral ministry—to spiritual ministry, because the latter seems closer to *Seelsorge*.[17]

WHAT DOES SOULCARE MEAN IN OUR LIVES TODAY? TRY SELF-CARE AND CAREGIVING!

In today's world, I believe there are two broad categories of soulcare. The first category focuses on care of and for the individual: self-care.[18] The second type is caregiving for others. Before I begin with a few examples of self-care, let me explain the paradox of caring for self versus caring for others. As biological beings, we are programmed to survive by exhibiting what theologian Reinhold Niebuhr called "self-seeking." Through families and others, we are gifted with security and trust. Therefore, we are also programmed to give to others, gracefully.[19] If this seems too idealistic or improbable to you, I ask you to reflect on societies that abandon or pervert legitimate care for self and others. Consider Margaret Atwood's *The Handmaid's Tale* and the cruel culture of William Golding's *Lord of the Flies*.

15. Rohr, *Immortal Diamond*, xiii. Elsewhere, he adds that while our self has many dimensions, such as emotional, physical, mental, the soul cannot be divided; it is a deep consciousness that "hums," our internal blueprint.

16. M. Miller and Miller, *Harper's Bible Dictionary*, 698; Reese, *Dictionary of Philosophy*, 541–42. For other sources on soul, see Prothero, *God Is Not One*; Biallas, *World Religions*; Wuthnow, *Acts of Compassion*; Putnam et al., *American Grace*; Diana Bass, *Grounded*.

17. Anderson, "Whatever Happened to *Seelsorge*," followed by Facebook comments, "What of *Seelsorge*?" by a Lutheran pastor, Aug. 25, 2012.

18. A resource for this self-care is Lawlor, *Home for the Soul*.

19. R. Niebuhr, *Man's Nature*, 106–10. Niebuhr cites Erik Erikson's research on the need for "basic trust" in Erikson's *Childhood and Society*, positing that the caring of others is a gift of grace.

When you recognize you are no longer participating in something you enjoy, or realize you are working more and neglecting other parts of your life, your soul needs care. Perhaps you may be spending so much time caring for others, you aren't caring for yourself sufficiently.

Another reason for self-care is a need for self-improvement. Join a congregation's book club or a craft group that is working in a medium you've always wanted to learn. Maybe there is a current issue about which you want to be informed, and you, along with others, can organize a group to study it. In 2020, the Black Lives Matter (BLM) movement became worldwide, and many who hadn't faced systematic racism learned about its depth.[20]

Of the types of self-care described above, let's single out one for now. In the current secular world, or postmodern world as some call it, younger and older adults alike are challenging the predominant worldviews with which they have grown up, even debating the efficacy of science. Observers say we are in an era of spiritual revolution.[21]

A poetic way to summarize this aspect of soulcare is expressed in the well-known Christmas carol "O Little Town of Bethlehem." Its third stanza suggests that humans are looking for a place, a setting "where yearning souls long to be whole."

ARE YOUR BELIEFS OPEN TO DOUBT, IMAGINATION, CURIOSITY?

Beliefs matter—or do they? In religions, historically and literally, they can be life and death. For persons who practice *engaged* spirituality, they are highly important for determining priorities. The political climate leading up to the January 6, 2021, incursion into the United States capitol and the ongoing white supremacist culture suggest they are critical. However, current researchers suggest that daily actions indicate beliefs are often left at home, that is, not significant in decision-making. Some minimize beliefs to avoid theological conflicts.[22]

20. Khabeer, *Muslim Cool*, 219–32, describes the founding of BLM and its significance. The book is pre-2020. Since 2020, a prime example of a continuing concern about racism is the debate over the inclusion of the 1619 Project in school curriculum.

21. Diana Bass, *Grounded*. Her thesis is that people experience God in their worlds, not in the three-tiered universe—God in heaven, the sky, and the earth—and are rejecting what she calls the "elevator" worldview.

22. How important are beliefs? As cited elsewhere, some argue beliefs are essential

Let's return to traditional big questions regarding beliefs. Do you believe in God or multiple gods, and, if so, how does the deity treat humans?[23] Does the Holy One act in history? Does that Being or Force cause suffering or permit it? Give you free will? Does God have a purpose for you? Your answers and your actions reflect your faith, which can be defined as a complete trust and confidence in a benevolent Creative Force or loving God.[24] If you don't believe in a divine being, you aren't exempt from contemplating stances on such questions as economic disparities, environmental dilemmas, and political decisions, including whether terrorism is permissible and if there is a force called evil.[25]

There are different kinds of beliefs, some observable from nature, which can be tested empirically: "I believe in gravity" or "The sun will come up tomorrow morning." Other belief statements are personal and experiential but harder to document: "I believe you will always tell the truth" or "I believe God controls the climate." The most difficult kind of belief statements are those which are not tangible, i.e., physically observable, which we read or hear about and accept as true. Rev. Dr. David Vasquez-Levy, president of Pacific School of Religion, posits that *theology*—in Greek, *theos* and *ology*, knowledge of God—is essentially stories humans tell about God; they become our beliefs.[26] As discussed in other chapters, researchers of teens and young adults make the following

for religion. See Chickering et al., *Encouraging Authenticity*, 221–22, on how beliefs motivate actions. Others say the right relationship with God or, for Christians, Jesus is more important than requirements or rewards, i.e., Marcus J. Borg, *Meeting Jesus Again*. Prothero, *God Is Not One*, 21, states that "belief is a part of most religions, but only a part, and in most cases, not the most important part." See Mercadante, *Belief without Borders*, 241.

23. Newberg et al., *Why God Won't Go Away*, argue that biologically humans are programmed to believe in the divine; see Weintraub, "Spirituality, Sense of Awe," and Froese and Bader, *America's Four Gods*.

24. Dillenberger, "Faith." Karl Barth, *Dogmatics in Outline*. and Paul Tillich, *The Dynamics of Faith*, are cited as other sources.

25. Sacks, *Dignity of Difference*; Stern, *Terror in the Name*. For an extended discussion on evil and evil differentiated from trauma, see Means with Nelson, *Trauma and Evil*, 97–99, 121–74, with examples on many other pages.

26. David Vasquez-Levy, in a presentation at the 2019 Theologian-in-Residence program, Ames, IA on Mar. 1, 2019. One does wonder what stories people recall about God, since 89 percent of emerging adults affiliated with a faith tradition say they believe in God (Denton and Flory, *Back-Pocket God*, 114).

consistent observations: they are willing to discuss beliefs with their peers, but the beliefs are not understood or articulated well.[27]

To the point. Whether you are a believer in God, an atheist, agnostic, or a searcher for the truth, sooner or later, you will have doubts about what is true—the big questions about the meaning of life, a relationship, sexuality, economic well-being, or a peace and justice issue. I've had those discussions with some who came from a faith tradition of absolute truths. Sooner or later, doubt will test you—after an unexpected stillbirth, a teenager diagnosed with terminal cancer, a partner unfairly fired, a community uprooted by a tornado, a country devastated by flood, a continent's residents dying of hunger due to drought, humanity's goodness/purpose, or, finally, your own mortality. You may believe but have doubts; call it "sacred ambiguity."[28]

Doubt has a long history, across many civilizations, and doubt isn't always about religious questions.[29] It's been said that the enemy of faith is not doubt but false certainty.[30] Uncertainty of beliefs and faith is a hallmarks of every formal religious tradition, but science and politics come in for their share of conflict about the truth. *The point I am making is that spiritual homes should accept your doubts as normal.* Doubt is not to be dismissed at any age of life. Your spiritual home should accept it, encourage it, and be ready to assist you as you struggle with it.[31] If you blame God for your parents' untimely deaths, for the grim tragedy of the World Trade Center's collapse on 9/11, or for the coronavirus pandemic, please believe you can find a caring, listening soul.

You may disagree with some or all of what I have just said. If you come from a historic faith, you may hold that one must believe/accept certain dogma as absolute truth. A Greek word, *dogma* refers to the

27. C. Smith with Lundquist, *Soul Searching*, 262.

28. Norris, *Amazing Grace*, 62. See also Holloway, *Leaving Alexandria*. Holloway is the former bishop of Edinburgh, who served Episcopal parishes in England and the United States.

29. Hecht, *Doubt*. The author's conclusion, 484–94, presents the case that doubters who have raised questions regarding truth can bring joy to life.

30. Irving, *Prayer for Owen Meany*. Daniel asserts her philosophy is that doubt is the essence of faith. See *Tired of Apologizing*, 102–14, for examples.

31. McLaren, *Faith after Doubt*, urges readers to use doubt as a vehicle to a mature faith through four stages: simplicity, complexity, perplexity, and harmony. See Kushner, *When Bad Things*, for a rabbi's grappling with the death of his young son. In discussing human tragedies, he reminds readers that the book title begins with when not why.

official doctrines of a religious body.[32] You may believe or have been told that it is essential that you accept every word of an inherited creed as "gospel."[33] I agree that disciples should be knowledgeable about the faith they proclaim, familiar with the texts and traditional views of its history, able to share its times of light and moments of darkness. These past tools should be helpful markers on today's spiritual journeys, but you should be able to challenge its worldview from time to time. Where you are should go beyond what is inherited from past holy men and women. Over a lifetime, worldviews change. You should periodically examine yours.[34]

To be clear, I know some denominations and non-affiliated houses of worship will not agree with me. They will insist that they have the ultimate truth(s). Their practices are to banish, shun, curse those who cannot accept those beliefs, and, in extreme cases, kill disbelievers.[35] From the 1890s to the 1920s, America saw a new wave of disputes over what were "fundamental beliefs." A movement began in opposition to European biblical scholarship that applied principles of literary criticism to the Bible. The battle lines, which still exist, were drawn over five key fundamentals.[36]

32. Pelikan, "Dogma."

33. Spong, *Unbelievable*. Rupp, in *Commitment and Community*, 70, captures the stereotype of faith communities that cite "infallible authorities, engage in uncritical propaganda, seeking blind conviction" that I would not join. They are the opposite of the communities of learning described in the last chapter.

34. Raman, "Worldviews." Factors in one's worldview: (1) the human condition, how we look upon the plight of other people and respond to it; (2) how we view and react to our national history and the history of other people, both positive and negative aspects. Attitudes: (1) *monodoxy:* conviction that one's own worldview is the only correct one; extreme version is *globodium*: hating everything, of which racism is an example; (2) AGA (Anything Goes Attitude), acceptance of everything as equally valid; (3) tolerance: respect of other views, but not necessarily acceptance of all views. Raman believes the US is in danger because it is in an AGA mood. See also Smart, *Worldviews*.

35. A case in point: the label "radical Islamic terrorists," is inaccurate. Many Muslim leaders criticize such groups, saying they are unfaithful to Islamic teachings.

36. Hudson, *Religion in America*, 283. These five fundamentals were developed at the Niagara, NY, Bible conferences of 1895: (1) the deity of Jesus Christ (John 1:1; John 20:28; Heb 1:8–9); (2) the virgin birth of Jesus to Mary (Isa 7:14; Matt 1:23; Luke 1:27); (3) Jesus's blood atonement, i.e., his sacrificial death on the cross (Acts 20:28; Rom 3:25, 5:9; Eph 1:7; Heb 9:12–14); (4) Jesus's bodily resurrection (Luke 24:36–46; 1 Cor 15:1–4, 15:14–15); (5) the inerrancy of the Hebrew and Christian Scriptures (Ps 12:6–7; Rom 15:4; 2 Tim 3:16–17; 2 Pet 1:20). Scholars have identified there were more than these five issues.

More recently, liberal churches have been attacked by religious fundamentalists because of such practices as approving of same-sex marriages, welcoming of LGBTQ persons to join the faith community, and ordaining women as ministers.[37] You will have to make your decision whether to choose a spiritual home that is opened or closed on such matters. Don't assume faith and doubt issues aren't important today. May I leave you with the words to an inherited hymn: "Teach me the struggles of the soul to bear, to check the rising doubt, the rebel sigh; teach me the patience of unanswered prayer."[38] These speak to the reality of doubt; I would rather say examine your rising doubt, not rein it in.

Does hearing about doubt scare you or at least trouble you? If so, would you say you have an active imagination? How often do you have a sliver of curiosity? Good teachers awaken our imaginations or, in other words, are artists who paint images for us that capture the past in a new way or create a world we hadn't conceived. Maria Harris suggests that we have times in our lives when we should "sit back in our souls," with periods of meditation, prayer, and stillness that will invite us to imagine.[39] When we care for ourselves this way, we become prophets of our own existence.[40] Do you really think outside the box? In 2021, the US Government admitted they cannot explain military plane numerous sightings of Unidentified Flying Objects (UFOs). Do you believe it is possible they could be space travelers? Even if not, what are the mathematical odds humanoids exist on some planet? How does that impact your belief in and trust of a divine Creator?

Sharon Daloz Parks argues that imagination is at the core of learning and the heart of leadership. A key to imagination is "paradoxical curiosity."[41] When we become curious, we take things apart, to help distinguish and clarify. But then we are driven to return to unity. In another book, Parks and three other authors speak of responsible imagination, positing that natal and spiritual homes can be sources of new images.[42]

---

37. Culver and Dorhauer, *Steeplejacking*. Attacks are often not spontaneous but strategic campaigns to remove ministers and to encourage congregations to withdraw from their liberal denominations.

38. George Croly, "Spirit of God, Descend Upon My Heart," #290, stanza 4, in United Church of Christ, *New Century Hymnal*.

39. M. Harris, *Teaching and Religious Imagination*, 160–61.

40. Ricoeur, *History and Truth*, 127; Brueggemann, *Prophetic Imagination*, xv.

41. Parks, *Big Questions*, 146–76; specifially on "curiosity," see 159–60.

42. Daloz et al., *Common Fire*, 125–53.

WHAT ARE CIRCLES OF CARING?

What about the caregiving side of soulcare? To answer that question, spiritual traveler, ask yourself, do I believe I have a duty to care for neighbors, the forgotten, the marginalized? If so, have I practiced my empathy recently? Do loved ones or friends trust me? If you need some guidance, read the petitions in the prayer of St. Francis (c. 1182–1226 CE) that begin "Lord, make me an instrument of Thy peace." They encapsulate the point of service above self.[43] I will stick with the word *caregiving*, although *compassion*—its root means "to suffer with"—would be an excellent alternative.[44]

To gain a perspective on caregiving overall within the United States, consider these statistics. In 2015, over 43 million Americans provided unpaid care to an adult or child within the last twelve months.[45] Almost half of that number were caring for a family member, about 15.7 million for someone with Alzheimer's disease or other dementia.[46] Other data indicate that it is not uncommon to have older care recipients to have spouses of equal or older age as their caregivers. Due to stress, caregivers often die before their care receivers do. If you want to understand what caregivers experience rather than study statistics, read stories in Gail Sheehy's classic, *Passages in Caregiving.*[47]

In the 1990s, a distinguished sociologist and scholar of American religion, Robert Wuthnow, wrote two books related to soulcare. The first, in 1991, was *Acts of Compassion.*[48] In it, he described compassion

43. Often called the Prayer of Saint Francis or the Make Me an Instrument of Your Peace Prayer. The Rotary motto, "service above self," is typical of mottos by civic organizations.

44. Nouwen, *Wounded Healer*, 40. The author believes compassion is an essential quality of a leader. The book contains several descriptions of acts of compassion.

45. National Alliance for Caregiving and AARP Public Policy Institute, "Caregiving in the United States 2015."

46. About 6 million Americans have Alzheimer's; by 2050, the estimate is 13 million (Alzheimer's Association, *Twenty-Twenty-One Alzheimer's Disease*).

47. Sheehy offers blunt descriptions of what happens after "the call"—the triggering event followed by the doctor's diagnosis. Early on, she includes a realistic job description of a caregiver (Sheehy, *Passages in Caregiving*, 10). A more extensive account is found in Sutton, *Stop and Smell*, 108.

48. Wuthnow, *Acts of Compassion*, 45. On p. 122, he notes that the world's major faiths all encourage compassion. For example, the Qur'an teaches those who practice charity guard themselves from evil. The Mayahana tradition of Buddhism holds compassion as the highest virtue.

as more than specific behaviors; it includes the language a person uses to describe his/her motivation and the cultural framework that makes it possible. In *Sharing the Journey* (1994), he estimated that 40 percent of adults participated in a support group.[49] In 2011, a Pew Research Center sample of two thousand-plus found that approximately half of adults join a group; about half (47 percent) indicated, as a rule, they trust other people; a larger percentage (50 percent), more non-joiners, say they generally don't trust others.[50] Wuthnow's statistics documented that religious institutions were the largest provider of support groups. Small groups, he acknowledged, are paradoxical; while they need formality—leaders, goals, and agendas—they also offer informality, warmth, encouragement, acceptance, with opportunities to share personal stories.[51] These groups of intimate strangers become the glue for individuals seeking emotional support for themselves but who also want community. Henri Nouwen is known for another paradoxical description of caregivers. His classic book *The Wounded Healer* describes ways to provide compassion in a dislocated world.[52]

This involvement may seem contrary to the phenomenon of growing alienation portrayed in the sociological classic *Bowling Alone*, by Robert D. Putnam.[53] Putnam, with David E. Campbell, in another book, addresses that issue.[54] They seem surprised by interviews and surveys describing how involved people are in caring for others. However, more recent research suggests that younger adults, sharing concerns for others as do other generations, express them in different ways.

Members of spiritual homes should be caregivers. What does that mean? To use the proverbial phrase, the devil is in the details. It is

---

49. Wuthnow, *Sharing the Journey*. See especially ch. 8, "The Spiritual Dimension: Personal Faith in Small Groups," 219–56.

50. Purcell and Smith, "State of Groups."

51. Wuthnow, *Sharing the Journey*, 158–59. He notes that small groups differ markedly from homes in one significant way: many have as their fundamental reason for existence the provision of offering deep intimate interpersonal support.

52. Means with Nelson, *Trauma and Evil*, 418–22, offer an insightful discussion about the meaning of therapists' work today and the appropriate times and ways they can share their wounded souls.

53. *Bowling Alone* is a 2000 nonfiction book. It was developed from Putnam's 1995 essay entitled "Bowling Alone: America's Declining Social Capital."

54. Putnam et al., *American Grace*. For data, see ch. 13, "Religion and Good Neighborliness," 443–92.

impossible, even with inspiring anecdotes, to describe the myriad opportunities that exist for spiritual caregiving.[55]

I'll focus on several familiar caregiving activities and describe several other areas I've come to believe need attention now. Rather than list hundreds of ways for you to offer support as an individual,[56] I will focus on four types of caregiving by small groups that are especially needed now. These four areas emphasize person-centered caregiving. The rationale is that groups can be more effective than individuals.[57] Let's call them circles of caring: 1) well-being of children and elders, 2) homeless services, 3) food and hospitality, and 4) civic participation.

Well-Being of Children and Elders

Can you think of any religious or spiritual tradition that does not value children? We know that perceptions about children have shifted over the centuries, from believing children needed minimal care and education to treating them like miniature adults; to recognizing them with changing physical, emotional, and moral stages of development.[58] Chapters 1 and 2 acknowledged the unfortunate truth that too many children have grown up in abusive homes.[59] Chapter 6 described a wide range of educational methods used to educate children. In rural areas especially, a key to improving childcare is broadband services. Religious institutions today would seem to have a golden opportunity to provide places for preschool

55. Although focused on hospital settings, an excellent overview of possibilities is provided by Carson and Koenig, *Spiritual Caregiving*. Drescher, *Choosing Our Religion*, 112, describes healing practices, including chanting drawn from Buddhist and Native American traditions. Mercadante, *Belief without Borders*, xv, describes different spiritual healing experiences from Native American drumming to Buddhist hand positions to qigong whole-body meditative exercises.

56. Blumberg and Hafiz, "Yes, Religion Can Still."

57. Brueggemann, *Prophetic Imagination*, xvi. Brueggemann believes a spiritual community that is effective has four qualities: a *long and available memory* of compassion, *a sense of pain* that is officially known and understood as unbearable in the future, *an active practice of hope*, and *effective mode of discourse* across generations.

58. Philippe, "Children and Religion"; a fascinating account from many countries and religious practices.

59. N. Harris, *Deepest Well*, is a wake-up call to social and psychological actions that result in medical conditions and social behaviors that need to be addressed. Her TED talk and this book speak to healing the long-term effects of childhood adversity. As Means with Nelson caution in *Trauma and Evil*, those of us who are spiritual caregivers are tempted to be problem-solvers of the soul sometimes too quickly, 2, 76, 145.

childcare.[60] In 2016, among children ages three to five who had employed mothers, 54 percent received center-based care, while 18 percent had home-based care from relatives, and 11 percent had home-based non-relative care.[61] The childcare issues that arise include its expenses: figures suggest families spent 12 percent to 20 percent of their income on it, while there is a declining number of licensed facilities (between 2005 and 2017, the number of small care facilities fell by 48 percent) and a reduction in qualified personnel.[62] Rural areas of the US are considered "deserts," because of the shortages of caregivers and distances to be traveled.[63] One of the realities of the US economy in 2021 is the recognition that employment isn't rebounding as fast as expected, because the cost of childcare is equal to or exceeds the income of the second parent. Faith-based agencies have a strong history in child welfare.[64]

Elders are at the fastest growing age cohort in the US; in the years just prior to 2020, persons over sixty-five jumped 34 percent, or 54 million, from the 2010 census. Other data reveals about 7 percent of that age group will need some medical assistance; another report indicates that one in ten adults reports being abused. Such statistics, like those of childcare, underscore the need for thinking about the nation's infrastructures of support. Understandably, most adults say they want to stay in their homes, but for medical and social well-being reasons, as they age, they will move to a residence with other seniors. Interestingly, some years ago, a corporation managing health-care facilities for retirement communities learned from focus groups that adults in the forty-five to sixty-five age bracket had negative feelings about the words *care* and *care plans*. Their self-image is that they don't see themselves as needing care, even as

60. Persons considered establishing care programs might find spaces available in houses of worship, those which were overbuilt in the 1950s–1970s. Wuthnow, *Sharing the Journey*, 170, indicates that 12 percent of volunteers in religious support groups are involved with childcare.

61. "Child Care."

62. "Decreasing Number."

63. Schochet, "Five Facts To Know." In rural areas, the average teacher salary is c. $23,000 anually, another factor in considering the decline.

64. Goodnow, "Role of Faith-Based Agencies." Dorothy Bass, *Practicing Our Faith*, 154–55, describes healing ministries of several religious congregations. See ch. 8 for a discussion on religious freedom. In Fulton vs. City of Philadelphia 593 U.S. _____ (2021), the US Supreme Court ruled that a Roman Catholic adoption agency refusing to place children with gay and lesbian couples had a right to do so consistent with their faith's beliefs.

they prepare for retirement. But with the escalating cost of living, including medical expenses, one estimate is that for every hundred persons of working age, almost fifty-four others will need support. Of those who move, some will go to independent facilities, others to assisted living, others to skilled nursing, and some to long-term care (LTC) or continuing care communities.[65] An estimated 80 percent of LTCs are affiliated with religious denominations.

These communities are faced with two significant trends. The first surfaced in the 2020 COVID-19 pandemic. Care facilities' physical arrangements and staff, like hospitals, were initially overwhelmed with high death rates of residents and staff.[66] A second trend was and is that hiring caring and competent staff has become more difficult. Being a resident and board member at a retirement community and having served on a county-wide senior services board, I can attest to elder service programs needing compassionate caregivers who provide wellness or well-being programs rather than focusing on end-of-life care.[67] If you search the phrase *dimensions of wellness* online, you will find a surprising variety of ways that senior communities identify wellness.[68] One component in that rainbow of opportunities will often be spiritual well-being. others dimensions of well-being include emotional, environmental, health services, intellectual, physical, social, and vocational.

I deliberately chose the words *wellness* and *well-being* for this segment, because I am not asking you to be pseudo-physicians or physician's assistants providing medical assistance to these two groups.[69] If

65. Tanzi, "Growth of Working-Age Adults." See also "Faith Based Assisted Living." The survey was conducted by Life Care Services, a retirement community management company headquartered in Des Moines, IA.

66. As of June 15, 2021, COVID-19 deaths in the United States exceeded 600,000. The Kaiser Foundation had estimated that one-third of the national deaths attributed to the 2020 coronavirus occurred in senior living communities; however, in 2022, one-half (51 percent) of all senior living communities reported no deaths due to COVID-19, according to a study by NORC at the University of Chicago.

67. At my retirement community, wellness-related topics are presented to employees, and they are encouraged, along with residents, to participate in well-being activities.

68. International Council on Active Aging, "Creating a Path," 15, highlights many wellness strategies for building cultures of positive aging. Another report from the same organization, *Future-Proof Your Senior Living*, 15–16, offers a broad definition of wellness and its many values.

69. Sanders, *Way of Imagination*, 207–18, states the word *well-being* is from the same root as the word *wealth*. How valuable do you consider your well-being?

you are gifted in these areas (medicine and healthcare), or feel drawn to those fields, bravo.[70] In rural and some urban areas, when older adults lose spouses and their closest neighbors move or don't drive anymore, the "olders" become "elder orphans." It's a cohort that needs friends and transportation to get groceries and prescriptions and go to medical appointments.

A trend in spiritual homes is to support faith community nursing programs.[71] In 2005, the American Nurses Association developed standards for this field, *Faith Community Nursing: Scope and Standards of Practice.* What do these nurses do? They care for the whole person—spiritual, physical, mental, emotional, social, and cultural, through health promotion. For example, following a worship service, a nurse can assist an older member with a blood pressure check, explain medications, or review a health insurance form. The nurse might accompany the elder to a medical appointment, should the elder have difficulty hearing or understanding.[72] Stephen Ministries is one well-known organization.[73] Perhaps you could be a mover and shaker to establish a group for family members and caregivers of those with autism, Alzheimer's, cancer, or addictions to alcohol or opioids.[74]

Services for the Homeless

Considering the importance of home, family, and spirituality that I've stressed, it would be ironic if the book didn't give serious consideration to

70. Wilke, *Creating the Caring Congregation.* I was privileged to meet Harold, a quadriplegic, born without hands. He was physically amazing and truly inspiring. Especially see ch. 5, "The Marks of a Caring Congregation," to see how he pioneered opportunities for volunteers in situations with the disabled.

71 Carson and Koenig, *Parish Nurse*, 6. Rev. Granger Westberg, a hospital chaplain, is considered the pioneer in beginning parish nurse programs. He preferred to say the nurses offered *holistic* care. Later some programs preferred to be known as faith-based community programs. For data on the scope of programs today, contact sources such as the Westberg Institute for Faith Community Nursing, https://westberginstitute.org; Health Ministries Association, https://hmassoc.org/; or Spiritual Care Association, https://spiritualcareassociation.org/new-york.html.

72. Sharon T. Hinton, Westberg Institute, phone interview, July 15, 2021, reported that the institute has trained over 15,000 faith community nurses in thirty-two countries. One emerging trend she noted is hospitals hiring nurses who are then assigned to work with congregations. Another is to work with COVID long-haulers.

73. https://www.stephenministries.org.

74. Sutton, *Stop and Smell*, is a vivid account by the wife of a doctor Alzheimer's. The author suggests that there were few who helped her.

the growing problem of homelessness in the United States. There are two ways to tackle it. The first, which on the surface seems like common sense yet sounds too radical, is to make more people homeowners or occupants of affordable, healthy rental units. The Pulitzer Prize-winning author of *Evicted*, Matthew Desmond, has real-world examples of how to make that happen. Noting that more than one out of five of *all* renting families spends 50 percent of their income on housing, he believes fundamental solutions need to occur, which will take time. One strategy is to establish publicly funded legal services for low-income families. It would result in decreased evictions and homelessness.[75] The book provides examples of persons who serve as support for or witnesses for those who are in house court disputes, i.e., eviction notices.

For other spiritual communities, their ministry would focus on assisting those who are homeless. That includes standing up when homeless persons, many elderly, are ignored, scammed, pushed to the margins.[76] It should be understood that being homeless doesn't mean only living under a bridge or bedding down in a car. It includes temporary housing, such as staying with friends or relatives or in a motel. Regardless, the stress of loss of the certainty of a home is what is critical.[77] One estimate is that on a single night, over 567,715 people in the United States experience homelessness, or 0.17 percent of the population. Their profiles represent every region of the country, every gender, racial/ethnic group, and family status.[78] Another disturbing trend is that major American cities have noticed 40 percent increases of homelessness in 2017 and 2019. Overall, there is somewhat of a decline in homelessness. But let's be clear: while 50 percent are in locations not fit for human habitation, the other 50 percent are staying in temporary commercial housing or with relatives or friends. Two shocking statistics are the homeless persons younger than nine years old, reflecting the fact of a parent's losing employment, an illness, or a spouse escaping an abusive situation; youth make up 20 percent of the homeless.[79] Even modest-sized school districts report that they

75. Desmond, *Evicted*, 303. Elsewhere, he describes how persons with jobs or who are job seeking lose work stability when they are in situations fighting evictions.

76. Klausner, "Vaccinate the Homeless."

77. Parks cites this in "To Venture and To Abide," 72. The article reinforces, with research findings, ways that *home* is a psychological foundation for life.

78. National Alliance to End Homelessness, "State of Homelessness."

79. Stasha, "State of Homelessness," point 10.

may have fifty to one hundred homeless children receiving instruction.[80] After the Great Depression of the 1930s, the Catholic Worker Movement began offering free housing, transportation, and job assistance. There are nearly 190 such houses around the world now. Some also help those transitioning from incarceration.[81]

Faith-based organizations provided nearly 60 percent of the emergency shelter beds in a 2017 study of eleven American cities.[82] Granted, not every single house of worship could provide such a service. Ninety churches in the Detroit area formed the Macomb County Rotating Emergency Shelter Team and pooled resources to assist the homeless. Some of the member communities provided housing, some vans, some meals.[83] Spiritual homes, as this makes clear, do not need to do everything. But some may have a history of providing clothing pantries or food kitchens that could be integrated in a new cooperative model. They can work in conjunction with local and regional governments as well as organizations like the Salvation Army and Habitat for Humanity for longer-term changes in homelessness.[84]

Food and Hospitality: Table and Hearth

Who likes to eat? Everyone! However, it is a cruel question for those not privileged to live in developed countries. Even in the United States, an estimated one out of eight persons and one out of six children is food insecure each day. Yet, in this country, we export $149 billion of food each year. In the United States, the average family of four wastes up to $2,275 per year in food; 25 percent of the food they purchase ends up in the garbage. An estimated nine million people in the world die annually of

80. Seventy percent of homeless are single; 30 percent are people in families with children. Over a three-year span, from 2014–2015 to 2016–2017, from 1.26 million to 1.36 million students experienced homelessness. In some states, the increase was over 20 percent (Camera, "Number of Homeless Students").

81. Rosario, "Catholic Worker House Opens."

82. Banks, "Homeless Find Rest." Data analyzed by the US Department of Housing and Urban Development estimated that there was $119 million in taxpayer savings by such shelters.

83. See https://www.mcrest.org. For a program set up to help persons with AIDS, see Bender, *Heaven's Kitchen*.

84. A problem related to homelessness is human trafficking. According to the United Nations, there are 40.1 million enslaved persons in the world; that includes many millions who are in forced marriages.

starvation; that is the equivalent of three 350 passenger airplanes crashing *each* hour of *each* day in a year![85]

Back down to earth and pleasant memories. For many, the most endearing recollections are from the table and around the fireplace or hearth.[86] Many traditions even consider preparing and sharing a meal a holy activity. Rabbi Abraham Joshua Heschel suggests that our tables at home can be an altar. A variety of foods are associated with ethnic religious traditions, and others have religious symbolism.[87] Religious holidays and seasons are associated with certain dishes to eat or avoid eating. I can't think of a house of worship I've been in that didn't have a kitchen and space for meals. In the book describing her spiritual journey, Diana Butler Bass came to the realization that the kitchen of a congregation more than the sanctuary is where members truly learn about each other, from setting up for meals to doing the dishes.[88] These many references to food, table, and hospitality gave me the thought that one image of an engaged spiritual person is as a "chef of soulcare."

Before the 2020 coronavirus brought more catastrophic changes, medically and economically, houses of worship were experiencing declining participation, in worship service attendance, in congregational dinners, from soup suppers to wedding receptions and after-memorial-service brunches. Smaller groups still prepare occasional meals or treats, but congregations now cancel fundraising annual events like Harvest Home dinners. Let's not forget perhaps the simplest form of showing caring for a member of one's fellowship—to take a plate of cookies to a home as a sign of welcome, or a dish when a death occurs.

85. Sentient Media, "Food Insecurity"; "Food Insecurity" (US Dept. of Veterans Affairs) mentions that 11 percent of U.S. households were food insecure at least some time during the year. In 2021 it was reported 13 million children are now food insecure (Suza, "Many Children").

86. Michael Pollan, *Cooked*, 4, as cited in Drescher, *Choosing Our Religion*, 120, provides historical perspectives suggesting cooking can be spiritually "magic," leading to family stories about food.

87. "List of Foods." The article lists foods for Taoism, Shinto, Judaism, Islam, Hinduism, and Christianity. See also Pérez, *Religion in the Kitchen*.

88. Diana Bass, *Strength for the Journey*, 146. A sad memory for me is when my wife and I hosted a potluck for graduate students at our home. All went well until we let our yapping toy poodle come upstairs. Upon seeing him, a student and his wife from Lebanon immediately stopped eating because a dog was in kitchen.

In some spiritual traditions, members show care by supporting a community food bank or pantry.[89] Think of the trust and hope exhibited in these accounts. A National Public Radio story described a business executive whose encore career was as CEO of a food bank. Would you consider being a volunteer in a food kitchen sponsored by one or more faith communities?[90] One congregation provided cards to "broke" persons so they could buy food at the supermarket.[91] That does not preclude having a coffee hour after a service along with some treats. A rural house of worship in Iowa offers a marvelous example of caring for members and friends that is the key to its vitality. Every Sunday it has a "not fancy" but delightful potluck following the service. Over the years, I found congregational potlucks of various traditions a common vehicle for persons who had grown up in the community to return to see old neighbors.

A final suggestion. Most cultures have bread. A unique event my grandchildren have at their New England school is a non-religious celebration on the last school day prior to Thanksgiving. It's called Bread Day. Families of current students, alumni, and neighbors bring a variety of breads that reflect their ethnic and religious heritages. A row of narrow tables goes across the gymnasium floor. Parents and guests tell the story about how and why their breads are made. One of my dreams is to spread, like butter, that mouth-watering and eye-opening event. See **activity 7.2**, Bread Together.

Civic Participation

In his autobiography *My Life*, Russian/French artist Marc Chagall recalled his village "as the centre of the world and the [house] the focus of his existence, around which life revolves."[92] Legend has it that the play/movie

89. Go to https://www.feedingamerica.org/find-your-local-foodbank to find food banks in your region. This website states that 4.3 billion meals are provided by food banks each year. Feedingamerica.org is the national network for food banks.

90. Call the USDA National Hunger Hotline, which operates from 7:00 AM to 10:00 PM Eastern Time, at 1–866–3–HUNGRY or 1–877–8–HAMBRE. If you need food assistance, you can speak with a representative who will find food resources such as meal sites, food banks, and other social services available near your location.

91. Baskette, *Real Good Church*, 74. According to the author, the governor of Massachusetts at that time suggested it is better to call people *broke*—considered a temporary condition—rather than *poor*—considered a permanent condition.

92. Marc Chagall, as cited in Frankel, "Home and the Holocaust," 345. The article is a poignant memory of the love, trust, and hope that hometowns provide, even though

Fiddler on the Roof was based on his numerous paintings, including *I and the Village*. The visual art messages of Chagall and poetry of Jewish Lithuanian-South African David Fram make clear how faith and spirituality bond communities, providing healing and rebirth even after unspeakable tragedies. Based on several surveys, Putnam and Campbell make the case that Americans who are involved in religious homes consistently are more likely to belong to community organizations, be actively involved with community problem-solving, take part in local civic and political projects, and advocate for political reforms. Further, the more involved people are in civic activity, the more supportive they are of civil liberties.[93] Diana Eck describes similar examples of Hindu and Buddhist involvement in what she calls bridge building.[94]

Putnam and Campbell point out a negative: religious people are less tolerant of dissent than their secular neighbors. Could that be related to their feelings of certainty about their beliefs? Peter Schmiechen, reflecting upon the meaning of compassion in the complex parable of the good Samaritan, noted that Jesus not only criticized practices of some religious practitioners of his day but made the hero a member of a despised ethnic group. Let us always be cautious about limiting who our neighbors are.[95]

Piazza and Trimble offer many examples of ways that churches can transform their communities through small groups. Scenario: you are considering joining a spiritual home. One of its requirements is that new members must serve as a member of one of the congregation's many small groups. [96] Would that give you pause? Let's say you are asked to serve on a dinner committee, or landscaping crew, or, yes, teaching rotation. Would you be game? Would you opt out?

---

wars decimated many such Russian small towns.

93. Putnam et al., *American Grace*, 444, 454–57, 452.

94. Eck, *New Religious America*, 364–66.

95. Schmiechen, *Words Unspoken*, 26–30. See Luke 10:25–37.

96. Piazza and Trimble, *Liberating Hope*. Their hope was the revitalization of mainstream congregations. While I applaud their recommendations, I see few examples of significant changes. Recall the example of Spiritual Locations, i.e., from MCC congregations placing new attendees in groups of mutual interests. See **activity 2.4**.

TRAVELER: READY TO BECOME A CHEF
OF SOULCARE?

Worn out? This third mark or quality of a healthy spiritual home is that it provides a place of trust for your soul to grow. That trust should be transformative, creating a "burning" that moves you to soulcare for others. When your soul catches its breath—pun intended—if you recall the description of the soul, ask yourself this: how well do I know my soul? If not well, consider Scott Sanders perspective that we have been so busy "saving our skins" that "few of us worry about saving our souls, and fewer still imagine that the condition of our souls has anything to do with the condition of our neighborhood."[97]

Take time to come up with the image that is you, a combination of body and spirit, how you listen and speak, what you like and dislike, what you are confident in doing and reluctant to try. When you feel comfortable, ask yourself, what questions have I asked and answered satisfactorily, and what are some I still have? And the other, bigger question, what are the dreams I have, shared and secret? When you have done this part, you are through with sitting back. Now it is on to stepping in. But a major question is, am I really helping someone else because it is a healing I still need? Am I, according to Nouwen's paradox, a "wounded healer"?[98]

Earlier in the chapter, one option I suggested was to become involved with others through food. It's quite common, harder with COVID, for a small group in a rural or small town, getting together periodically with each individual or partner bringing a dish. In many communities of faith, at a time of grief or serious illnesses, members provide meals. Chefs of soulcare.

A healthy spiritual home will ask you to choose to be a caregiver for others. In time, you will have intimate strangers—another paradox—who help you achieve your worthy dream of caregiving. In either case, you will be transformed by trust. An outcome of that trust is likely to be hope. Find "the room for hope"[99] that brings a feeling of certainly that allows you and those you are for to face the future regardless of how it will turn out.

97. Sanders, *Staying Put*, 117.

98. Nouwen, *Wounded Healer*, 81–100.

99. Shirley Erena Murray, "Come and Find the Quiet Center," a 1989 hymn text that urges persons to have hope. For more details, go to https://hymnary.org/text/come_and_find_the_quiet_center.

Chapter 7 Activities

ACTIVITY 7.1: SOULCARE

Based on the description in the text, what do I understand to be soulcare? Start with key words or phrases.

What type(s) of soulcare might I need now?

Who might be able to help me find such care?

What kind of soulcare have I received in the past?

What gifts do I have for extending soulcare to others?

What limits do I have in providing soulcare for others?

Consider the importance of trust in answering each of these questions!

ACTIVITY 7.2: BREAD TOGETHER

Purpose: Your spiritual home or group within the community must decide the purpose of the event. Is it informational, to simply introduce those attending to types of breads and the recipes of the cultures they represent? Is it to learn more about the symbolism of the bread and any links to specific traditions and holidays? Is it to become better acquainted with individuals and groups from specific cultures, such as international students? Is it to build awareness of the diversity within your community and foster better relationships? Will you want one or more guests to speak about the bread(s) they bring?

Settings: Pick a place suitable for the number of persons invited. Determine if all the breads should be baked in advance or could be completed on site. Do you want to have warming appliances? Or do you need a kitchen for preparation or cleanup? What drinks will you have to go with the bread? Anticipate how many tables you will need for the breads, including any gluten-free. Will it be informal, such as in a gymnasium, where small groups can sit on the floor?

(*Activity 7.2 continued*)

Program: If the event is associated with a holiday, such as Thanksgiving, will you have any special music? Speakers?

Publicity and advance notices: This type of event should be planned well in advance. Attendees may need to purchase special baking ingredients.

A select list of breads and one other food with religious significance (limited to two each):

Hinduism: modak—sweet dumpling filled with fresh coconut and jaggery, for Ganesh; chaturthi

Islam: halva—on the seventh and fortieth days and first anniversary following the death of a Muslim, the semolina or flour helva is offered to visitors by relatives of the deceased; ketupat—packed rice wrapped in a woven palm leaf—associated with Eid al-Fitr in SE Asia

Shinto: tofu—the abura-age (soybean curd) is a favorite food of the foxes associated with the deity Inari

Taoism: noodle—symbolizes longevity, usually served on Chinese New Year's Eve

Judaism: sufganiyot, eaten on Hanukkah, a fried pastry filled with sweet jelly symbolizing the miracle of oil; matzo—unleavened bread eaten at the Passover seder, recalling the Jews leaving Egypt in haste.

Christianity: pretzel—Southern France monks (610 CE) baked thick strips of dough into the shape of a child's arms folded in prayer; hot cross bun—traditionally eaten on Good Friday—to break the fast required for that day. Prepare eggs for Easter Sunday.

FOR ADDITIONAL CONVERSATIONS

First things first. In your own words, can you describe what a soul or, more important, your soul is? Can you relate it to soul food or soul music or the soul of a nation? Second, how do you visualize caring for family, neighbors, and communities?

- A starting point is Richard Rohr's *Falling Upward: A Spirituality for the Two Halves of Life*. Look at his descriptions soul, then immerse yourself in reflecting on "the second half of your life."

- The subtitle of J. Jeffrey Means with Mary Anne Nelson's *Trauma and Evil* is *Healing the Wounded Soul*. If that image fits you or others you know, this somber collection of stories may offer you both comfort and confrontation.

- A classic for those who raise doubts about faith when tragedies occur is Harold S. Kushner's *When Bad Things Happen to Good People*.

- A best-seller in years past, Gail Sheehy's *Passages in Caregiving: Turning Chaos into Confidence* centers around her care for her dying husband. It includes many other insights into caring for others and the burdens and rewards of caregiving.

- A focus of chapter 7 is the importance of trust. Small-town and rural Americans feel forgotten and leery about trusting those who hold power over them, whether in business or government. Robert Wuthnow, a sociologist of religion, from a small Kansas town, offers a stunning view in *The Left Behind: Decline and Rage in Small-Town America*.

- Another sociologist, Courtney Bender, tells the story of a non-religious program begun in New York City to help AIDS victims and their families. Amazing dialogues occur between volunteers who come with different motives to *Heaven's Kitchen*, whose motto is "God's Love We Deliver."

- Homelessness can't be ignored. Matthew Desmond's *Evicted: Poverty and Profit in the American City*, a Pulitzer Prize winner, offers innovative strategies to assist those in need.

8

Service—"Trans-Formed" by Love

I know my Christian pasture so well. I know where the briars are along with the piles of turds. I also know where the springs of living water are, but when I look over the fence at the neighbor's spread, it looks so flawless, so unblemished, and perfectly tended, at least from where I stand.

—Barbara Brown Taylor, *Holy Envy*, 64

There are still other lands and countries, beautiful and deep, longing and asking for the good and the bright.

—Avesta, The Creation, the Zoroastrian Avesta

For the primary task before us, both women and men, is not that of becoming a fulfilled self (or a fulfilled nation) but rather to become a faithful people, members of a whole human family, developing together in our small planet home, guests to each other "in the household of God."

—Sharon Daloz Parks, "Home and Pilgrimage," 7.

Love is the fulfillment and highest form of the spirit of justice.

—Reinhold Niebuhr, *Love and Justice*, 25

YESS: <u>Y</u>OUR <u>E</u>VERYDAY <u>S</u>OULCARE AND <u>S</u>UPPORT

- ◆ Invitation: to become part of a community of turning, "trans-formed" by love

- ◆ What does "speaking truth to power" mean—past, present, future?

- ◆ Three worldviews: redemption, regeneration, and reconciliation

- ◆ A world of justice: what does environmental stewardship mean?

- ◆ A world of neighbors: how do we make race and refugees matter?

- ◆ A world with freedom of conscience: whose boundaries?

- ◆ Traveler: ready to be a world neighbor?

- ◆ For Additional Conversations

Recall your trail to find a healthy spiritual home. In the first four chapters, you gained insights to prepare for a spiritual venture. I hoped your natal home provided you with protection and an openness to travel. In chapters 2 and 3, you inspected yourself, your roles, talents, and abilities to grapple with the big questions of life and voices tempting the identity you were forming. Alone and together, whispering and shouting, you have framed worthy dreams you want to turn into reality.[1] Concluding part I, chapter 4 described what your destination should be, a spiritual home offering both comfort and confrontation.

Earlier chapters of part II assisted you in assessing three qualities of a healthy spiritual home. That eventual home, I hope, will support you in a "trans-formative" spiritual growth. Did some activities make your trip up close and vibrant rather than distant and hollow? Chapter 5's intent was to describe ways a spiritual home enhances your yearnings for life's mysteries. Are you becoming aware of or reconnecting with ways to celebrate the awe-fullness of life and gaining support to wrestle with its awful-ness? Chapter 6 examined a backpack full of learning strategies and practices, individually and communally, that can make spiritual growth exciting as well as informative. Chapter 7 assumed you've experienced doubts along your spiritual trip. Have you? If you did, you're not alone. Caring for your soul's questions should lead to a burning sensation of caregiving for others; that's soulcare. Ready for the last big step now?

Back to the analogy of finding the right house. It will have outdoor as well as indoor features that make it a home to which you invite neighbors. Picture a backyard where you and yours relax, maybe do some gardening, a front porch where you wave to neighbors, and a deck where you serve ice cream to gaggles of guests.

---

1. Parks, *Big Questions*, 246–47, proposes that in these uncertain times, the dream of justice with liberty for all is further broken. The increasingly global perspective we must have needs to overcome "the poverty of 'the self alone' culture," and through wisdom, maturity, and faith, "we come to realize the 'other' is needed to complete our dreams." My advice: don't give up on dreams. A Broadway musical, *South Pacific*, set in World War II, has a character singing that you can never have a dream come true if you never have a dream.

INVITATION: TO BECOME PART OF A COMMUNITY OF TURNING, "TRANS-FORMED" BY LOVE

The last stop on this spiritual journey involves turning to a new perspective. From your spiritual home's window, look out and view yourself as a visionary embracing a world of neighbors. Become a planet patriot! Too much, you say. Recall the story of Grover's Corners, New Hampshire, in Thornton Wilder's play *Our Town*. In a quaint village of 2,642 souls, Emily, who dies giving birth, returns unseen to witness precious scenes of love and service in ordinary conversations and deeds. Returning to the afterlife, she grieves that humans cannot appreciate that there are no boundaries of time and space for their simple behaviors. Another character in the play, Rebecca, reinforces Wilder's universal message. She tells the story of a letter to a town resident whose envelope address goes beyond town, state, and country to include: "Continent of North America; Western Hemisphere; the Earth; the Solar System; the Universe; the Mind of God."[2]

Spirituality, like religion, should make differences. Chapters 5–7 have shared narratives of three transformative spiritual qualities—joy, truth, and trust—that could be potential outcomes for you. With chapter 8, I propose love-based justice as an imperative. To be blunt, spirituality without justice isn't worth squat. Love is the foundation of all spirituality; justice is its ultimate instrument.[3] As Dirk Ficca reminded me, when we are in solidarity with others, from pulling up the roots of inequality to planting the seeds of justice and peace, that's when "trans-formation" flowers. In many faith traditions, justice is linked to peace—*shalom*. Children sense fairness. Perhaps there will never be absolute equality in our families, communities, tribes, or nations. But isn't that our vision? Look at the text of the hymn "This Is My Song" and paintings such as *Peaceable Kingdom*: worthy dreams of love-based justice rooting out the weeds of obscene inequities.[4]

2. T. Wilder, *Our Town*, end of act 1, 936. Long, "Is Our Town," discusses a book by Sherman, *Another Day's Begun*, about the reasons this 1938 play remains so popular.

3. Attributed to Reinhold Niebuhr. See ch. 6. Patton, "Love and Justice," contains a reframing of the opening quotation of the chapter.

4. The first two stanzas of "This Is My Song," were written by Lloyd Stone in 1934, and the third stanza was written by Georgia Harkness, c. 1939; see https://hymnary.org/text/this_is_my_song_o_god_of_all_the_nations. *Peaceable Kingdom* has over a hundred renditions painted by Edward Hicks, c. 1820–1849.

Chapter 8 offers an outlook on what earth's inhabitants need in three critical arenas: environmental stewardship, refugee resettlement,[5] and freedom of conscience. You may not wish to be politically active now,[6] but I implore you to think globally and act locally in these three areas. As world neighbors, united, we can make a difference.

WHAT DOES "SPEAKING TRUTH TO POWER" MEAN—PAST, PRESENT, FUTURE?

Sister Joan Chittister offers this brisk summary: "What the world needs now, respects now, demands now, understands now is not poverty, chastity, and obedience; it is generous justice, reckless love, and limitless listening."[7] I would add nonviolent protest, using Martin Luther King Jr. and Congressman John Lewis as models of dissent. Exchange rancor for righteousness, leave familiar ground for foreign soils, and replace ignorant and incompetent actions with informed and insightful service. Some call this radical or revolutionary. Really? Our world changes. Pandemics and wars, corporate globalization, wealth disparities, and political corruption see to that.[8]

We need to create new paradigms, transforming spheres of suspicion into world neighborhoods.[9] Begin by examining these traditional paradigms for speaking truth to power by speaking out, providing relief, and challenging systems.

5. Recent figures estimate there are 80 million refugees and 270 million migrants (Reuters, "Number of Refugees Worldwide").

6. Mercadante, *Belief without Borders*, 299, with citations, describes where different generations are in views of what I call social justice.

7. Kielsmeier-Cook, *Blessed are the Nones*, 147–48.

8. Rupp, *Globalization Challenged*, 9, cites Paul Krugman's statistics that almost 40 percent of the wealth of the country is in the hands of 1 percent of the population. Even in the 1970s, the very top tier in terms of total income—one-hundredth of 1 percent of the population—received seventy times as much as the average family. By the early 2000s, the top tier received three hundred times as much.

9. Rupp, *Globalization Challenged*, 26, emphasizes the financial imbalances as the chief atrocious outcomes of other policies that must be countered by conviction, conflicts, and neighbor-focused communities.

Past

In the past, we emphasized speaking out. We assumed our portfolios of persuasion, in letters written to editors and legislators, and our signed petitions, buttressed by occasional appearances at city halls and state capitals, were enough. Admirably, we joined others in cornucopias of relief efforts by contributing canned goods, donating clothing, building Habitat for Humanity homes, and cleaning up after floods and tornadoes. Far less frequently, we confronted the systemic reasons behind poverty and economic disparities, racism and its debacles regarding minority health and education, and the gnawing growth of water and air pollution. When the civil rights battle of the 1960s required a direct confrontation of racial discrimination, Rabbi Abraham Joshua Heschel informed US president John Kennedy that it would require moral grandeur and spiritual audacity.[10]

Present

Where are we now? We could say, for example, that the 1965 civil rights legislation provided relief and challenged the system, but enforcement was slow. Key provisions of the 1965 civil rights legislation were gutted in the US Supreme Court decision Shelby County v. Holder, 570 U.S. 529 (2013). Unfortunately, violence against Black people has a four-hundred-year history in America; change is slow in coming. In the US, police killings of minorities have sparked protest movements like Black Lives Matter (BLM). While protests are an acceptable, even prophetic, form of speech, some state legislatures have limited them. The idea that dissent should always be civil is disputed by some, with evidence that it is a norm too often favoring the privileged.[11] Who will listen to religious institutions or spiritual communities if their pamphlets, pew sitters, or pulpiteers fail to address blatant half-truths of government leaders or ignore injustices in their neighborhoods? While few disagree that we should be involved in serving others, the dilemma is how to keep from becoming too cozy

---

10. Telegram sent from Heschel to Kennedy, June 16, 1963. Heschel recommended clergy donate a month's salary to the civil rights cause (Heschel, *Moral Grandeur*, vii).

11. Cone, *Black Theology of Liberation*, argues as did Malcom X, that the dominant culture "sets the rules," including matters of civility, that must be challenged if changes are to be made.

with corrupt or inept powers. As Martin Luther King Jr. remarked, we begin to die the day we become silent about acting on significant issues.

Too often, the stained glass windows of spiritual homes become stained glass walls.

Labels act like walls. How? Stereotypes like "radical," "far right," "socialist," or "fundamentalist" allow us to stop thinking, to avoid seeing complexity. I agree with Jeff Means, who describes evil as a process with continuing actions that separates us from interacting with others. Ultimately, actions that are morally indefensible, harmful, injurious, disastrous, and deliberately ignore those in need are evil.[12]

I admit I'm moving to a stage beyond what I said in chapter 4 about confrontation. But if we are speaking about addressing major inequities and injustices, don't spiritual homes have a responsibility to speak out when governments or even private foundations commit serious breaches in their responsibilities to protect and defend?[13] On the level of what we do not do, can we plead not guilty to Saint Basil the Great's charge: "The bread in your cupboard belongs to the hungry; the coat unused in your closet belongs to the one who needs it; the shoes rotting in your closet belong to the one who has no shoes; the money which you hoard up belongs to the poor."[14] On what we, or our governments do, I know of no religious tradition or moral system that approves of putting migrant children in cages. I believe engaged spirituality strategies must include challenging systems with public actions.[15]

12. Means with Nelson, *Trauma and Evil*, 92–94, for their definition of evil, but see also 12, 15, 23, 25, 34 for additional discussion. They include a quote from a James Poling book of 1996: "Genuine evil is the abuse of power that destroys bodies and spirits; evil is produced by personal actions and intentions which are denied and dissociated by individuals; evil is organized by economic forces, institutions, and ideologies, but mystified by appeals to necessity and truth; evil is sanctioned by religion, but masked by claims to virtue, love, and justice" (Means with Nelson, *Trauma and Evil*, 110).

13. Wuthnow, *Restructuring American Religion*, 6–7, cites those who recognized years ago that government agencies would take over civic responsibilities that churches had abandoned or become inadequate to manage.

14. As cited in Good Reads, https://www.goodreads.com/author/quotes/1823057. Basil_the_Great.

15. Basil the Great (c. 313–379 CE), founder of monasteries and a bishop of the Christian church. These words are similar in intent to those of William of Ockham (c. 1285–1348 CE), English philosopher, Franciscan friar, who believed evil was doing one thing while under obligation to do another. Consider how significant this definition should be for political and religious leaders today!

Future

For the world that is coming, new paradigms are needed. Agreed? Sweetly spoken or even heated words aren't enough. Action or service, relief, must better link passion with realistic planning and logistics to deliver love-infused justice effectively to neighbors in need. Charismatic leaders may surface, but it will take spiritual homes joining together to dismantle evil systems, including empires in business, media, politics, and religion. Evil is a perennial pandemic found in all geographies, engaged by all political systems, about which spiritual beings must develop righteous rage.[16] Again, don't believe your community has to do it alone! See the notes for inspiring accounts of persons of various faiths working together.[17] First understand the goals of world systems, then develop strategies for changing what is dangerous and dysfunctional to what is fruitful and positive.

Be forewarned: you will be criticized. Develop thick skin. As my university dean said repeatedly, "The wolves will always howl, but the wagon train moves on."

THREE WORLDVIEWS: REDEMPTION, REGENERATION, AND RECONCILIATION

Worldviews determine actions. You have a worldview, and so do I. For example, I'll wager you have an opinion whether or not the coronavirus was God's warning to humans to change their ways. Several media reports allege that half of survey respondents believed it was a sign from God. This worldview affects whether individuals get vaccinated or not. Another example: should governments actively work to control climate effects? This chapter takes past and current worldviews seriously; perceptions influence decisions made. I want you to turn your spiritual attention to how you feel about other parts of the world, especially your attitude about interacting with the neighbors you are not likely to ever meet or see, even with Zoom. Begin by deciding whether your worldview is like one of the three described below. Over the past two hundred years,

16. Wuthnow, *Left Behind*. R. Jones, *End of White Christian*, provides numerous examples.

17. Beadle and Haskins, *Acting on Faith*. Nangle, *Engaged Spirituality*, uses experiences in Latin America to propose spiritual responses "in the heart of the empire."

people in developed Western cultures have tended to hold one of these three widely accepted worldviews about other cultures.[18]

Redemption, the first, from approximately 1850 to 1950, was one of superiority. We—the presumed civilized and privileged—should redeem the world. The word *redemption* has an inspiring root meaning: "to set free." On the downside, it implies that receiving cultures are inferior, flawed, and should pay a price, a ransom, or make some type of reparation or sacrifice, as Haiti did to France.

With limited travel and technology, people then were "innocents abroad," as Mark Twain described international tourists in 1869. In 1892, William Fremantle, an English clergyman, concluded missionaries could redeem the world by taking the gospel to foreign shores, especially to Africa and Asia.[19] His best-selling book inspired thousands of college students to become missionaries. Freemantle and others genuinely believed they would improve the lives of the unchurched not only through preaching but also through building schools and medical clinics and providing social services.[20]

The second worldview, regeneration, gradually replaced the redemption model in the decades after World War II and the Cold War. Spiritually, *regeneration* means to be reborn; mechanically, it signifies restoring to an original condition and, in physics, to reestablish a process. In political terms, it signaled a willingness to be partners, with the greater nations helping the lesser countries. The Marshall Plan was its signature program, which prevailed until the computer era took root. The dominance of the United States allowed the US to control the repair of broken world economies. However, the sunshine achievements of the Space Age could not hide the shadows cast by the war in Vietnam, racial

18. I acknowledge that *worldview* for philosophers and theologians generates comprehensive definitions with detailed components, including the nature of human beings, concepts of life and death, theories of knowledge and consciousness, etc. In German, worldview is *Weltanschauung*. Here, it refers to common, widespread understandings of the purposes of life, relationships to others, and right and wrong, including the "guardrails" of behavior. Worldviews may or may not have religious components. See also Smart, *Worldviews*.

19. Freemantle, *World as Subject*. Freemantle (1831–1919), a clergyman or canon in the Church of England, turned his series of lectures given at Oxford University in 1883 into this book.

20. An organization begun in the same era—the 1893 World's Fair event—the Parliament of World Religions, focused on sharing sacred scriptures from world religions. See Barrows, *World's Parliament of Religions*.

disparities, disquieted youth, and the growing horrors of opioid addiction and terrorism. Religious communities joined others in proposing solutions. Their strategies included speaking out, demonstrating, and providing legal relief to the downtrodden. Once again, those in power made minimal attempts to fix systemic problems.

The 9/11 terrorist attack on the World Trade Center in New York City, ironically, signaled a new worldview: *reconciliation*. Nation "actors" now viewed themselves as independent partners. This perspective is not about the traditional definition of reconciliation;[21] it involves moving from finding cause and laying blame to problem-solving, locating sufficient resources, and sustaining commitments remedies.[22] This worldview emphasizes critical thinking skills, planning, and flexibility.[23] Paradoxically, with as much knowledge as we have at our fingertips with smartphones and tablets, many of us know relatively little about the world; what we think we know is often factually incorrect.[24] That said, most of us recognize that there are huge disparities of natural resources, wealth, education, and access to healthcare between and within countries. In this digital age, we have almost too much information at hand. Speaking out is more narrowly focused.

The scale and scope of protest is changing. News of disasters and diseases halfway around the world are broadcast within seconds. Political as well as social borders and boundaries are broken or vanishing. The killing of George Floyd sparked worldwide repercussions in 2020. Slowly, the trials of those responsible for his and similar murders are taking place. Despite this, too many resist systematic and global responses to cataclysmic events. Not responding will result in regrettable consequences. These changes require a worldview that acknowledges that hostilities exist between nations, religions, and races, which must be mediated

21. M. Miller and Miller, *Harper's Bible Dictionary*, "Reconciliation," 603–4. Brueggemann, *Practice of Homefulness*, describes the elements in reconciliation and concludes with a chapter called "'The Family as World-Maker," 84–94.

22. Brands and Edel, two veteran diplomats, using historical and contemporary evidence, argue persuasively that the "winners" of wars must help "losers" recover if future conflicts are to be diminished. See their *Lessons of Tragedy*.

23. College students should be challenged to examine their worldviews, from both secular as well as religious perspectives, argues Brett, "Religious and Scientific Concept Integration." See also Kim, "'Think Christianity, Think Critically."

24. Haass, *World*, xv–xvi, and Rosling, *Factfulness*. Cone, Black *Theology of Liberation*, ix, challenges reconciliation as a worldview if its conditions are set by the dominant culture.

through genuine reconciliation rather than a "we know what is best for you" redemption model.[25]

Where are you now with your worldview? Do any of these voices resonate with your perspective? Robin Kimmerer says our human kinships can be transformed if we see the natural world as a gift.[26] Speaking from a Christian perspective, but with references to other faith traditions, Arnold Come believes God expects fallible humans to live with truth and love, expressed through honesty and compassion. Human responsibility is not to reject the world but to live in it as agents of reconciliation, with judgment and encouragement.[27]

Too abstract? How then do you describe service? I strongly urge you, consistent with your engaged faith or spiritual worldview, to become involved. See **activity 8.1.** You may feel you can best do service by speaking out or by acting to provide relief for others. I urge you to put your effort into one of three systemic strategies for three global issues: environment, migration especially related to refugees, and freedom of conscience.

Speaking out and truth-seeking: 1) study abroad opportunities, where students and faculty absorb, experience, and share their languages and cultures; 2) occupational and professional seminars where legislators, farmers, and business leaders exchange ideas and discuss policy issues; 3) and so-called soft power strategies, including cultural exchange programs, such as professional artists—where performances are given by instrumentalists, dancers, painters, and storytellers.[28]

Relief programs: 1) volunteer teams and locals establish freshwater wells and build schools;[29] 2) chefs like José Andrés create nonconventional

25. Rupp, *Globalization Challenged*, 3–40 and 85–108, advocates for inclusive communities. In another work he calls them communities of particularities that are concerned for others. Within *Globalization Challenged*, three scholars respond to Rudd's worldview: Jagdish Bhagwati (41–51), Jeremy Waldron (52–67), and Wayne Proudfoot (68–82)..

26. Kimmerer, *Braiding Sweetgrass*. I was alerted to this book by Linda Sandman of Oak Park, IL, who cited it as a transformative source.

27. Come, *Agents of Reconciliation*, ch. 7, especially 148–49.

28. In governmental and political terms, cultural exchange activities are "soft" power and are a more effective tactic against terrorism than hard military power. See Nye, *Future of Power*, 81–112, and xiii: "Smart power is the combination of the hard power of coercion and payment with the soft power of persuasion and attraction."

29. The best intentions can have unintended consequences, as reported in Lupton, *Toxic Charity*. One example is the Rotary Foundation, which, through individual

ways to feed thousands following hurricanes and earthquakes;[30] 3) a Midwestern grain bin manufacturing company develops a hurricane-resistant structure that can be erected quickly—the kits include tools—to be used for birthing clinics, schools, and shelters for up to thirty people.[31]

Systemic change: 1) Eboo Patel established Interfaith Youth Core, an ecumenical organization resolving sensitive community issues;[32] 2) rural and small-town residents, often acting from anger, use data from university extension research to counter agribusiness trends, address meatpacking plant abuses, and find remedies to become "smart-shrinking towns."[33] They, like their urban counterparts, strive to be "moral communities."[34] Granted, making systemic changes is like moving tectonic plates, which requires spiritual homes to use the techniques of strategic planning, change management, and evaluation to bring about productive, cooperative results. Can we as individual spiritual persons make a difference? Certainly. The documentary *Sweet Adversity* tells the story of actor Marsha Hunt, who became an advocate for the United Nations and a fundraiser for causes like world hunger, refugees, the homeless, and climate change. She phrased it this way: "After a trip around the world, I became a planet patriot."[35]

We, like her, must recognize the importance of working with others. Wuthnow, cited above, indicates that small-town leaders increasingly learn that solving problems requires working diligently with others at the regional, state, and national levels. Here are my choices for three world

---

clubs, has installed wells and water systems in Africa. A key is the partnership with local clubs to prepare individuals and communities for management and maintenance.

30. Chef José Andrés, who founded World Central Kitchen, a non-profit program. His program began in 2019 after Hurricane Dorian struck the Bahamas. In response to the 2020 coronavirus, he, food pantries and other organizations, with volunteers, distributed 800,000 pounds of food daily in Houston, TX.

31. Sukup Manufacturing, Sheffield, IA, has placed over 450 Safe T Houses in Haiti and other countries. See https://www.sukup.com. or GoServ Global (www.goserv-global.org), the agency who makes arrangements for volunteers.

32. Patel, *Interfaith Leadership*, 39. Patel describes himself as a social entrepreneur. The sample actions described above he would call "civil interfaith activities." He prefers *faith* to *religious* because such leaders are not primarily concerned with abstract religious systems.

33. Wuthnow, *Left Behind*. See also Peters, "Shrink-Smart Small Towns."

34. Wuthnow, *Left Behind*, 43. See also, for his findings on "makeshift solutions," 66–67, 80–94, and 116–40.

35. As heard in Memos, *Marsha Hunt's Sweet Adversity*.

issues that need to be addressed by spiritual homes. Only when ordinary folks are involved will extraordinary changes occur. May these stories and accounts give you hope and courage.

A WORLD OF JUSTICE: WHAT DOES ENVIRONMENTAL STEWARDSHIP MEAN?

"One touch of nature makes the whole world kin," Shakespeare observed.[36] Whatever you call it—climate change, global warming, environmental crisis—and whether it is just a long natural cycle or human activity, the climate affects all of us. Consider the action of Greta Thunberg, a Swedish fifteen-year-old, in 2018: she traveled the world and gave a speech at the United Nations that energized efforts to make the world less polluted. She may well have acted out of no specific religious or spiritual reasons, but the theologies and leaders of many world religions support her.[37] Perhaps she chose to act because she had heard the words of a past UN leader, Dag Hammarskjöld, who said, "Never for the sake of peace and quiet deny your own experiences and convictions."[38]

Faith traditions describe a divine Creator in sacred texts through myths.[39] These stories portray the earth as a gift of the Almighty to humans. In turn, humans are to be responsible stewards of the natural and animal worlds, hence my preference for calling this issue environmental stewardship. In Genesis 1–4, in stories such as the garden of Eden, humans are instructed not to waste the planet's precious resources. The moral of mythical creation accounts is that it is folly to assume we can control the forces of nature. Over time, hymns, poems, and stories tell

---

36. Shakespeare, *Troilus and Cressida*, act 3, scene 3.

37. Berndt, *Cathedral on Fire*, 3, begins his book with the account that Greta Thunberg spoke to the European Parliament the day after the Notre Dame fire, arguing that the parliament should act as if "their house was on fire."

38. Hammarskjöld, *Markings*, 84.

39. Myths here are reference to the literary style in which they are written. Willis, *Religion Book*, "Creationism," 148–53, includes brief summaries of Hinduism, Buddhism, Confucianism, Daoism, which are quite different from Christian and Judaic traditions. Also, Willis includes discussion of nonreligious origin theories. See also Gill, "Native Americans and Their Religions." An interesting concept of a God who was not present at creation but who evolves is in Abrams, *God That Could Be*.

of the mystery and majesty of the natural world.[40] **Activity 8.2** provides a way to share your thoughts/feelings about environmental stewardship.

Voices in the Roman Catholic tradition speak of the whole universe as God's dwelling, and Earth as a corner of it. We humans, as Pope Francis proclaimed in 2015, are united with "brother sun, sister moon, brother river and mother earth."[41] Diana Butler Bass's book *Grounded* is a litany of calls to a spiritual vocation of finding God through working with dirt, water, and sky. I recommend it if you wish to learn specific ways you as an individual or as part of your spiritual home can turn or return to the soil, improve water quality, and reduce pollution. How long, for example, can we ignore such monstrosities as a plastic island twice the size of Texas floating in the Pacific Ocean? It is more than an embarrassing blemish on the global face; it kills marine life and endangers human health. We must end such pollution![42]

Based on your location, personal circumstances, and your spirituality or religious beliefs, how do you respond to what Richard Haass calls the "climate kaleidoscope"?[43] Haass, a former career diplomat and president of the nonpartisan think tank, the Council on Foreign Relations, presents data, then offers measured, realistic outcomes. David Wallace-Wells, a journalist, speaks in a more strident tone, citing a variety of scientific sources and government reports. His blunt book title, *The Uninhabitable Earth*, tells you the harsh conclusion he has reached: the earth will be uninhabitable if we refuse to take care of the warming now occurring.[44] There are numerous reports and resources to spur public action.[45]

---

40. For example, the hymn "Joyful, Joyful, We Adore Thee," by Henry Van Dyke (1907); see https://hymnary.org/text/joyful_joyful_we_adore_thee.

41. Diana Bass, *Grounded*, opening page.

42. B. Gates, *How to Avoid*, for example, focuses on reducing air pollution through electric vehicles. Griffith, *Electrify*, offers numerous ways to reduce our carbon-footprint.

43. Haass, *World*, "Climate Change," 183–92.

44. Wallace-Wells, *Uninhabitable Earth*. A leading academic scholar on climate who has an evangelical background is Katharine Hayhoe, who wrote the foreword to Karelas's *Climate Courage*. Bullitt-Jonas and Schade, *Rooted and Rising*, offer theological perspectives on climate issues.

45. Antal, *Climate Church, Climate World*, and Berndt, *Cathedral on Fire*. While not rejecting individual and local responses, public actions are critical; he asserts "it is difficult to fight a forest fire with a garden hose." See also https://en.wikipedia.org/wiki/Environmental justice.

The sources just cited point us toward needed systemic changes.[46] We can differ on the causes or extent of climate change but agree pollution is present, severely endangering our lives. Because pollution disproportionately impacts the health of poor and racial minorities, it is a matter of environmental justice. For example, if you are part of a minority, you are much more likely to be living near a chemical plant.[47] In what part of your city are chemical and processing plants located? It is hard to dispute the world's average annual temperature is rising and contributing to natural disasters, since deadly winds, floods, and wildfires are increasing. Data show fossil fuel use contributes to poorer air quality. Haass projects it is only a matter of time before climate change becomes the greatest cause of refugee flow, due to a reduction in the amount of land that can support human life. There are programs and agencies that aim to sustain farmlands and assist in rural development in many countries. They are responding to dramatically increasing starvation rates, with 9 million people, 3.1 million of them who are children, dying annually.[48]

If these climate change trends are true, what does that demand engaged spiritual persons do?[49] Earlier I urged you to think globally and act locally. Consider these two actual situations and contemplate what systemic remedies should be implemented. Years ago, my wife and I were walking one evening in her Nebraska hometown. On a farm field at the edge of town, thousands of gallons of clear water from the massive Ogallala aquifer were gushing from an irrigation pipe, flooding paved streets. Now severely depleted, how can that aquifer be restored? Second, Iowa farmers make extensive use of herbicides and fertilizers to increase yields on its rich soils. The result is pollution of many rivers, including

46. B. Gates, *How to Avoid*, exemplifies an approach that requires huge changes in attitudes and a "buy-in" by the general population, businesses, and the government.

47. Bruggers, "Report: Chemical Stockpiles," states 134 million Americans of disproportionately black and brown populations are exposed to unhealthy air levels at 3,400 sites.

48. Practical Farmers of Iowa creates a system of on-farm research and information sharing on low-cost, environmentally friendly practices. The organization formerly known as Foods Resource Bank, now Growing Hope Globally, engages funds for agricultural development by building a coalition of farms and farm supply businesses to produce those funds by growing crops in this country, selling them in normal markets, and donating the proceeds. These programs work with established and trusted agencies such as Church World Service.

49. Beadle and Haskins, *Acting on Faith*, "Care for the Environment," 7–20, contain examples of multi-faith projects. See Karelas, *Climate Courage*, "Faith Communities in Action," 89–108, for specific program narratives.

the Mississippi. What must be done to save fresh water and make ocean waters healthier?

A WORLD OF NEIGHBORS: HOW DO WE MAKE RACE AND REFUGEES MATTER?

Human migration is a constant in world history.[50] No surprise then that based on generations of tender and tragic experiences, in stories shared and recorded, cultures around the world developed etiquettes and admonitions for of welcoming or rejecting strangers.[51] The Roman Catholic Trappist monk and missionary Thomas Merton (1915–1968) asserted, "God speaks to us in three places: in scripture, in our deepest selves, and in the voice of the stranger."[52] How willing are countries today to relocate strangers? Based on what you've heard or read, are you reluctant to accept immigrants?[53] In previous chapters, I have mentioned the spiritual practice of coping with diversity. Our world too often has responded with genocides.[54] Religious voices call today's spiritual bodies to face this issue squarely.[55]

Diversity refers most often to race. In the United States, race flows easily into caste.[56] Caste or race are like viruses. The virus of racial prejudice, at least four hundred years old, is still active. To believe that racism is not a current problem is delusional.[57] Videos of police brutality starkly

50. Manning and Trimmer, *Migration in World History.*

51. Eck, *New Religious America*, and Richardson, *Strangers in This Land.* For ethical issues of pluralism, Niles, *Doing Theology with Humility.*

52. Merton, as cited by Taylor, *Holy Envy,* 101.

53. Dartagnan, "Here's What Happens," describes how conservative political parties and leaders, with media companies, use misinformation regarding employment figures, violent crime statistics, to build fear about immigrants.

54. Power, *Problem from Hell.* Her main topic is genocide.

55. Pavlovitz, *Bigger Table,* asserts that the Christian faith must be more open by having a "bigger table." Two of its four legs need to be "radical hospitality" and "true diversity." Beadle and Haskins, *Acting on Faith,* 36–37, offer actual examples of how strangers are welcomed and involved with interfaith program construction projects, 40–51.

56. Wilkerson, *Caste,* 18–19, indicates race and caste in the US are "neither synonymous mutually exclusive." They coexist and reinforce each other.

57. C. Wilder, *Ebony and Ivy,* has an eye-opening history of how the oldest colleges in the country were funded by slave ship owners; some of their sons became plantation owners. Describing recent examples of racism are Kendi and Blain, *Four Hundred*

revealed that the symptoms of segregated malpractice were real, not illusions. The murder of George Floyd in Minneapolis, following too many others throughout the country, could not be ignored. How did you react to that event?[58] **Activity 8.3** reveals how misleading our racial stereotypes can be. Much could also be said about the related issue of religious pluralism, because so many faith traditions are linked to race.[59]

Justice is demanded. It is not enough to say that progress has been made. Celebrating Juneteenth on June 19 to commemorate President Abraham Lincoln's 1863 Emancipation Proclamation, now a national holiday, is important but not sufficient. Spiritual leaders and spiritual homes should encourage thorough historical studies.. White people need to understand the abuse of centuries brought by white supremacy. Ultimately, they must join people of color in pursuing justice.[60] Some may regard tearing down Confederate statues as a necessary step to offset misguided patriotic loyalties, while others defend their placement. The concern about inappropriate police treatment of minorities will not be resolved quickly; sustained conversations and actions are required. Citizens need to speak out for meaningful legislation to correct systemic racism. Some say the most effective remedy for racism, however, is face-to-face conversations with our neighbors, old and new. Films like *Just Mercy* (2019) demonstrate racism is far too pervasive.

Let's deliberately narrow the focus now to the pressing matter of migration of refugees.[61] In the United States, three days after President

---

Souls, and Bush, *Out of Many, One*, contain stories of trial and triumph.

58. In American legislatures battle lines are drawn about critical race theory (CRT) that asserts systemic racism has always been and is currently active in society. Critics, including organized parents groups, argue the US is not racist now ("Editorial").

59. Ariarajah, *Not without My Neighbour*. Eck, *New Religious America*, 2, describes the Pluralism Project and on pp. 70–77 defends the concept of and richness of pluralism. For more on religious pluralism, see Niles, *Doing Theology with Humility*.

60. See Diangelo, *White Fragility*; Metzl, *Dying of Whiteness*; R. Jones, *End of White Christian*; Koppelman with Goodhart, *Understanding Human Differences*, "Race and Oppression: The Experiences of People of Color in America," 101–30 and "Racism: Confronting a Legacy of White Domination in America," 188–210.

61. Koppelman with Goodhart, *Understanding Human Differences*, a multicultural textbook for future teachers; for this topic, "Immigrants and Oppression," 72–90. Another textbook, Nacoste, *Taking on Diversity*, concludes that confronting diversity truthfully moves us from anxiety to respect. For demographic information about migrants, see Frey, *Diversity Explosion*. Lewis and Cantor, *Our Compelling Interests*, document the different results in a democracy that come from diverse economic and social values.

Donald Trump issued an executive order reducing US Refugee Resettlement Program admissions, Pope Francis published an encyclical, *Fratelli tutti* (*Our Brothers*), prescribing how the world needed to care for the displaced in a time of pandemic.[62]

The commonsense definition of the term *migrant* is someone who moves away from his or her place of usual residence, whether within a country or across an international border, temporarily or permanently, and for a variety of reasons. Using that definition, the United Nations estimates there are 272 million international migrants in the world. Most often, people move for economic reasons, to find a job or a better job. Another reason is hunger; when crops can't be grown or food isn't available locally, families move. The variety of reasons includes forced relocations due to war, political chaos, and increasing drug cartels. The term *refugees* applies to those migrants forced to leave their homeland. It's shocking that in 2019 there were almost 80 million refugees, and an estimated 37,000 persons were forced to flee their homes each day.[63] That is about 1 percent of the world's population. An evil practice, noted earlier, is separating families and putting children in cages.[64] Economic injustice has spawned a related problem—human trafficking.[65]

We could debate the appropriateness and effectiveness of building anti-immigrant walls. I would rather spend space sharing two stories with you about positive programs for immigrants and refugees.[66] The first describes what happened at a large plant whose workforce was primarily from Central American countries.[67] In the largest raid ever done

62. Marty, "US Is Failing Refugees." The previous high number of refugees admitted per year was 110,000. Trump slashed the number to 15,000 annually.

63. Haass, *World*, 184. Updated by *New York Times* data June 2, 2020. In 2021, an Amnesty International brochure stated that of the 80 million total refugees, 26.3 million were fleeing war, violence, and persecution. The major regions were Syria, Afghanistan, Myanmar, South Sudan, Venezuela, and three Central America countries.

64. Soboroff, *Separated*.

65. Kelly, "Enormity of Global Sex." There are more than four million victims of sex trafficking global; 99 percent are women and girls; one in seven runways in the U.S. in 2018 is likely a victim of child sex trafficking. National Human Trafficking Hotline: 1–888–373–7888. Other figures indicate that if forced child marriages are included, the total number of victims could be thirty to forty million persons.

66. Rupp, *Globalization*, 16–18, 18–20, 27–29, and elsewhere explains the work of the International Rescue Committee, of which he was the president at the time the book was published. The potential of a World Migration Organization (WMO) is described on p. 50.

67. Bloom, *Postville*. Postville was the Iowa town that was the site of a meatpacking

at that time, US government forces swooped in, arrested the workers, and deported many back to Guatemala. The results were catastrophic not only for the families of workers but for the community and region. Over time, the work of multiple faith traditions—Jewish, Roman Catholic, Quaker, Lutheran—resulted in immigrant families being reunited and new jobs found and proposed legislation.[68]

The second, more recent, story is of refugees seeking safe homes in new lands. Called "the world of neighbors," it was begun by the current Lutheran Archbishop of Sweden.[69] When in 2015 the civil war in Syria became intolerable, nearly five million citizens left the country, traveling through Turkey and the Baltics in search of a European destination. Of those forced to flee, 163,000 Syrians walked to Sweden, with an estimated 39,000 unaccompanied minors among them. Though their right to seek asylum was guaranteed, nevertheless, Sweden was overwhelmed by their sudden presence. So, the government turned to the Church of Sweden to help with the initial reception. In response, nearly 70 percent of 1,440 Lutheran parishes provided support of one kind or another, such as housing, meals, clothing, and accompaniment in those first few weeks after arrival. The experience had a transformative impact on those congregations, many of which maintained the close relationships that were formed. Over time, the "humanitarian honeymoon" inevitably waned, and criticism emerged. Archbishop Antje Jackelén continues to be a voice advocating for the welcome and embrace of "people on the move" for humanitarian, ethical, and religious grounds.[70] Bottom line: refugee resettlement challenges can be met with positive outcomes.

---

plant, owned by Hasidic Jews and the producer of Kosher products, that employed close to nine hundred workers when it was raided.

68. Stories told by David Vasquez-Levy and others, Theologian-in-Residence program in Ames, IA, 2019. Immigration attorney Sonia Parras Konrad of Des Moines, IA, provided pro bono assistance to two hundred detainees from Postville. For powerful descriptions of diverse spiritual traditions working together see Beadle and Haskins, *Acting on Faith*, "Race and Privilege," 21–34, and "Immigration and Refugees," 35–50.

69. See "World Neighbors" at https://www.wn.org. Nouwen observed, *Wounded Healer*, 41, that compassion can break "through the boundaries between languages and countries, rich and poor, educated and illiterate. [Compassion] pulls people away from the fearful clique into the large world where they can see that every human face is the face of a neighbor."

70. Account by Rev. Dirk Ficca, Oak Park, IL. The study, *A Time of Encounter*, was completed by the Church of Sweden in 2017.

A WORLD WITH FREEDOM OF CONSCIENCE: WHOSE BOUNDARIES?

I am torn about which modifier to use with freedom—is it civic or political freedom, religious freedom, personal freedom, spiritual freedom? In the late 1990s, there was much discussion and many court battles about religious freedom; in the 2020s, the subject surfaced again. While my feeling is both religion and spirituality are vitally important in life, surveys, and interviews of the growing number of "None of the aboves" say religion is not a major factor in their daily decision-making,[71] I conclude the most inclusive term for our discussion is freedom of conscience. That said, it is difficult to separate conscience from religion.[72] Many would argue history has examples of religion being a life-or-death matter. Individuals were and are martyred because of beliefs. Religious genocides continue to occur.[73] While we can debate organized religion's importance, the sheer number of adherents requires us, if for no other reason, to acknowledge its significance around the world. While no religion can assert that it has the majority of the world's people, and more than one billion have no religion, here are the impressive numbers:

- 2.3 billion are Christian
- 1.8 billion Muslim
- 1.0+ billion are Hindu
- 500 million are Buddhist
- 15 million are Jewish[74]

A key issue throughout human history, and especially in Western cultures, is the relation of the government or state to religious bodies. In the United States, the long-standing legal view has been that there should

---

71. Oakes, *Nones Are Alright*, 17–31; Mercadante, *Belief Without Borders*, 229; Denton and Flory, *Back-Pocket God*, 57–91. Also, Burge, *Nones*, 35-67.

72. Nelson, *Conscience*, provides numerous theological and psychological descriptions by distinguished experts in their fields.

73. Waldman, *Sacred Liberty*, focuses on the two-hundred-plus years in the United States, offering many illustrations of violence against those expressing minority religious opinions. Also, he describes religious genocides.

74. Haass, *World*, 63. The Muslim population is expected to grow the fastest, possibly reaching three billion by 2050.

be a "wall of separation between church and state."[75] The United States includes such laws as there can be no religious test for a person seeking a public office and that public schools must be neutral regarding religion, i.e., they cannot favor one religious tradition over another, or religion over non-religion.

In the United States, freedom of conscience matters relate to First Amendment rights, which include freedom of speech and religious freedom.[76] Because "religious freedom" has taken on special connotations in recent years, I need to refer to some of its recent debates.[77] I have former colleagues on both sides of the issue today. Consider: if I am a business owner or professional serving the public, when am I allowed to not serve them because of my religious convictions? Examples: as a pharmacist, can I refuse to honor a prescription for birth control? If the principle is that the First Amendment protects religious rights but also prohibits religion from getting special privileges, why should houses of worship be exempt from public health measures?[78] Voting is a form of freedom of speech. Under the guise of voter integrity to eliminate voter fraud, voter suppression is occurring.[79] Currently, proponents of a movement called religious or Christian nationalism are instrumental in placing judges in federal courts that favor individuals, businesses, organizations, and agencies denying services, employment, or insurance benefits to others

75. Balmer, *Solemn Reverence*, 81, cites Justice Sandra Day O'Connor's final church-state opinion: "Those who would renegotiate the boundaries between church and state must answer a difficult question: Why would we trade a system that has served us so well for one that has served others so poorly?"

76. Wuthnow, *Left Behind*, 121. Small town and rural interviewees clearly believed that not allowing school prayer and not teaching the Ten Commandments contribute to moral decline. Supreme Court decisions do not prohibit individuals from praying or expressing their religious views, but public school teachers and administrators, as "government" officials cannot appear to favor certain faith traditions. See **activity 8.4** and fn99 sources.

77. Boston, *Taking Liberties*, provides chapters on various issues. A counter stance is taken by Charles J. Russo, a Catholic law school attorney, in "Does Religion Have Place."

78. Hayes, "Radical Reaction," reports that more than sixty bills granting religious exceptions were introduced in more than half the states in spring 2021. Countering such efforts was an Apr. 12, 2021, statement from twenty-seven faith-based organization.

79. In his conclusion, Waldman, *Sacred Liberty*, 301–21, offers his advice to keep the nation's religious freedom principles intact. If you want to keep your faith, you must allow others to keep their faith. To oppose their practices or to impose your beliefs on others endangers you sustaining yours. The same principle applies to voting.

based on their religious beliefs and practices. Is this religious freedom or discrimination?[80] A recent case in point: a Roman Catholic adoption agency was allowed to not accept a gay couple's application.[81]

See **activity 8.4** for references as well as examples of recent controversial freedom of conscience cases.

Barry Lynn, a lawyer and a minister, has spent his career fighting for freedom of conscience. He graciously provided this perspective on why it is critical for all of us:[82]

> In many ways, the absence of "freedom of belief," religious and non-religious, is a repudiation of the crux of human rights. Every person must deal with central questions of human existence like why the world even exists and what if anything follows the life we have on earth. Similarly, she or he must construct, even if imperfectly, a moral center for their lives, determining how those values relate to interaction with others around them.
>
> When any government refuses to allow a broad latitude to citizens for their articulating and, within reason, practicing their beliefs, beliefs become tyrannical according to the government. When a nation chooses to turn its majority religious tradition—worse, as its leaders interpret that tradition—into legal mandates, it invariably represses the rights of those who disagree with that understanding and interpretation. It also diminishes the possibility that the nation will grow intellectually, finding itself trapped in a vise of complacency in its conduct that tends to ignore new ideas that are based on other philosophies or religious traditions. Freedom of belief of course does not guarantee that the "best" solution to questions of ethics or governance will always be found, but it does make those solutions increasingly likely.
>
> Some would argue that since "religious traditions" tend to be rooted in absolutes they inhibit free dialogue and searches

---

80. Whitehead and Perry, *Taking America Back*, offer an extensive analysis of the Christian Nationalism movement. See also Stewart, *Power Worshippers*. Two journals—*Report from the Capital* (published by the Baptist Joint Committee) and *Church & State* (published by Americans United)—are sources for articles on Christian Nationalism. The Robert Nusbaum Center at Virginia Wesleyan University, formerly the Center for the Study of Religious Freedom, is another source of information on this and related topics.

81. Fulton vs. City of Philadelphia 593 U.S. ____ (2021).

82. Barry W. Lynn, email to author, early 2000. Rev. Lynn was the CEO of Americans United for Separation of Church and State and prior to that worked for the American Civil Liberties Union. He authored *God and Government*.

for "common ground." This view neglects the reality that people who have a deep and abiding sense of what guides them often feel more willing to have their ideas challenged and to alter beliefs after they examine alternative viewpoints.

The world I see is trending toward more autocratic, tyrannical governments.[83] Will such governments allow spiritual/religious persons to proclaim their broader beliefs and conduct their practices? Multiple stories from the past tell us when faith adherents proclaim their "good news" they are either eliminated or assimilated into the dominant culture, becoming the state's officially recognized church. In our time and culture, the media and pollsters have made serious errors defining individuals and churches who are identified as Evangelicals.[84] As I shared earlier, I come from a mainline Protestant background. I am a proponent of secondary school study about religion as discussed in chapter 6. I want the ability to live my faith and for you to live yours.[85] That requires some understanding of various traditions. Here we are speaking about religion/spirituality in the public square. Are we free to express our conscience? Where is the line to be drawn? Can it be done without becoming the proverbial red line?[86] I urge you to consider political discourse essential, that at its core we rigorously search for the truth, treating others with respect, because all deserve dignity.[87] From that perspective, civility and safety should be the norms when we and our elected representatives express

83. Snyder, *On Tyranny*.

84. Balmer, a former Evangelical, now an Episcopal priest and college chaplain is well known for his critiques of the political involvement of Evangelicals in American politics. His works include *Mine Eyes Have Seen the Glory*, *Thy Kingdom Come*, and *Evangelicalism in America*. Another observer is Frances Fitzgerald, *Evangelicals*. For a personal account of a change of heart, see Rob Schenck, *Costly Grace*.

85. My position is to minimize my religious and spiritual backgrounds, to minimize influencing readers. That doesn't satisfy some, especially those who feel their religious approach believes in Jesus as a divine being. I believe it mirrors Barbara Brown Taylor's perspective as a world religions teacher in *Holy Envy*.

86. As the U.S. Supreme Court declared in the Abington v. Schempp 374 U.S. 203 (1963) decision, "It can be said one's education is not complete without a study of religion." As Beadle and Haskins, *Acting on Faith*, "Interfaith Conflict and Extremism," 83–98, suggest, we need to face the issues realistically so that cooperative results still occur.

87. Wehner, *Death of Politics*, citing Aristotle, John Locke, and Abraham Lincoln, in "What Politics Is," 33–60, and "Politics and Faith," 61–96, advocates that those with faith perspectives should be involved in politics. He is a self-identified conservative Christian who advocates criticism by Evangelicals of corrupt political leaders.

public opinions. Sadly, a too frequent occurrence has been intolerance of spiritual minorities. That said, I agree with Martin Luther King Jr. that the role of religion should be as a guide and conscience of the state, never its master or slave.[88]

Having lived in a country with a dictatorship but, thankfully, most of my life in a democratic nation, as a religious person, I prefer the latter. My point here is not to argue the merits/demerits of democracy, socialism, communism, fascism, or authoritarianism. Rather, it is to urge that any society benefits from having certain civil norms in place. These norms include insistence of equal treatment of all under its rules, the legitimacy of political opponents, intolerance of violence against others, and opposition to the curtailment of civil liberties of opponents, including the media.[89] Lose these, and soon freedom to act and speak are in jeopardy if you don't mimic what the "official religion" demands. Stephen Carter, in *The Dissent of the Governed*, argues that dissent is also in this country's DNA. Someone quipped, "Dissent is as American as apple pie."[90] Carter provides provocative arguments for when one should consent and when one should dissent. Robert Nash and others have developed guidelines for moral conversations that include ways to diminish remarks that shut down "hot topic" dialogues.[91]

In closing, I will be specific. The terrible realities the Hebrew prophets experienced are with us again. As with Isaiah, Amos, Jeremiah, and Elijah, so it is with the United States and other countries today. The closer some religious leaders and their traditions are to political leaders, the softer and smaller their voices of courage become. Why do people embrace national leaders who did too little and too late for the death machine of the 2020 coronavirus? Why are there no indictments for "murdering the truth" repeatedly?[92] Perhaps the answer is found in the story of the

88. King, *Strength to Love*, 59, from the sermon "A Knock at Midnight." He adds that churches who do not speak with prophetic zeal should be forgotten.

89. Levitsky and Ziblatt, *How Democracies Die*, 23–24. For a provocative case study regarding the pros and cons of forcing the US's First Amendment rights on religion in other countries, see Marzouki, *Islam*, 168–94.

90. Carter, *Dissent of the Governed*. In summer 2018, the Chautauqua Institution had a weeklong series of lectures on "The Ethics of Dissent." Contact the institution for more information: https://chq.org.

91. Nash et al., *How to Talk*. See also Franklin and Zartman, *Belovedness*.

92. Wehner, *Death of Politics*, "Why Words Matter," 117. A speech writer in several Republican administrations, he is appalled that Evangelicals didn't speak out against Trump.

calling of the young prophet Isaiah (Isa 6: 9–12) following the death of a righteous king. Even though God tells him to deliver a message to change their behavior, God adds, the people will ignore it.[93] An equivalent in today's world is the voice of a young woman from Hong Kong I heard on a National Public Radio broadcast. Prophetically, she pleads with older generations to recognize how their government is stifling the freedoms to assemble, to speak out: "Be brave enough to open your eyes to what is going on." So may we be open and when necessary, be morally courageous.

TRAVELER: READY TO BE A WORLD NEIGHBOR?

Change happens. I can't predict what changes will have occurred between the time these words were published and the time you read this book. What progress will be made regarding worldwide climate catastrophes, health pandemics, and economic disparities? Will national and state politics become less vitriolic? How will you feel about the changes in your family, your community? How will you have changed? By now you know my position is that healthy spiritual beings and religious individuals must be engaged in service, activated by love, eager to bring justice and peace to world neighbors. Otherwise, we are spiritual couch potatoes.

It's tempting, I know, to want to return to a nostalgic past that is better in our memories than it was; recall *The Matrix* (1999). As a spiritual difference-maker, you can operate only in your present. You will make your share of mistakes. Hopefully, you won't assume you can solve problems by throwing money at them. That is another paradox, toxic charity.[94] You will either speak truth to power or pander to the popular. The final practice I see essential to the spiritual life is the practice of reconciliation. Consider it a blend of the traditional religious practices of discernment, mercy, and justice. My hope is that you begin to have a perspective of being a world citizen or neighbor.

Ask yourself periodically: how have I responded to one of the systemic issues with the environment, migration, or religious freedom? Is

---

93. Isaiah 6:9–12: "Go and say to this people: Keep listening, but do not comprehend; keep looking, but do not understand. Make the mind of this people dull, and stop their ears, and shut their eyes, so that they may not look with their eyes, and listen with their ears, and comprehend with their minds. Then I said, 'How long, O Lord?' And he said: 'Until cities lie waste without inhabitant, and houses without people, and the land is utterly desolate; . . . and vast is the emptiness in the midst of the land.'"

94. Lupton, *Toxic Charity*.

it with a tough love that is nudging the world toward justice? Let's be honest. Love is not a spoonful of magic that makes the injustice go away. It takes persistence. As we know from parenting, love may bring about a temporary change or no change at all.

This capstone chapter of the book anticipates a yes answer or, preferably, YESS (commitment to yearning, education, soulcare, service). Don't take that to mean all your questions are answered. I hope that you do better understand and narrate stories about yourself and have a stronger grasp of the story you are now living. I hope you are better at discerning truth from falsehood in daily conversations, in digital encounters, and from whatever secular and sacred voices entice you with their wares. I hope your spiritual practices have brought a song of confidence to your soul, drowning out the drumming of anti-intellectual, anti-science powers. I hope you are empowered by this and other chapters to become involved with an interfaith venture, a dream team, that connects to the wider world. To that world, you and your current spiritual home can bring hope. If you want some specifics about how a spiritual community can take on one of the issues mentioned or one which is more pertinent for you, let me suggest as a starter to read the epilogue of the book *Common Fire*.[95]

Continue to do these things in the future, and you will gain answers to your big questions. More importantly, you will have constructed one or more worthy dreams that will be fulfilled.

95. Daloz, *Common Fire*, 213–32.

Chapter 8 Activities

ACTIVITY 8.1: SERVICE PROJECT

If you agree with the purpose of this chapter that spirituality involves gaining a new world perspective that includes service to others, what are some ideas you have for service projects?

You can do one individually or in a group. Here's how to make it a success.

Step 1: Learn what the project involves, so you can *prepare* to do what is needed. In other words, determine what is realistic and what makes it complete.

Step 2: Do the task called for with passion, accuracy, and thoroughness.

Step 3: Clean up! Don't waste supplies or time. Help the next volunteers succeed.

Regarding your decision on a spiritual home, choose one that takes service beyond its walls seriously. Not only should your spiritual home be committed to service, but it should also help you and others involved through careful planning and preparation. You should be able to say clearly what your purpose is when you do the service project. Then, your spiritual home should provide you with the proper tools so that you can accomplish your mission effectively. You should feel confident that you are working in the proper "supply chain." Ultimately, with prayer and discernment, you should be able to clean up your mission. By doing that, you will be able to share with future disciples how they can best bring honor to the service yet to be done.

Your service project: _____

What is its purpose? What will you specifically bring to the project?

Date begun: _____ Date completed: _____

ACTIVITY 8.2: ENVIRONMENTAL STEWARDSHIP

What is your impression of planet Earth? Do you see it as a divine creation or a small pebble in a universe? Do humans have an obligation, sacred or secular, to improve the natural world? Some say we must do something; we don't have a Plan B—there is no Plan-et B! The song text that follows is one I've written. Would your text be similar? Or quite different?

"A WORLD OF TIME AND SPACE"[96]

Stanza 1: A changing world requires stewardship decisions.

A world of time and space
Before our eyes unfolds,
Creating choices we must face,
Decisions new and bold.
Earth will not be the same.
Foul air brings warming land.
Green fields are gone. Whom do we blame
When high hills turn to sand?

Stanza 2: Human disasters signal a need for new ethical solutions.

Ice flows and rivers rise,
Jeweled jungles disappear,
Koalas lose their homes and cry,
Less birdsong year to year.
Missed mountains veined with coal,
Now stripped by greed, are bare.
Oiled oceans claim a frightful toll.
Please, guide our quest to care.

96. Text by Charles R. Kniker, music by Lynn J. Zeigler (tune: TIME AND SPACE). The lines are acrostic; each contains the letters of the English alphabet in order. Can be sung to tune TERRA BEATA,"This Is My Father's World." A similar hymn is "O God of Earth and Space," by Jane Parker Huber, 1980.

(Activity 8.2 continued)

Stanza 3: Creator God calls humans to restore a vibrant, sustaining world.

Rule us with loving deeds.
Shelter us both night and day.
Thanks for the rest and food we need,
All under your grand way.
Vast mysteries unfold
When we explore your sphere.
Your name, O God, be ever told;
With zeal, we praise, draw near!

ACTIVITY 8.3: SUBWAY PICTURE

In the late 1960s, a psychological test attempted to illustrate the power of stereotypes to shape one's view of reality. One technique showed study participants a series of drawings of ordinary scenes in rapid order. Later, the participants were asked to describe what they recalled from specific scenes. One of the pictures was a group of people waiting for a subway. One person was an African American man in a business suit holding a briefcase. Several persons away was a white man, shabbily dressed, with an open knife or switchblade in one hand. Result: many respondents reported a black man with the knife.

The subway picture is found in Kent Koppelman, *Understanding Human Differences*. Koppelman offers a technique used with groups. Have a group sit in a circle. Show the picture to one person and ask that person to whisper what he/she saw to the next person. See what comes out when the last person to hear the description shares with the group what supposedly occurred.

What would you interpret that to mean? Would you go so far as to say that it indicates that humans want to hear, see, remember what they already believe or want to believe? As the German poet-philosopher Johann Wolfgang Goethe (1749–1832) observed, "Every man hears only what he understands."[97]

97. Goethe, *Maxims and Reflections*, 143.

(*Activity 8.3 continued*)

We like to say we are not racists. We don't want to disparage others. But do our minds retain stereotypical images?[98]

If this is a human characteristic, how do you have a dialogue with someone whose mind is made up, who can't accept the truth and the facts that you believe are true?

How do you feel when someone says you are misinterpreting the facts?

ACTIVITY 8.4: SPEAKING OUT ABOUT RELIGIOUS FREEDOM

The First Amendment of the Constitution begins with two clauses, the so-called Establishment Clause and the Free Exercise Clause. Some think they are somewhat contradictory, because the first forbids an establishment of religion, while the second seems to encourage a person or group to act upon their religious faith (note: neither includes a definition of religion). Over time, political leaders and the courts have weighed in on this, so that the general interpretation is that federal and state governments must be neutral, neither favoring specific religions nor being hostile to religion or anyone for not having a religion.

As discussed in this chapter, an emerging issue is how much religious freedom—speech or practice—do I or you or does any entity—religious organization, family-owned business, etc.—have if it discriminates against or is otherwise harmful to others? Congress passed the Religious Freedom Restoration Act in 1993, in response to incidents where individuals were having difficulty expressing or practicing their faith. Other cases have emerged that suggest the opposite—that owners of public businesses or religious orders with hospitals, for example, claim that their religious convictions would be violated by providing the services their customers wish.

Here are several examples.[99] If you were a Supreme Court judge, what would be your thinking?

98. Sue, *Microaggressions.*

99. Eastland, *Religious Liberty in Supreme Court*; B. Lynn, *God and Government*; Walker, *Church State Matters*; *Church and State* (journal of Americans United); *Report*

(Activity 8.4 continued)

1. You own a restaurant. Your faith interprets the Bible as saying that African American people are inferior to white people. You refuse to serve them (Newman v. Piggie Park Enterprises, Inc., 390 U.S. 400 [1968]).

2. You and your partner have a cake catering business. A gay couple asks you to prepare a wedding cake for their marriage ceremony. You decline (Masterpiece Cakeshop v. Colorado Civil Rights Commission, 584 U.S. ___ [2018]).

3. You own a large business. Your health insurance plans does not cover birth control prescriptions for employees based on your religious views (Burwell v. Hobby Lobby Stores, 573 U.S. 682 [2014]).

4. You hear a case from a state whose constitution is based on the principle of the separation of church and state. It does not permit any public tax money to be given to religious schools. Your colleagues in the US Supreme Court are divided, some believing that whenever any public tax money is given to private schools (non-religious), such funds should also be given to religious schools. Do you agree or disagree (Espinoza v. Montana Department of Revenue, 591 U.S. ___ [2020])?

from the Capital (journal of Baptist Joint Committee).

FOR ADDITIONAL CONVERSATIONS

Because this is the wrap-up chapter, which emphasizes an engaged spirituality, motivated by love, to speak out and serve others, I offer more suggested readings than other chapters. Most are mentioned in the text with publication details in the bibliography.

- Saul Griffith, *Electrify*, challenges readers to move to carbon-free living as soon as possible. He offers practical suggestions and potent actions. Richard Haass, *The World: A Brief History*. Remarkable range of topics and significant global data.

- Stephen Cope, *The Great Work of Your Life: A Guide to the Journey for Your True Calling*. Can you say you know your life's purpose, your dharma?

- Scott Russell Sanders, *The Way of Imagination: Essays*. A bountiful garden of ideas and proposals, expressed exquisitely, about paying attention to a changing world.

- Joseph Nangle, *Engaged Spirituality: Faith Life in the Heart of the Empire*. A Christian's experience with confronting empires.

- Diane Faires Beadle and Jamie Lynn Haskins, *Acting on Faith: Stories of Courage, Activism, and Hope across Religions*. Inspiring stories of constructive projects done by interfaith groups.

- James H. Cone, *A Black Theology of Liberation*. An essential profile from Cone and others offering insights related to working for justice and equality for all.

◆ Andreas Karelas, *Climate Courage: How Tackling Climate Change Can Build Community, Transform the Economy, and Bridge the Political Divide in America.* The title says it all.

◆ David Wallace-Wells, *The Uninhabitable Earth: Life after Warming.* Are his assertions accurate? You can compare with actualities you and others are experiencing.

◆ Steven Levitsky and Daniel Ziblatt, *How Democracies Die: What History Reveals about Our Future.* Prophetic insights about the fragility of democracies and the signs of coming autocracy.

◆ Randall Balmer, *Solemn Reverence: The Separation of Church and State in American Life.* A fundamental understanding of the importance of church/state separation and clarification about the US founded as a Christian nation.

◆ Robert Boston, *Taking Liberties: Why Religious Freedom Doesn't Give You the Right to Tell Other People What to Do.* Clearly stated assertions about what religious freedom permits and does not permit.

Final Conversation

The goal in sacred story is always to come back home, after getting the protagonist to leave home in the first place! A contradiction? A paradox? Yes, but now home has a whole new meaning, never imagined before. As always, it transcends but includes one's initial experience of home.

—Father Richard Rohr, *Falling Upward*, 87–88

Trust in dreams, for in them is hidden the gate to eternity.

—Khalil Gibran

The only people who don't need heaven are people who have not known grief, suffering, and injustice that is larger than a lifetime.

—Howard Thurman

"And then"... (*vahz*) was a favorite literary tool of Hebrew writers to extend their narratives of the human and divine. With the diverse beliefs and doubts and life after death, that may be the best way to end our conversation and for me to ask you. And then?

—Rachel Held Evans, *Inspired*, epilogue

GOING HOME

- ◆ Circumstances for writing the book

- ◆ Homes and spiritual homes are meaning-makers

- ◆ Homecoming

- ◆ My questions to you—time for a grilling

- ◆ Your questions to me about going home

- ◆ Future possibilities

- ◆ Goodbye . . . and then?

Convention says an epilogue is appropriate for a literary work. Convention says an afterword or afterward is appropriate for a postbook comment of an academic treatise. Since this is neither one, let's dub this our final conversation. Confession: Barbara Brown Taylor's epilogue in *Holy Envy* is my template. I'll describe what prompted me to write this book, ask questions about your finding or still searching for a spiritual home, then share some future possibilities I'm considering.

If we had a face-to-face final conversation, we might begin by both giving thanks for thoughts shared and support given, apologize for intemperate words and deeds, probe with a few questions about future ventures, and end with words of affection, possibly "I love you." My brother, Dr. Ted, did that in his last years.

CIRCUMSTANCES FOR WRITING THE BOOK

In 2019, life was fine. The calendar was full, busy with activities at my retirement community. Volunteer work with churches rewarding, visits with families on the East Coast fun. The highlight was a bucket list checkoff—a land and sea tour of Alaska with my granddaughter. By mid-2019, a gnawing feeling about national and world conditions prompted me to return to a manuscript begun twenty years earlier—why people were turning from organized religion to what seemed numerous strategies for addressing spiritual matters. Then, COVID-19.

I lost my excuse for not writing. No travel. My retirement community was "locked down." With the help of friends, fantastic and faithful friends—new and old—I soaked up knowledge from books, journals, and media. Online contacts with so many wonderful persons affirmed, challenged, directed me. Blessings to so many for the book! But what to say?

World conditions were worsening. Blaming it on politicians was tempting. Throw in media empires force-feeding us unhealthy doses of chemical wonder drugs and businesses seducing us with non-chemical pills such as sports, beauty products, entertainment, vehicles, and furniture. Prophet-like, I wanted to roar about our plundered planet's loss of beauty and resources, the power grabs by international corporations with budgets larger than countries, the perversions of cyber terrorists and military mercenaries. World governments seem uncommitted and inept in fighting climate change as well as racial, sexual, and religious discrimination. The consequences, a pandemic—God's judgment?

Tempting to blame our despair on religion, too. Atrophied moral and spiritual values. Historically and currently, traditional religious faiths have offered much positive but also failed miserably. Inept and corrupt leadership from spiritual and secular organizations holding on to power, unjust structures, and property under scandalous conditions. No wonder younger generations view religious creeds and past spiritual practices as outdated and largely irrelevant. Is there a correlation between the spread of cruelty and hate and the increase of greed, superstition, and ignorance?

Is SBNR spirituality a possible savior? Partially—but to me, it offers the supremacy of the individual at the cost of the common good. It speaks of "love," but it has cheapened love, which ought to apply only to humans—OK, pets, too—and not to face creams, pizzas, and constipation medications. People assign "spiritual" to family, company, team, party, and country. Some adherents co-opt science and technology to their brand of spirituality. Too few voices listened to those saying spirituality is demanding, with the best changes coming from group support.

It was time to get off the soapbox and put passion to paper.

HOMES AND SPIRITUAL HOMES ARE MEANING-MAKERS

What I learned is that, rightly or wrongly, organized religion—its traditional beliefs, practices, and language—doesn't connect for many people. It's still OK for some; great. The vocabulary to use is spirituality, meaning-making. It starts at home, a transformation process.

Our beginning, our ending begins with being formed in love, then being "in-formed." Our social images are influenced by many: relatives, peers, schools, houses of worship, social media. Our spiritual growth includes "re-forming" and "con-forming" over years from links and bonds with individuals, groups, and communities. Many of us have or are currently experimenting with some unhealthy non-religious communities of belonging. That may be why, reader, you are open to becoming a part of a healthy spiritual home.

HOMECOMING

The book hopes to offer you ways, not one way, to make a difference in your spiritual life. A key is to be with others who comfort and confront you; that's what makes your search with a spiritual community transformational. If you are part of a community that makes you feel you have come home spiritually: congratulations! If not there: keep exploring, traveler. I believe what makes a difference includes a never fully satisfied yearning, commitment to lifelong learning, daily spiritual practices, and engagement in loving soulcare for yourself and others. Your traveling companions or catalysts will be joy, truth, trust, and love, whose offspring should be generosity, courage, care, and justice. Finally, the book has the audacity to hope you can turn dreams of justice and well-being into reality for this planet of neighbors we call home. To get to that homecoming, I've suggested you mirror the strategies you employed when you searched for a new house. Please take my suggestions and resource references as gutsy guides, not dusty mandates.

MY QUESTIONS TO YOU—TIME FOR A GRILLING

Do you recall the story of my wife's ritual of grilling our sons when they came home from college? It became a cherished memory. Let me grill you; then you can grill me. My first question is, where are you on your journey? Others I could ask, have you gained a new appreciation of your natal/primary home? Its benefits and shortcomings? Recall Sharon Daloz Parks and Richard Rohr reminded us, spiritually speaking, we yearn to return to our first home. True?

Consider the rest of these questions a checklist. Answer only those that are relevant in helping you determine where you are spiritually now. If you attend yearning services, are they joyful? Do you consistently engage in a spiritual practice? If you have been a longtime church, synagogue, or mosque member, were you upset about not attending services in person during the pandemic? What did you do during that time?

Have you gained new information and insights about spirituality? Enjoy being a questioning truth-teller? New perspective on storytelling? Do you handle doubt better? Easier to trust others now? Changed your attitude about food and table? More of a world neighbor now? Honestly, I still find it hard to believe we live on a blue marble where orders at a McDonalds can be taken in another state, a PowerPoint can be massaged overnight in India, an international school in Costa Rica can host a model UN program with participants from numerous countries.[1] Your attitude on pandemics? Weather extremes? Feel comfortable sharing your worldview?

YOUR QUESTIONS TO ME ABOUT GOING HOME

Enough, you say. It's my turn, Charles, to ask *you* a big question or two. First and second, what are your images of a healthy primary home and healthy spiritual home on earth? Third, what about an eternal life, i.e., going home?

First Home?—Backyard Streetcar

OK. On a primary home. I have gained a deeper appreciation of my Seguin, Texas, home—not perfect, but it gave my brothers and me comfort and confrontation in one unusual way. We had a real streetcar in our backyard. Mind you, we weren't a rich family. Mom and Dad had purchased one for twenty-five dollars from the city of Austin. Stripped of all wires, batteries, lights, and wheels, it still had seats, windows, and an outside ladder that allowed us to climb to its roof. Our imaginations quickly turned to unlimited possibilities—a castle, fort, submarine, train, church, refuge, club house, laboratory for chemistry experiments. A hideaway to puff a first cigarette butt. A refuge for boys discussing the mysteries of girls. A military headquarters where peers plotted rubber-gun battles against other neighborhood gangs. At day's end, we took questions and dreams, alright, most of them from that pitted, faded orange-and-white wheelless beast to our parents at the dinner table or on the open porch. The result: we were creatively yet realistically prepared for what was achievable.

---

1. The McDonalds story from Cape Girardeau, MO, and the PowerPoint narrative from New York are found in Friedman, *World Is Flat*; the model UN program was supplied by a friend's daughter, Jayne Hutchcroft, a teacher at Lincoln International School, San José, Costa Rica.

Second Home?—Spiritual Home

As chapter 1 remarked, home is thought of as a place. Sharon Daloz Parks reminds us it is paradoxical: we both abide in and venture from it, often to return. From friends and colleagues, I have a new appreciation of the diverse ways various faiths and spiritualties construct their spiritual homes. I like Buddhist monk Thich Nhat Hanh's image: home is like an ocean wave. When we find our true home, it is where we are now, with a feeling of peace and joy that we deserve, but open to constant change.[2] Home is an uncountable composite of past, present, and future experiences, a melding of memories of those gone and those with us, topped by the foam of our spiritual beliefs and practices, rushing to shore in ever-changing ways.

From my religious past, my spiritual mantra is, "Always be prepared to make a defense [I prefer explanation] to anyone who calls you to account for the hope that is in you, yet do it with gentleness and reverence" (1 Pet 3:15).

I hope when I have spoken of any historic faith tradition or spiritual practice that I have done it with gentleness and reverence. I apologize if I have misstated or omitted critically important perspectives. My intent has been to offer some wisdom with humor.

Third Home?—Eternal Home, Going Home

As I'll mention in closing, when I discuss some future possibilities, one of them relates to writing about the concept of the afterlife. Let me share with you two stories with a different perspective.

The first story I experienced in a tiny Honduran village in 1960. A villager died. Neighbors crafted a mahogany casket from local timber. They screwed in brass handles. A two-hour service. No hearse. Friends traded off carrying the coffin to the cemetery some distance away. Final words. The brass handles removed for the next service. Dirt shoveled in. Walking back to the village, several voices said, "He has gone home." To this visitor, what was most touching was friends sharing in carrying him to his final earthly home.

At my sister-in-law's funeral in Lincoln, Nebraska, the minister offered this story. The company president whose firm had just opened

2. Hanh, *Going Home*, 41–42.

a new branch office called a florist shop. "A terrible mistake," he said with alarm, "One of the celebratory floral arrangements is an obvious mix up—its ribbon reads 'Condolences.'" The florist quickly phoned the grieving family that had received the incorrect bouquet and offered to send an appropriate replacement. The family member chuckled and said, no, they were quite pleased with what had been delivered. Its message? "Congratulations on your new location."

After Heaven by Robert Wuthnow provides a sociologist's conclusion that our images of heaven are based on our ethnic groups, circumstances (such as having immigrated), and geographical location.[3] Rather than focus on details, Protestant reformer Martin Luther's advice was don't worry about the details of the afterlife. It's enough if you believe in a loving God. If you push me on the meaning of an eternal home, my response will begin with the sentiment of a hymn, "I Was There to Hear Your Borning Cry." Its text depicts the voice of God describing the stages of life in which God is always present, including the promise of "just one more surprise."[4]

FUTURE POSSIBILITIES

What's next? Based on the trends happening now and if interest from this book supports it, one option would be a book on spiritual trends that are working. By *working*, I don't mean most popular. What are those making the most constructive differences morally and spiritually? Are the truth issues described in chapter 6 being addressed? What about the climate changes and economic inequities discussed in chapter 8? Two specific concerns: 1) *Telling the whole truth, even when uncomfortable.* As a university professor in education, I did a statewide survey of social studies teachers. I learned that one of the easiest ways the teachers could get student participation on an ethics or values question was to offer accounts of how their ancestors and other groups emigrated to this country—reasons for coming, passage experiences, acceptance or rejection, hardships of their occupations. Imagine the truths from those stories. In many states now, certain parents and organizations want legislation that prohibits making their children "uncomfortable." 2) *Becoming less knowledgeable and empathic due to gated-ness—my word.* The latest estimate I find is

3. Wuthnow, *After Heaven*, 7, 9, 28–29, 106.
4. John Ylvisaker (1937–2017), "I Was There to Hear Your Borning Cry" (1985).

that the United States now has an estimated 2 million gated communities. I concede that in this country and in other countries, there can be economic and physical safety reasons for such communities. My concern is the social or psychological attitude spawned by those of us who live even in non-gated but "think-alike" communities: we can't imagine what other lifestyles are like. Our gated-ness is a virus that destroys empathy.

If I were to do another book on engaged spirituality, it would be called *How Spirituality Works*.

Second possibility. Down to earth, so to speak. I am a member of a congregation that celebrated its 150th anniversary a few years ago. The historian in me began to compile the stories and statistics for a comprehensive history. Unfortunately, I ran out of time to complete it. That project calls.

GOODBYE . . . AND THEN?

By now, you know you are free to choose another term than my choice, *traveler*: seeker, searcher, nomad, pilgrim, tourist, or refugee. The journey through this book is done. Our conversations are over. My hope is that if you were searching for a spiritual home, you have found it, or if you are still in the process, you are more confident about continuing the venture. If you are more of a stayer (you never left your family's house of worship) involved in revitalizing your current spiritual home, I hope you learned some practices that can transform your life and those of your loved ones—with joy, truth, trust, and love.

You know I am not a salesman of a sticky-sweet spiritual serenity. The paradox of both our primary home and our spiritual home is that they support us with comfort but challenge us with confrontations. These two homes, when stable, sharpen our big questions and steel us to set and implement worthy dreams. If I or others jar you by saying a meaningful spirituality is not a pillow of puffy pronouncements softening the edges of daily life, your reactions can range from shock to disappointment to anger. Hopefully, the message is that a structured life of saying YESS—yearning, education (learning), soulcare (burning), and service (turning)—makes sense. To hear that your journey has changed you from traveler to disciple to friend, and, yes, even to moral servant leader would merit a loud shout from me.

Let's end by recalling where we began: the word *home* is the most powerful word in the English language. As we discovered, the major religious and spiritual traditions have diverse images of both earthly and heavenly homes.[5] To cite Thich Nhat Hanh again, an afterlife homecoming is a symbol of reconciliation for the separation of the world's people and their faiths.[6]

YESS! AND THEN?

May you have a safe but exciting trip as you go home. And then? (*v'ahz*)

5. Diana Bass, *Grounded*, 163–92, especially 169.

6. Hanh, *Going Home*.

Appendices

Resources for Spiritual Travelers

CHAPTER ONE

Appendix 1A: Three Kinds of Mysteries[1]

The human mind is confronted with three kinds of mysteries: trivial, significant, and grand.

Trivial mysteries include simple confusions, wonderments, and riddles. Where is the key I had just placed on my table cluttered with so many things? A little careful search will find the key. Why has my friend not yet arrived for dinner? We may find out that there was a huge traffic jam on the way. Which travels faster, heat or cold? Heat, because we can catch cold! Trivial mysteries are easily solved.

Significant mysteries relate to natural phenomena. How is the rainbow formed? How do mirages arise? Why is the sky blue? These are some instances of significant mysteries. Significant mysteries are resolved by scientific investigation and analysis. Indeed, science may be defined as a collective transnational effort to resolve significant mysteries by working in a collectively agreed-upon framework that relies on reason, experimentation, instruments, and well-defined concepts.

Grand mysteries relate to the perennial puzzles that have tormented human minds since time immemorial. What is the purpose of human life in

1. V. V. Raman, January 6, 2000. Reprinted with permission of the author.

253

a cold and vast cosmos? What, if any, is the ultimate meaning of life? Is there postmortem persistence? What is the source of suffering and evil in the world? How can one know the day one will die and how it will happen? These are some grand mysteries. No science or search, no poet or philosopher can resolve grand mysteries to everyone's satisfaction.

There can be three reactions to grand mysteries.

The first is to provide some reasonable and persuasive answer that will be accepted by a vast number of people. This is usually done by charismatic individuals in various cultures who gradually manage to acquire a significant number of followers. That is how the religions of humankind have arisen and continue to do. Indeed, a religion is a culturally significant framework that provides answers to grand mysteries, which are meaningful and fulfilling to large numbers of people.

A second reaction to grand mysteries is to concede that the human mind cannot provide logical, rational, and incontrovertible answers to them; then, contemplate them periodically with reverence and humility. One may look upon this reaction to grand mysteries as spiritual experience. Spiritual experience may be regarded as a serious and deeply fulfilling response to the grand mysteries that human minds confront.

Conflicts between science and religion arise when religions go beyond answering grand mysteries and attempt also to answer significant mysteries—and when science asserts that grand mysteries are irrelevant and trivial.

The third reaction to grand mysteries is simply to ignore them as an irrelevant and unproductive waster of time, somewhat like the fox in Aesop's fable who, after a couple of unsuccessful attempts to reach the grapes, declared them to be sour anyway.

CHAPTER FOUR

Appendix 4A: Six Values—A Statement Prepared by an Ecumenical Group, Ames, IA (2005)

Love: We *believe* God is love, and, in that love, Christ calls us to love God, self, neighbors, and our enemies; thus, we embrace and celebrate all humanity.

> *Scripture:* We *know* that God is love and God calls us to love (1 John 4:7). Love is fundamental in our relationships with family, community, and the world (1 Cor 13). Our Christian traditions expect us to be welcoming to "strangers" (Matt 25:35).

Reconciliation and Peace: We *believe* that all people are separated from God, both by the things we do and by the things we choose not to do. Reconciled with God through Jesus Christ, we seek always to be reconciled with our neighbor.

> *Scripture:* We *know* as Christians that Jesus's life and death were God's action to bring humanity into a renewed relationship with God marked by love and blessing (John 3:16). Our faith in Jesus, in turn, leads us as well to a new kind of relationship with others. Jesus said to his disciples, for example, "You have heard that it was said, 'An eye for an eye, a tooth for a tooth.' But I say to you, 'Do not resist an evildoer . . . . If anyone strikes you on the right cheek, turn the other also . . . . Love your enemies and pray for those who persecute you'" (Matt 5:38–48).

Compassion for the Vulnerable and Outcast: We *believe* that Christ calls us to extend ourselves in special, active compassion for the vulnerable and outcast in society.

> *Scripture:* Of many relevant stories, sayings, and parables, we cite three. In Luke's gospel, Jesus reminded his listeners to love one's neighbor as one loves oneself. In the story of the good Samaritan, Jesus defined a neighbor as simply one who has need, whatever the circumstance. In Matthew 25, Jesus identified as righteous those who minister to the hungry, the thirsty, the stranger, the naked, the sick, and the prisoner. Throughout Jesus's own ministry, we see the model of healing the sick, feeding the hungry, listening to the children, and embracing society's outcast.

Environmental Stewardship: We *believe* that a Divine Force created the universe, including the beautiful and bountiful natural world in which we live. Created in the divine image, we are called to be stewards of earth.

Scripture: Throughout the Scriptures, and especially in the Psalms, God is praised as the Creator (Ps 104:13). Numerous biblical accounts emphasize the importance of the land—"The earth is the Lord's, and the fullness thereof" (Ps 24:1)—and the responsibility of humans to be faithful stewards of its products—"The fruit of the land shall be the pride and glory of the survivors of Israel" (Isa 4:2). Genesis 1 and 2 underscore the creation of the natural world as "good." Jesus's life was a model of servanthood. In such a context, we see that humanity's "domination over" nature is not a license to exploit but a responsibility to serve.

Truth and Accountability: We *believe* in a transforming God who gives individuals and groups the freedom to learn the truth, the ability to make choices, and the duty to be accountable.

Scripture: We *hold* that the past and its truths are to be respected. However, God promises a world that will change, where "all things will be made new" (Rev 21:8). Hence, our imperative is to search for truth that sets us free (John 8:32). We view personal and social responsibility as gifts of God, and we assume that God will ultimately judge all our actions. God expects truth in our "inward being" (Ps 51:6), and God's prophets and leaders instructed people "to serve God in sincerity and in truth" (Josh 24:14). In his teaching, Jesus frequently used questions and parables to aid hearers to discern truth.

Family: We *believe* that as a fundamental unit of social structure, families deserve special recognition and support. In families, we, children and adults, can be protected and nurtured. We must learn to love, sacrifice, and support one another. In families, we may form moral and social values that guide our lives. In healthy families, we have opportunities to be intimately known and unconditionally accepted. As Christians, we believe that the church is called to be "the household of God," a spiritual family with purposes like those of all families.

Scripture: We *hold* that the Bible does not advocate a single model for family structure. Indeed, the family configurations of biblical times would be quite out of place in the United States of the twenty-first century. Instead of structure, Scripture provides us with guidance and values that effectively cross cultures and centuries. For example, the commandment to honor our parents is universal. There is a sacred trust between husband and wife that should not be broken through adultery. The parable of the prodigal son stresses the father's welcoming home the wayward child—and calls the elder son also to forgive.

APPENDIX 4B: HOLDING MORAL CONVERSATIONS[2]

Background: On February 8, 2010, two authors of the book cited below held a noon forum on the Iowa State University campus. The following are the major points made by Professor Robert J. Nash—a long-time faculty member at the University of Vermont, who also served as the applied ethicist for the campus—and Dr. DeMethra LaSha Bradley, a staff member from the provost's office at the University of Vermont.

Purpose and Application: All of us engage in difficult dialogues from time to time. They occur in our personal relationships, work environments, and in our social networks. The three virtues described below may result in interactions with others that lead to constructive results, especially when there are differences, real or perceived, in values, priorities, and performance.

Why Moral Conversations? The Latin and Greek roots of the word *moral* focus on patterns or standards. The implication is that discussions are based on treating the other with dignity.

Virtue of Humility: The first virtue is *humility*. The implications here are that: 1) we are willing to find the truth in what we oppose or, said another way, that as much as we may oppose someone else's view, we recognize he/she has some merit; 2) we are willing to admit that we may have an error in what we espouse. In the academic world (and business?), our behavior is contestation rather than conversation. We challenge, we debate, we are like boxers in a ring. *An appropriate analogy for behavior here is to raise a barn together.*

Virtue of Respect: The second virtue is *respect.* If we respect the other, we will evoke rather than invoke or provoke. *Evoke* means to "call forth," to make a connection, to truly listen to the other's voice. When we *provoke*, we are either attempting to put down the other or discredit the person, which usually promotes anger. When we *invoke*, we cite experts or examples that say my way is better than yours. This encourages the other to pit his or her experts against yours.

When this happens in discussion, be willing to look again at where each party is. Ask clarifying questions that "do no harm" or intentionally

2. Summarized by Charles R. Kniker, Feb. 19, 2010. Based on the book by Nash et al., *How to Talk.* Permission granted by Robert J. Nash.

are not meant to shut down the other. Conversation starters: What do you mean? How did you come to hold that position? Do I understand your opinion to be . . .? I want to understand your position. Am I correct in believing you support . . .? Conversation stoppers: You won't give in, will you? How could you hold that position?

We may assume that the other won't negotiate. Ask yourself on what issues would I be non-negotiable? On what issues will I be flexible?

Virtue of Generosity: The third virtue of *generosity* begins with the belief that the other can be an ally, not an enemy. Yes, with individuals we should respect the others as people, although we can be critical of their ideas. Gossip is really being critical of the individual. The opposite of generosity is selfishness. I am right. I am important. I want decisions that please me, even if it is at your expense.

Generous persons will engage in dialogue rather than monologue. Make the moral conversation about what is best for both of us (individuals, groups, and the wider community).

CHAPTER FIVE

Appendix 5A: The Meanings of Spiritual Music[3]

Confucius: Allegedly a music teacher and excellent musician, he said, "If one should desire to know whether a kingdom is well governed, if its morals are good or bad, the quality of its music will furnish the answer." "Be aroused by poetry; structure yourself with propriety; refine yourself with music."

Hindu: A *bhajan* is a Hindu devotional song, in lyrical language expressing emotions of love for the divine, whether for a single god/goddess or many divinities. Hindus may achieve *moksha* (release from the cycle of rebirth) through their special music to God. The Sage Yajnavalkya wrote a famous verse after hearing the wife of Yajnavalkya playing a *veena* (lute or harp): "*Veena Vadana Tatvagnaha, Sruthi Jathi Visharada, Talagnanacha Aprayasena, Mokshamargam Gachachati.*" Translation: "All who are adept at the Venna and are versed in tonal components and musical measures attain musical ecstasy effortlessly."

Buddhism: "Our melodies can be described as being strong, but not fierce; soft but not weak; pure but not dry; still, but not sluggish, and able to help purify the hearts of listeners."

In the *Amitabha Sutra*, "Heavenly singing and chanting is heard all day and night in the world around us: as flowers softly rain down from the heavens; as birds produce beautiful and harmonious music; the blowing of a gentle breeze; the movements of jewel trees . . . all being played together in harmony, in order to guide sentients belongs to enlightenment."

Taoism: Its priests use chanting and singing to find harmony and simplicity in all things. Most of its music is based on the ying tone (standing for the female and soft) and the yang tone (male and hard). Some ceremonies are for the benefit of the priests and god, spirits, and gods, while others are for the general population.

Judaism: Historically, Jewish religious music was focused on the cantors, synagogues, and the temple. According to the *Mishnah*, the temple orchestra had twelve instruments and twelve male singers. Its music began with cantors singing *piyyutim* (liturgical poems). Over the centuries, some of these were preserved to be used with the reading of Scripture. As

---

3. Many of the descriptions of these forms of religious music are paraphrased from Wikipedia articles.

Judaism spread, it integrated music and musical instruments from various cultures for various holidays and milestone events.

Christian: The forms of music from the Jewish tradition were continued, then expanded. "Joined together in harmony and having received the godly melody in unison, you might sing in one voice through Jesus Christ . . . that you might always partake of God."—Ignatius of Antioch, c. 35–107 CE, citing Eph 4.

"Apart from those moments when the scriptures are being read or a sermon is preached, when the bishop is praying aloud or the deacon is speaking the intention of the litany of community prayer, is there any time when the faithful assembled are not singing?"—Augustine, fourth century.

"This precious gift [music] has been bestowed on men alone to remind them that they are created to praise and magnify the Lord. But when natural music is sharpened and polished by art, then one begins to see with amazement the great and perfect wisdom of God in his wonderful work of music . . . . He who does not find this an inexpressible miracle of the Lord is truly a clod and is not worthy to be considered a man."—Martin Luther, preface to a 1538 hymnal.

Islam: Since its founding and spread throughout the world, Muslim music has taken many forms. Some religious songs, *nasheeds*, have moral messages and are sung without instruments.

Sufi services are widely known for their chanting and rhythmic dancing of whirling dervishes. In South Asia, in countries like India, Pakistan, and Bangladesh, a popular program of religious music is *qawwali*. It includes a *hamd*, a song in praise of Allah; a *na'at*, a song praising Muhammad; *manqabats*, songs for the brotherhood the singers; and *ghazals*, songs of yearning and intoxication, romantic language wishing for union with the divine.

Appendix 5B: A Variety of Religious and Spiritual Practices[4]

Animal sacrifice

Scripture reading

Communal fellowship

Observing sacred laws

Human sacrifice

Sharing sacred meals

Hospitality

Wearing amulets or talismans

Plant harvest sacrifice

Reciting mantras

Sacred dancing

Observing rites of passage

Spoken prayers

Giving alms

Lighting candles

Observing sacred calendrical times

Spirit possession

Fasting from food

Burning incense

Making offerings

Meditation

Sexual abstinence

Blessing of fields

Consulting oracles

Pilgrimages

Ritual water on skin

Blessing of houses

Conducting exorcisms

Singing worship songs

Studying sacred texts

Blessings of marriages

Celebrating festivals

Water baptisms

Proselytizing

Genuflecting

Wearing prescribed clothing

Religious conversion

Taking oaths

Celebrating worship liturgies

Observing holy days

Possessions

Conducting crusades

Requesting prayer support

Practicing pacifism

Visiting shrines

Praying to ancestors

Venerating sacred objects

Constructing monuments

Kneeling

Keeping silence

Receiving visions, apparitions

Giving public testimony

Laying on hands

Closing one's eyes

Folding hands

Raising arms

Trusting a divinity

Waving plant branches

Obeying divine commands

Holy kisses

Political blessings

4. C. Smith, *Religion*, 29. Permission granted to reprint this list.

Housing divine statues

Contemplating icons

Spiritual journaling

Phallus worship

Spiritual direction

Ordination for office

Spinning prayer wheels

Reciting the Rosary

Penance

Attending religious services

Confession of sin

Believing the gospel

Ashes on forehead

Endowing religious homes

Praying to patron saints

Buying indulgences

Teaching religion

Performing sacred dramas

Hanging images on walls

Self-flagellation

Consecrating objects

Coming forward down the aisle

Using prayer beads

Memorizing scripture

Divination

Observing dietary restrictions

Conducting funerals

Making sacred art

Walking labyrinths

Preserving bodies of the dead

Reciting oral histories

Venerating animals

Using hallucinogens

Retelling sacred narratives

Offering food to priests

Ritual sexual acts

Feeding spirits

Observing dietary restrictions

Covering body parts

Revering names of deities

Ritual breathing exercises

Abstaining from unclean words

Ritual physical exercises

Avoiding taking any life

Renunciation of clothing

Reenacting cosmic mythologies

Pastoral discipline

Water purification rites

Casting of spells

Refusal of professional medicine

Pronouncing of curses

Positioning talismans

Coloring bodies

Burning dedicated objects

Keeping vigils

Pouring libations

Eucharistic adoration

Family visits with ancestors present

CHAPTER SIX

Appendix 6A: Sacred Texts (selected)[5]

+ Hinduism—teachers (c. 2000 BCE?)—*The Rig-Vedas, Yajur-Veda, Sama-Veda, Atharva-Veda; Bhagavad Gita, Upanishads*

+ Buddhism—Gautama, the Buddha (800–600 BCE)—*The Dhammapada, Buddaghosha's Parables, The Lotus of the True Law, The Diamond Sutra, Asvaghosha's Awakening of Faith*

+ Confucianism—(551–479 BCE)—*Wujing (or Five Classics), The Li Ki, The Shih King, The Analects of Confucius, The Great Learning, The Doctrine of the Steadfast Mean, The Works of Mencius, The Book of Filial Piety*

+ Judeo-Christian—(1000 BCE–200 CE)—*Hebrew Scriptures, Christian Testaments*

+ Taoist/Daoist—Tao Te Ching (5000 BCE?)—*The Tao-Te King, The Works of Chuang Tzu*

+ Zoroastrianism—Zoroaster (c. 628 BCE–c. 551 BCE)—*The Bundahis, The Vendidad, The Zendavesta, The Pahlavi Texts, The Gathas*

+ Islam—Muhammad (b. 570 CE)—*The Qur'an (Koran), Masnavi, The Forty-Two Traditions of An-Nawawi*

5. Ballou, *Portable World Bible*; Neusner, *World Religions in America*; Willis, *Religion Book*. It should go without saying that there are many other historic religions and that those traditions listed above have branches. The intent is to show a sampling of sacred texts and significant teachings.

Bibliography

Abrams, Nancy Ellen. *A God That Could Be Real: Spirituality, Science, and the Future of the Planet*. Boston: Beacon, 2015.

Ackerman, James S., and Thayer S. Warshaw, eds. *The Bible as/in Literature*. 2nd ed. Glenview, IL: Scott Foresman, 1997.

Adams, Marilee. *Change Your Questions, Change Your Life: Twelve Powerful Tools for Leadership, Coaching, and Life*. 3rd ed. San Francisco: Barrett-Koehler, 2016.

Adler, Felix. *The Essentials of Spirituality*. 1905. Reprint, n.p.: Franklin Classics Trade, n.d.

Albanese, Catherine L., ed. *American Spiritualities: A Reader*. Bloomington: Indiana University Press, 2001.

Aleshire, Daniel. "Finding Eagles in the Turkey's Nest: Pastoral Theology and Christian Education." *Review and Expositor* 85 (1988) 699–702.

Allers, Roger, and Rob Minkoff, dirs. *The Lion King*. Burbank, CA: Buena Vista, 1994.

Alzheimer's Association. *Twenty-Twenty-One Alzheimer's Disease Facts and Figures*. https://www.alz.org/media/Documents/alzheimers-facts-and-figures.pdf.

Andersen, Ericka. "How to Boost Your Mental Health: Attend Worship." *Des Moines Register*, Mar. 31, 2021.

Anderson, Herbert. "Whatever Happened to *Seelsorge*?" *Word and World* 21, no. 1 (Winter 2001) 32–41.

Andrus, Chip. "Contemporary Worship: Past, Present, and Future." Call to Worship, 48, no. 4 (2011) 35-38.

Andrus, Chip. "The Emerging Worship Initiative." Emerging Worship, Dec. 25, 2007. http://www.emergingworship.org/ewinitiative.htm. Site discontinued.

Angelou, Maya. *All God's Children Need Traveling Shoes*. New York: Random House, 1986.

Antal, Jim. *Climate Church, Climate World: How People of Faith Must Work for Change*. Lanham, MD: Rowman & Littlefield, 2018.

Applebaum, Anne. *Twilight of Democracy: The Seductive Lure of Authoritarianism*. New York: Random House, 2020.

Ariarajah, S. Wesley. *Not without My Neighbour: Issues in Interfaith Relations*. Risk. Geneva: World Council of Churches, 1999.

Armstrong, Karen. *The Spiral Staircase: My Climb out of Darkness*. New York: Knopf, 2004.

Astin, Alexander W., et al. *Cultivating the Spirit: How College Can Enhance Students' Inner Lives*. San Francisco: Jossey-Bass, 2011.

Astyk, Sharon. *Making Home: Adapting Our Homes and Our Lives*. Philadelphia: New Society, 2012.

Augsburger, David W. *Pastoral Counseling across Cultures*. Philadelphia: Westminster, 1986.

Augustine. *The Confession of St. Augustine*. Edited and translated by E. B. Pusey. New York: Dutton, 1951.

Autry, James A. *Looking Around for God: The Oddly Reverent Observations of an Unconventionl Christian*. Macon, GA: Smith & Helwys, 2007.

Avalos, Hector. "Imagine." *Ames Tribune*, Jan. 29, 2021.

Bachelard, Gaston. *The Poetics of Space*. Translated by Maria Jolas. Boston: Beacon, 1994.

Bainton, Roland H. *Christianity*. Boston: Houghton Mifflin, 2000.

Baldwin, James. *Collected Essays*. New York: Library of America, 1998.

———. *Giovanni's Room*. New York: Knopf, 2016.

Ballou, Robert O., ed. *The World Bible*. Viking Portable Library. New York: Viking, 1995.

Balmer, Randall Herbert. *Evangelicalism in America*. Waco, TX: Baylor University Press, 2016.

———. *Mine Eyes Have Seen the Glory: A Look into the Evangelical Subculture in America*. 4th ed. New York: Oxford University Press, 2006.

———. *Solemn Reverence: The Separation of Church and State in American Life*. Lebanon, NH: Steerforth, 2021.

———. *Thy Kingdom Come: How the Religious Right Distorts the Faith and Threatens America; An Evangelical's Lament*. New York: Basic, 2006.

Banks, Adelle M. "Homeless Find Rest in Faith-Based Shelters More than Others." *Deseret News*, Feb. 1, 2017. https://www.deseret.com/2017/2/1/20605260/homeless-find-rest-in-faith-based-shelters-more-than-others.

Barber, Nigel. "Are Religious People Healthier?" Psychology Today, Dec. 22, 2012. https://www.psychologytoday.com/us/blog/the-human-beast/201212/are-religious-people-healthier.

Barrows, John Henry, ed. *The World's Parliament of Religions: An Illustrated and Popular Story of the World's First Parliament of Religions, Held in Chicago in Connection with the Columbian Exposition of 1893*. 2 vols. Chicago: Parliament, 1893.

Baskette, Molly Phinney. *Real Good Church: How Our Church Came Back from the Dead, and Yours Can, Too*. Cleveland: Pilgrim, 2014.

Bass, Diana Butler. *Christianity after Religion: The End of Church and the Birth of a New Spiritual Awakening*. New York: HarperOne, 2012.

———. *Christianity for the Rest of Us*. San Francisco: Harper, 2006.

———. *Grounded: Finding God in the World—A Spiritual Revolution*. New York: HarperOne, 2015.

———. *The Practicing Congregation: Imagining a New Old Church*. Herndon, VA: Alban Institute, 2004.

———. *Strength for the Journey: A Pilgrimage of Faith in Community*. San Francisco: Jossey-Bass, 2002.

Bass, Dorothy C., ed. *Practicing Our Faith: A Way of Life for a Searching People*. San Francisco: Jossey-Bass, 1997.

"Be a Part of Our Musical Worship Leadership." Worship and Church Music. worshipandchurchmusic.com/kierkegaard.html.

Beadle, Diane Faires, and Jamie Lynn Haskins, eds. *Acting on Faith: Stories of Courage, Activism, and Hope across Religions.* St. Louis: Chalice, 2020.

Belitsos, Byron. "Religious Beliefs of the Trump Movement." *Evolving Souls*, Mar. 14, 2020. http://evolving-souls.org/religious-beliefs-behind-the-trump-phenomenon/.

Bell, John L. *The Singing Thing Too: Enabling Congregations to Sing.* Chicago: GIA, 2007.

Bellah, Robert N., et al. *Habits of the Heart: Individualism and Commitment in American Life.* Berkeley: University of California Press, 1985.

Bender, Courtney. *Heaven's Kitchen: Living Religion at God's Love We Deliver.* Chicago: University of Chicago Press, 2003.

Bennis, Warren G., and Robert J. Thomas. *Geeks and Geezers: How Era, Values, and Defining Moments Shape Leaders.* Boston: Harvard Business School Press, 2002.

Berger, Peter L. *The Sacred Canopy: Elements of a Sociological Theory of Religion.* Garden City, NY: Anchor Books, 1967.

Berndt, Brooks. *Cathedral on Fire: A Church Handbook for the Climate Crisis.* Cleveland: United Church of Christ, 2020.

Berryman, Jerome W. *Teaching Godly Play: How to Mentor the Spiritual Development of Children.* Denver: Morehouse Education Resources, 2009.

Biallas, Leonard J. *World Religions: A Story Approach.* Mystic, CT: Twenty-Third, 1991.

Bishop, Bill, with Robert G. Cushing. *The Big Sort: Why the Clustering of Like-Minded America Is Tearing Us Apart.* Boston: Houghton Mifflin, 2008.

Bishop, James. "Ninian Smart's Seven Dimensions of Religion and Why It Is Helpful." *Bishop's Encyclopedia of Religion*, Society and Philosophy, Jan. 11, 2020. https://jamesbishopblog.com/2020/01/11/ninian-smarts-seven-dimensions-of-religion-and-why-is-it-helpful/.

Bloom, Stephen G. *Postville: A Clash of Cultures in the Heartland.* New York: Harcourt, 2000.

Blumberg, Antonia, and Yasmine Hafiz. "Yes, Religion Can Still Be a Force for Good in the World. Here Are One Hundred Examples How." *HuffPost*, June 17, 2014; updated Dec. 6, 2017. https://www.huffpost.com/entry/100-religious-groups-doing-good_n_5460739.

Bonhoeffer, Dietrich. *Discipleship.* Edited by Eberhard Bethge et al. Dietrich Bonhoeffer Werke 4. Minneapolis: Fortress, 2003.

Borg, Marcus J. *Meeting Jesus Again for the First Time: The Historical Jesus and the Heart of Contemporary Faith.* San Francisco: HarperSanFrancisco, 1994.

———. *Speaking Christian: Why Christian Words Have Lost Their Meaning and Power—and How They Can Be Restored.* New York: HarperOne, 1989.

Borgo, Lacy Finn. *Spiritual Conversations with Children.* Downer Grove, IL: IVP, 2020.

Boston, Robert. "Inside Information." *Church and State* (June 2020) 10–11.

———. *Taking Liberties: Why Religious Freedom Doesn't Give You the Right to Tell Other People What to Do.* Amherst, NY: Prometheus, 2014.

Boyd, Jeffrey H. *Reclaiming the Soul: The Search for Meaning in a Self-Centered World.* Cleveland: Pilgrim, 1996.

Boyett, Jason. *Twelve Major World Religions: The Beliefs, Rituals, and Traditions of Humanity's Most Influential Faiths.* Berkeley, CA: Zephyros, 2016.

Bracke, John M., and Karen B. Tye. *Teaching the Bible in the Church.* St. Louis: Chalice, 2003.

Brands, Hal, and Charles Edel. *The Lessons of Tragedy: Statecraft and World Order.* New Haven, CT: Yale University Press, 2019.

Brett, Brandon. "Religious and Scientific Concept Integration in Developmental, Cultural, and Educational Context." *Religion & Education* 47, no. 3 (2020) 257–72.

Bridge, Andrew. *Hope's Boy.* New York: Hyperion, 2008.

Brooks, David. "The Rise of the Haphazard Self." *Ames Tribune*, May 15, 2019.

Brueggemann, Walter. *A Glad Obedience: What and Why We Sing.* Louisville: Westminster John Knox, 2019.

———. *Journey to the Common Good.* 2nd ed. Louisville: Westminster John Knox, 2021.

———. *The Practice of Homefulness.* Eugene, OR: Cascade, 2014.

———. *The Prophetic Imagination.* 2nd ed. Minneapolis: Fortress, 2001.

———. *Virus as a Summons to Faith: Biblical Reflections in a Time of Loss, Grief, and Uncertainty.* Eugene, OR: Cascade, 2020.

Bruggers, James. "Report: Chemical Stockpiles Endanger Poor, Minorities." *USA Today*, May 1, 2014. https://www.usatoday.com/story/news/nation/2014/05/01/chemical-stockpiles-endanger-poor-minorities/8583849/.

Bryson, Bill. *At Home: A Short History of Private Life.* New York: Anchor, 2010.

Buber, Martin. *Between Man and Man.* New York: Macmillan, 1967.

———. *God in Search of Man.* Cleveland: World Publishing, 1955.

———. *I and Thou.* 2nd ed. New York: Charles Scribner's Sons, 1958.

Buechner, Frederick. *A Room Called Remember.* San Francisco: Harper & Row, 1984.

Bullit-Jonas, Margaret, and Leah Schade, eds. *The Rooted and Rising: Voices of Courage in a Time of Climate Crisis.* Lanham, MD: Rowman & Littlefield, 2019.

Burge, Ryan P. *The Nones: Where They Came From, Who They Are, and Where They Are Going.* Minneapolis: Fortress, 2021.

Bush, George W. *Out of Many, One: Portraits of America's Immigrants.* New York: Crown, 2021.

Camera, Lauren. "Number of Homeless Students Soars." *U.S. News and World Report*, Feb. 21, 2019. https://www.usnews.com/news/education-news/articles/2019-02-21/number-of-homeless-students-soars.

Campbell, David P. *If You Don't Know Where You're Going, You'll Probably End Up Somewhere Else.* Notre Dame, IN: Sorin Books, 2007.

Campbell, J. Y. "Disciple." In *Theological Word Book of the Bible*, edited by Alan Richardson, 69–70. New York: Macmillan, 1950.

———. "Perfection." In *The Interpreter's Dictionary of the Bible*, edited by George A. Buttrick, 3:730. New York: Abingdon, 1962.

Carper, James C., and Thomas C. Hunt, eds. *The Praeger Handbook of Religion and Education in the United States.* 2 vols. Westport, CT: Praeger, 2009.

Carson, Verna Benner, and Harold G. Koenig. *Parish Nursing: Stories of Service and Care.* West Conshohocken, PA: Templeton, 2011.

———. *Spiritual Caregiving: Healthcare as a Ministry.* Philadelphia: Templeton Foundation, 2004.

Carter, Stephen L. *The Dissent of the Governed: A Meditation on Law, Religion, and Loyalty.* Cambridge, MA: Harvard University Press, 2008.

Chaves, Mark. *How Do We Worship?* Herndon, VA: Alban Institute, 1991.

Cherry, Constance M. *The Worship Architect: A Blueprint for Designing Culturally Relevant and Biblically Faithful Services.* Grand Rapids: Baker Academic, 2010.

Chesterton, G. K. *What I Saw in America.* In *Collected Works of G. K. Chesterton*, edited by George J. Marlin et al., 21:35–264. San Franciso: Ignatius, 1990.

Chickering, Arthur W. *Education and Identity*. San Francisco: Jossey-Bass, 1969.

Chickering, Arthur W., et al. *Education and Identity*. 2nd ed. San Francisco: Jossey-Bass, 2011.

———. *Encouraging Authenticity and Spirituality in Higher Education*. San Francisco: Jossey-Bass, 2006.

"Child Care." Child Stats, 2021. https://www.childstats.gov/americaschildren/family3.asp.

Chödrön, Pema. "Tonglen Meditation: News We Can Use." YouTube, June 23, 2016. https://www.youtube.com/watch?v=j_XPJhGwjbU.

Clark, Timothy R. *EPIC Change: How to Lead Change in a Global Age*. San Francisco: Jossey-Bass, 2008.

Cole-Turner, Ronald. *The New Genesis: Theology and the Genetic Revolution*. Louisville: Westminster John Knox, 1993.

Coles, Robert. *Lives of Moral Leadership*. New York: Random House, 2001.

———. *The Spiritual Life of Children*. Boston: Houghton Mifflin, 1990.

Come, Arnold B. *Agents of Reconciliation*. Philadelphia: Westminster, 1964.

———. *Human Spirit and Holy Spirit*. Philadelphia: Westminster, 1959.

Communauté de Taizé. *The Eucharistic Liturgy of Taizé*. Translated by John Arnold. London: Faith, 1962.

Cone, James H. *A Black Theology of Liberation*. Maryknoll, NY: Orbis, 2004.

Conwell, Russell H. *Acres of Diamonds*. 1921. Project Gutenberg, Nov. 9, 2010. https://www.gutenberg.org/ebooks/34258.

Cook, Harry T. *Christianity beyond Creeds*. Clawson, MI: Center for Rational Christianity, 1997.

———. *What a Friend They Had in Jesus*. Salem, OR: Polebridge, 2013.

Cooper, Betsy, et. al. "Exodus: Why Americans Are Leaving Religion—and Why They're Unlikely to Come Back." PRRI, Sept. 22, 2016. https://www.prri.org/research/prri-rns-poll-nones-atheist-leaving-religion/.

Cope, Stephen. *The Great Work of Your Life: A Guide to the Journey for Your True Calling*. New York: Random House, 2015.

Cox, Daniel A., et al. "The Decline of Religion in American Family Life: Findings from the November 2019 American Perspectives Survey." American Enterprise Institute, Dec. 11, 2019. https://www.aei.org/research-products/report/the-decline-of-religion-in-american-family-life/.

Cox, Harvey. *The Future of Faith*. New York: HarperOne, 2009.

Cox, Meg. *The Book of New Family Traditions: How to Create Great Rituals for Holidays and Every Day*. Philadelphia: Running, 2012.

Cramer-Flood, Ethan. "US Time Spent with Media 2021 Update: Pivotal Moments for TV, Subscription OTT, Digital Audio, and Social Media." eMarketer, Feb. 4, 2021. https://www.emarketer.com/content/us-time-spent-with-media-2021-update.

Cremin, Lawrence A., ed. *The Republic and the School: Horace Mann on the Education of Free Men*. New York: Teachers College Press, 1962.

———. *The Transformation of the School*. New York: Vintage, 1961.

Crossan, John Dominic. *The Greatest Prayer: Rediscovering the Revolutionary Message of the Lord's Prayer*. San Francisco: HarperOne, 2010.

Csinos, David M. *Children's Ministry That Fits: Beyond One-Size-Fits-All Approaches to Nurturing Children's Spirituality*. Eugene, OR: Wipf & Stock, 2011.

Csinos, David M., and Ivy Beckwith. *Children's Ministry in the Way of Jesus.* Downers Grove, IL: IVP, 2013.

Csinos, David M., and Melvin Bray, eds. *Faith Forward: A Dialogue on Children, Youth, and a New Kind of Christianity.* Kelowna, Can.: CopperHouse, 2013.

Cully, Iris V. *Education for Spiritual Growth.* San Francisco: Harper & Row, 1984.

Culver, Sheldon, and John Dorhauer. *Steeplejacking: How the Christian Right Is Hijacking Mainstream Religion.* Brooklyn: IG, 2007.

Daloz, Laurent A. Parks, et al. *Common Fire: Leading Lives of Commitment in a Complex World.* Boston: Beacon, 1996.

Daniel, Lillian. "The Insights of Isolation." (June 17, 2018). https://www.ucc.org/daily-devotional/daily_devotional_the insights_of_isolation/ Daniel, Lillian. *Tired of Apologizing for a House of Worship I Don't Belong To.* New York: Faith Words, 2016.

———. *When "Spiritual but Not Religious" Is Not Enough: Seeing God in Surprising Places, Even the Church.* New York: Jericho, 2013.

Dartagnan. "Here's What Happens When a Developed Nation Lets in 'Too Many' Immigrants." Daily Kos, Apr. 4, 2021. https://www.dailykos.com/stories/2021/4/4/2024315/-Here-s-what-happens-when-a-developed-nation-lets-in-too-many-immigrants.

Davie, Grace. *Religion in Britain Since 1945: Believing without Belonging.* London: Blackwell, 1994.

Davies, J. G., ed. *The Westminster Dictionary of Worship.* Philadelphia: Westminster, 1972.

Dawn, Marva J. *Reaching Out without Dumbing Down: A Theology of Worship for This Urgent Time.* Grand Rapids: Eerdmans, 1995.

"Decreasing Number of Family Child Care Providers in the United States." Office of Child Care, Dec. 19, 2019. https://www.acf.hhs.gov/occ/news/decreasing-number-family-child-care-providers-united-states.

Denton, Melinda Lundquist, and Richard Flory. *Back-Pocket God: Religion and Spirituality in the Lives of Emerging Adults.* New York: Oxford University Press, 2020.

———. "A DIY Religious Outlook." *Christian Century* 137, no. 8 (Apr. 8, 2020) 30–31, 33.

DePaulo, Bella. *Singled Out: How Singles Are Stereotyped, Stigmatized, and Ignored and Still Live Happily Ever After.* New York: St. Martin, 2006.

Deresiewicz, William. *Excellent Sheep: The Miseducation of the American Elite and the Way to a Meaningful Life.* New York: Free Press, 2014.

Desmond, Matthew. *Evicted: Poverty and Profit in the American City.* New York: Broadway, 2016.

De Waal Malefyt, Norma, and Howard Vanderwall. *Designing Worship Together: Models and Strategies for Worship Planning.* Herndon, VA: Alban Institute, 2005.

DiAngelo, Robin. *White Fragility: Why It's So Hard for White People to Talk About Racism.* Boston: Beacon, 2018.

Dillenberger, John. "Faith." In *A Handbook of Christian Theology: Definition Essays on Concepts and Movements of Thought in Contemporary Protestantism,* edited by Marvin Halverson and Arthur A. Cohen, 128–32. Cleveland: World, 1963.

Dollahite, David C, et al. "Why Religion Helps and Harms Families: A Conceptual Model of a System of Dualities at the Nexus of Faith and Family Life." *Journal of*

Family Theory and Review 10, no. 1 (Mar. 2018) 219–41. https://doi.org/10.1111/jftr.12242.

Donahue, Bill, and Russ Robinson. *Building a Church of Small Groups: A Place Where Nobody Stands Alone*. Grand Rapids: Zondervan, 2001.

Doucleff, Michaeleen. *Hunt, Gather, Parent: What Ancient Cultures Can Teach Us about the Lost Art of Raising Happy, Helpful Little Humans*. New York: Avid Reader, 2021.

Dowley, Tim. *Christian Music: A Global History*. Minneapolis: Fortress, 2011.

Drescher, Elaine. *Choosing Our Religion: The Spiritual Lives of American Nones*. New York: Oxford University Press, 2016.

Driver, Thomas. *Liberating Rites: Understanding the Transforming Power of Ritual*. Boulder, CO: Westview, 1998.

Drury, Keith. *Spiritual Disciplines for Ordinary People*. Grand Rapids: Zondervan, 1991.

Duck, Ruth C. *Worship for the Whole People of God: Vital Worship for the Twenty-First Century*. Louisville: Westminster John Knox, 2013.

Dunkelman, Marc J. *The Vanishing Neighbor: The Transformation of American Community*. New York: Norton, 2014.

Dykstra, Craig. *Growing in the Life of Faith: Education and Christian Practices*. Louisville: Geneva, 1999.

Eastland, Terry, ed. *Religious Liberty in the Supreme Court: The Cases That Define the Debate over Church and State*. Washington, DC: Ethics and Public Policy Center, 1993.

Eck, Diana L. *A New Religious America: How a "Christian Country" Has Now Become the World's Most Religiously Diverse Nation*. HarperSanFrancisco, 2001.

Ecumenical Consultation on Protocols for Worship, Fellowship, and Sacraments. "Resuming Care-Filled Worship and Sacramental Life during a Pandemic." https://drive.google.com/file/d/1DhfgclYRUomeWApWtRGPr_tZJ4pe5ew6/view.

Edelman, Marian Wright. *The Measure of Our Success: A Letter to My Children and Yours*. New York: Harper Perennial, 1993.

"Editorial." *Des Moines Register*, May 23, 2021.

Eliade, Mircea. *From Gautama Buddha to the Triumph of Christianity*. Vol. 2 of *A History of Religious Ideas*. Chicago: University of Chicago Press, 1982.

Esack, Farid. *On Being a Muslim*. Oxford, UK: Oneworld, 1999.

Evangelical Lutheran Church in America (ELCA). *Evangelical Lutheran Worship Book*. Minneapolis: Augsburg Fortress, 2006.

———. *With One Voice: A Lutheran Resource for Worship*. Minneapolis: Augsburg Fortress, 1995.

Evans, Alice Frazer, et al. *Pedagogies for the Non-Poor*. Maryknoll, NY: Orbis, 1994.

Evans, Rachel Held. *Faith Unraveled: How a Girl Who Knew All the Answers Learned to Ask the Questions*. Grand Rapids: Zondervan, 2010.

———. *Inspired: Slaying Giants, Walking on Water, and Loving the Bible Again*. New York: Thomas Nelson, 2018.

"Faith Based Assisted Living and Communities." Senior Guidance. https://www.seniorguidance.org/senior-living/faith-assisted-living-retirement-communities/.

Farabaugh, Tim. *Lay Pastoral Care Giving*. Nashville: Cokesbury, 2009.

"Fast Facts about American Religion." Hartford Institute for Religion Research. hirr.hartsem.edu/research/fastfacts/fast_facts.html.

Felicetti, Elizabeth. Review of *God Land: A Story of Faith, Loss, and Renewal in Middle America*, by Lyz Lenz. *Christian Century* 136, no. 24 (Nov. 20, 2019) 42–43.

Ficca, Dirk. "Problems That Solve Us: An Opportunity for Interreligious Experience." Paper given at Interfaith Association, Lubbock, TX, Apr. 21, 2018.

Fine, Debra. "The First Art of Small Talk." *Rotarian* (July 2020) 13.

Fitzgerald, Frances. *The Evangelicals: The Struggle to Shape America*. New York: Simon and Schuster, 2017.

Flory, Richard W., and Donald E. Miller. *Finding Faith: The Spiritual Quest of the Post-Boomer Generation*. New Brunswick, NJ: Rutgers University Press, 2008.

"Food Insecurity." U.S. Department of Veterans Affairs. https://www.nutrition.va.gov/ Food_Insecurity.asp.

Fosdick, Harry Emerson. *The Meaning of Prayer*. New York: Association, 1950.

Fowler, James, et al., eds. *Stages of Faith and Religious Development: Implications for Church, Education, and Society*. New York: Crossroad, 1991.

Frankel, Hazel. "Home and the Holocaust in Selected Paintings of Marc Chagall and Yiddish Poems of David Fram." *Soundings* 101, no. 4 (2018) 341–59.

Franklin, James, and Becky Zartman, eds. *Belovedness: Finding God (and Self) on Campus*. New York: Church, 2020.

Freedman, David Noel, and Michael J. McClymond, eds. *The Rivers of Paradise: Moses, Buddha, Confucius, Jesus, and Muhammad as Religious Founders*. Grand Rapids: Eerdmans, 2001.

Freemantle, William Henry. *The World as the Subject of Redemption*. New York: Longmans, Green, 1892.

Freud, Sigmund. *The Future of an Illusion*. Revised and edited by James Strachey. Translated by W. D. Robson-Scott. Garden City, NY: Anchor, 1964.

Frey, William H. *Diversity Explosion: How New Racial Demographics Are Remaking America*. Washington, DC: Brookings Institution, 2015.

Friedman, Thomas L. *The World Is Flat: A Brief History of the Twenty-First Century*. New York: Farrar, Straus and Giroux, 2005.

Froese, Paul, and Christopher Bader. *America's Four Gods: What We Say about God and What That Says about Us*. New York: Oxford University Press, 2010.

Fryholm, Amy. "A Strange, Humble Ritual." *Christian Century* 137, no. 7 (Mar. 25, 2020) 22–25.

Fulghum, Robert. *All I Really Need to Know I Learned in Kindergarten*. New York: Villard, 1989.

Gallup, George, Jr., and Timothy Jones. *The Saints among Us*. Ridgefield, CT: Morehouse, 2007.

Gates, Bill. *How to Avoid a Climate Disaster: The Solutions We Have and the Breakthroughs We Need*. New York: Knopf, 2021.

Gates, Henry Louis, Jr. "How Black Churches Became a Creative Force." *AARP the Magazine* 64, no. 2C (Feb./Mar. 2021) 14.

Gehman, Herman S., ed. *Dictionary of the Bible*. Philadelphia: Westminster, 1970.

Gergen, Kenneth J. *The Saturated Self: Dilemmas of Identity in Contemporary Life*. New York: Basic, 2000.

Gibran, Kahlil. *The Prophet*. New York: Knopf, 1995. (orig. 1923)

Gill, Sam. "Native Americans and Their Religions." In *World Religions in America*, edited by Jacob Neusner, 11–32. Louisville: Westminster John Knox, 1993.

Gilligan, Carol. *In a Different Voice: Psychological Theory and Women's Development*. 2nd ed. Cambridge, MA: Harvard University Press, 1993.

Gilligan, Carol, and Naomi Snider. *Why Does Patriarchy Persist?* New York: Polity, 2018.

Gillis, Martha, ed. *Let Us Pray: Reformed Prayers for Christian Worship.* Louisville: Geneva, 2002.

Gladwell, Malcolm. *David and Goliath: Underdogs, Misfits, and the Art of Battling Giants.* New York: Little, Brown, 2013.

Glick, Robert P. *With All Thy Mind: Worship That Honors the Way God Made Us.* Herndon, VA: Alban Institute, 2006.

Goethe, Johann Wolfgang von. *Maxims and Reflections by Johann Wolfgang von Goethe.* Translated by Thomas Bailey Saunders. New York: Macmillan, 1906.

Good Body, The. "Twenty-Four Meditation Statistics: Data and Trends Revealed for 2021." Good Body, updated Jan. 25, 2021. https://www.thegoodbody.com/meditation-statistics/.

Goodnow, Natalie. "The Role of Faith-Based Agencies in Child Welfare." *Heritage Foundation Backgrounder* 3320, May 22, 2018.

Grant, Tobin. "The Great Decline: Sixty Years of Religion in One Graph." Religion New Service, Jan. 27, 2014. https://religionnews.com/2014/01/27/great-decline-religion-united-states-one-graph/.

Gray, Kurt. "Personal Stories, Not Facts, Bridge America's Political Divisions." *Des Moines Register*, Jan. 28, 2021.

Greeley, Andrew. *Religion as Poetry.* New Brunswick, NJ: Transaction, 1995.

Greenleaf, Robert K. *On Becoming a Servant-Leader.* San Francisco: Jossey-Bass, 1996.

Griffith, Saul. *Electrify: An Optimist's Playbook for Our Clean Energy Future.* Cambridge, MA: MIT Press, 2021.

Grundy, Christopher. "Stepping In." N.p.: Hand and Soil Music, 2011. http://www.christophergrundy.com/stepping-in-lyrics/.

Guralnik, David, ed. *Webster's New World Dictionary of the American Language.* 2nd college ed. New York: Simon & Schuster, 1984.

Haass, Richard N. *The World: A Brief History.* New York: Penguin, 2020.

Hammarskjöld, Dag. *Markings.* Translated by Leif Sjöberg and W. H. Auden. New York: Knopf, 1978.

Hanh, Thich Nhat. *Going Home: Jesus and Buddha as Brothers.* New York: Riverhead, 1999.

———. "What Is Sangha?" Lion's Roar: Buddhist Wisdom for Our Time. https://www.lionsroar.com/the-practice-of-sangha/.

Hanh, Thich Nhat, and Elaine Pagels. *Living Buddha, Living Christ.* New York: Riverhead, 1995.

Harasim, Linda. *Learning Theory and Online Technologies.* 2nd ed. London: Taylor and Francis, 2017.

Harris, Maria. *Teaching and Religious Imagination: An Essay in the Theology of Teaching.* San Francisco: HarperSan Francisco, 1987.

Harris, Nadine Burke. *The Deepest Well: Healing the Long-Term Effects of Childhood Adversity.* Boston: Houghton Mifflin Harcourt, 2019.

Harris, Sam. *Waking Up: A Guide to Spirituality without Religion.* New York: Simon & Schuster, 2014.

Harvey, Andrew. *The Direct Path: Creating a Personal Journey to the Divine Using the World's Spiritual Traditions.* New York: Broadway, 2000.

Hauerwas, Stanley, and William H. Willimon. *Resident Aliens: A Provocative Christian Assessment of Culture and Ministry for People Who Know That Something Is Wrong.* Nashville: Abingdon, 1989.

Hawn, C. Michael, ed. *New Songs of Celebration Render: Congregational Song in the Twenty-First Century.* Chicago: GIA, 2013.

Hayes, Liz. "Radical Reaction." *Church and State* 74, no. 5 (May 2021) 4–5.

Hayhoe, Katharine. "Foreword." In *Climate Courage: How Tackling Climate Change Can Build Community, Transform the Economy, and Bridge the Political Divide in America*, by Andreas Karelas, ix–xii. Boston: Beacon, 2020.

Heath, Emily C. *Glorify: Reclaiming the Heart of Progressive Christianity.* Cleveland: Pilgrim, 2016.

Hecht, Jennifer Michael. *Doubt: A History.* San Francisco: HarperSanFrancisco, 2003.

Heifetz, Ronald A. *Leadership without Easy Answers.* Cambridge, MA: Harvard University Press, 1994.

Heifetz, Ronald A., and Marty Linsky. *Leadership on the Line: Staying Alive through the Dangers of Change.* Boston: Harvard Business Review Press, 2011.

Heim, David. "Peter Berger's Rumors of Transcendence." *Christian Century*, July 7, 2017. https://www.christiancentury.org/blog-post/editors-post/peter-bergers-rumors-transcendence.

Hervieu-Léger, Danièle. *Religion as a Chain of Memory*, Translated by Simon Lee. New Brunswick, NY: Rutgers University Press, 2000.

Herwees, Tasbeeh. "Housing Insecure." *ACLU Magazine* (Winter 2021) 17–23.

Heschel, Abraham Joshua. *God in Search of Man.* Cleveland: World, 1964.

———. *Man's Quest for God.* New York: Charles Scribner's Sons, 1954.

———. *Moral Grandeur and Spiritual Audacity.* New York: Farrar, Straus, and Giroux, 1996.

———. "Prayer." *Review of Religion* 9, no. 2 (Jan. 1945) 153–68.

Hickam, Homer H., Jr. *Rocket Boys: A Memoir.* New York: Delacorte, 1998.

Highet, Gilbert. *The Art of Teaching.* New York: Knopf, 1950.

Hitchens, Christopher. *God Is Not Great: How Religion Poisons Everything.* New York: Hachette, 2009.

Hobb, Robin. *Fool's Fate.* Vol. 3 of *The Tawny Man.* New York: Bantam, 2004.

Hoge, Dean R., et al. *Vanishing Boundaries: The Religion of Mainline Protestant Baby Boomers.* Louisville: Westminster John Knox, 1994.

Hollman, Holly. "Fighting for Religious Freedom on All Fronts." *Report from the Capital* 74, no. 4 (Winter 2019) 5.

Holloway, Richard. *Leaving Alexandria: A Memoir of Faith and Doubt.* Edinburgh: Canongate, 2012.

———. *A Little History of Religion.* New Haven, CT: Yale University Press, 2016.

Horn, Edward T., III. *The Christian Year.* Philadelphia: Fortress, 1957.

Howard, Wilbers F. "The Fellowship of Love and the Call to Service." In *The Interpreter's Bible*, edited by George A. Buttrick, 8:723–25. New York: Abingdon, 1952.

Hudson, Winthrop S. *Religion in America: An Historical Account of the Development of American Religious Life.* New York: Charles Scribner's Sons, 1965.

Hunter, James C. *The Servant: A Simple Story about the Truth of Leadership.* New York: Crown Business, 1998.

International Council on Active Aging COVID-19 Senior Living Task Force. "Creating a Path Towards the 'Next Normal' in Senior Living." International Council on Active Aging, Aug. 2020. https://in2l.com/wp-content/uploads/2020/09/COVIDTask-Force.pdf.

────. *Future-Proof Your Senior Living Community: Summary and Action Report.* Vancouver, Can.: ICAA, 2021.

Irving, John. *A Prayer for Owen Meany.* New York: HarperCollins, 2012.

Irwin, Alfreda L. *Three Taps of the Gavel: Pledge to the Future.* Chautauqua, NY: Chautauqua Institution, 1987.

Jackson, Michael. *The Politics of Storytelling: Variations on a Theme by Hannah Arendt,* 2nd ed. Copenhagen: Museum Tusculanum, 2013. Jaffee, Martin S. "Discipleship." Encyclopedia, 2005. https://www.encyclopedia.com/environment/encyclopedias-almanacs-transcripts-and-maps/discipleship.

Johnston, William M., ed. *Encyclopedia of Monasticism.* 2 vols. Chicago: Fitzroy Dearborn, 2000.

Jones, Jeffrey M. "U.S. Church Membership Falls below Majority for First Time." Gallup, Mar. 29, 2021. https://news.gallup.com/poll/341963/church-membership-falls-below-majority-first-time.aspx.

Jones, Robert P. *The End of White Christian America.* New York: Simon & Schuster, 2016.

Jung, Joanne J. *The Lost Discipline of Conversation.* Grand Rapids: Zondervan, 2018.

Karelas, Andreas. *Climate Courage: How Tackling Climate Change Can Build Community, Transform the Economy, and Bridge the Political Divide in America.* Boston: Beacon, 2020.

Katz, Michael S., et al. *Justice and Caring: The Search for Common Ground in Education.* Professional Ethics in Education. New York: Teachers College Press, 1999.

Kea, Kaila. "Skills That Make a Good Leader." *Des Moines Register,* Oct. 11, 2020.

Kegan, Robert. *The Evolving Self.* Cambridge, MA: Harvard University Press, 1982.

Kegan, Robert, and Lisa Laskow Lahey. *Immunity to Change: How to Overcome It and Unlock Potential in Yourself and Your Organization.* Boston: Harvard Business Press, 2009.

"Keisaku." Wikipedia, last edited Aug. 10, 2021. https://en.wikipedia.org/wiki/Keisaku.

Kelly, Cara. "The Enormity of the Global Sex Trade." *USA Today,* July 29, 2019.

Kendi, Ibram X., and Keisha N. Blain. *Four Hundred Souls: A Community History of African America, 1619–2019.* New York: One World, 2021.

Khabeer, Su'ad Abdul. *Muslim Cool: Race, Religion, and Hip Hop in the United States.* New York: New York University Press, 2016.

Kielsmeier-Cook, Stina. *Blessed are the Nones: Mixed-Faith Marriage and My Search for Spiritual Community.* Downers Grove, IL: IVP, 2020.

Kim, Young K. "Think Christianity, Think Critically: Faith-Learning Integration, Critical Thinking, and Perceived Importance of Worldview Development among Students in Christian Higher Education." *Religion & Education* 47, no. 3 (2020) 273–99.

Kimmerer, Robin Wall. *Braiding Sweetgrass: Indigenous Wisdom, Scientific Knowledge, and the Teachings of Plants.* Minneapolis: Milkweed, 2013.

King, Martin Luther, Jr. *Strength to Love.* Minneapolis: Fortress, 2010.

Klausner, Brian. "Vaccinate the Homeless. They're Ignored Enough." *Des Moines Register,* Feb. 25, 2021.

Kniker, Charles R. "Reflections." In *Religious Schooling in America,* edited by James C. Carper and Thomas C. Hunt, 169–206. Birmingham: Religious Education, 1984.

————. "Religious Pluralism in the Public School Curriculum." In *Religion and Schooling in Contemporary America*, edited by Thomas C. Hunt and James C. Carper, 3–30. New York: Garland, 1997.

————. "Songs of Disciples." Unpublished manuscript, in possession of author, 2013.

————. "Spirituality." In *The Praeger Handbook of Religion and Education in the United States*, edited by James C. Carper and Thomas C. Hunt, 2:431–32. Westport, CT: Praeger, 2009.

————. *You and Values Education.* Columbus: Charles E. Merrill, 1977.

Koppelman, Kent L., with R. Lee Goodhart. *Understanding Human Differences: Multicultural Education for a Diverse America.* 3rd ed. Boston: Pearson, 2011.

Kulgowski, Susan. "How Many Orphans in the U.S.?" Adoption, Apr. 26, 2019. https://adoption.com/how-many-orphans-in-the-US.

Kurtz, Ernest, and Katherine Ketcham. *The Spirituality of Imperfection: Storytelling and the Search for Meaning.* New York: Bantam Books, 1992.

Kushner, Harold S. When Bad Things Happen to Good People. New York: Avon, 1981.

Lama, Dalai, and Desmond Tutu. *The Book of Joy.* New York: Avery, 2016.

Lawlor, Anthony. *A Home for the Soul: A Guide for Dwelling with Spirit and Imagination.* New York: Clarkson Potter, 1997.

Latourette, Kenneth Scott. *A History of Christianity.* New York: Harper & Brothers, 1953.

Lear, Bruce. "GOP Should Cut Its Losses, Ditch Gas Station Sushi." *Des Moines Register*, May 22, 2021.

Leder, Steve. *The Beauty of What Remains: How Our Greatest Fear Becomes Our Greatest Gift.* New York: Avery, 2021.

Levitsky, Steven, and Daniel Ziblatt. *How Democracies Die: What History Reveals about Our Future.* New York: Viking, 2018.

Lewis, C.S. *Surprised by Joy.* Glasgow: Collins Sons, 1955.

Lewis, Earl, and Nancy Cantor. *Our Compelling Interests: The Value of Diversity for Democracy and a Prosperous Society.* Princeton, NJ: Princeton University Press, 2016.

"List of Countries by Number of Households." Wikipedia, last edited Oct. 27, 2021. https://en.wikipedia.org/wiki/list_of_countries_by_number_of_households.

"List of Foods with Religious Symbolism." Wikipedia, last edited Apr. 21, 2021. https://en.wikipedia.org/wiki/List_of_foods_with_religious_symbolism.

Loder, James E. *The Transforming Moment.* 2nd ed. Colorado Springs, CO: Helmers & Howard, 1989.

Long, Thomas G. *Beyond the Worship Wars: Building Vital and Faithful Worship.* Herndon, VA: Alban Institute, 2001.

————. "Is Our Town Everybody's Town?" *Christian Century* 138, no. 10 (May 19, 2021) 38–41.

Lowell, James Russell. *Among My Books.* Boston: Toughton, Osgood, 1879.

Lupton, Robert D. *Toxic Charity: How Churches and Charities Hurt Those They Help.* New York: HarperOne, 2011.

Lynn, Barry W. *God and Government: Twenty-Five Years of Fighting for Equality, Secularism, and Freedom of Conscience.* Amherst, NY: Prometheus, 2015.

Lynn, Robert W., and Elliot Wright. *The Big Little School.* 2nd ed. Birmingham: Religious Education, 1980.

Magida, Arthur J., and Stuart M. Matlins, eds. *How to Be a Perfect Stranger: A Guide to Etiquette in Other People's Religious Ceremonies.* Vol. 1. Woodstock, VT: Skylight Paths, 2011.

———. *How to Be a Perfect Stranger: A Guide to Etiquette In Other People's Religious Ceremonies.* Vol. 2. Woodstock, VT: Jewish Rights, 1997.

Mahn, Jason A. "Taking Religion to Heart: Faith Formation in My World Religions Classroom." *Christian Century* 137, no. 4 (Feb. 12, 2020) 20–25. https://www.christiancentury.org/article/first-person/faith-formation-my-world-religions-classroom.

Manning, Patrick, and Tiffany Trimmer. *Migration in World History.* 3rd ed. New York: Routledge, 2020.

Manseau, Peter. *One Nation, Under Gods: A New American History.* New York: Little, Brown, 2015.

Manskar, Steven W. *Accountable Discipleship: Living in God's Household.* Nashville: Discipleship Resources, 2000.

"Marital Status by Religious Group." Pew Research Center, n.d. https:www.pewforum.org/religious-landscape-study/marital-status.

Martin, James. *Between Heaven and Mirth: Why Joy, Humor, and Laughter Are at the Heart of the Spiritual Life.* New York: HarperOne, 1989.

Marty, Martin E. *Baptism.* Philadelphia: Fortress, 1962.

Marty, Peter (attributed to "The Editors"). "The US Is Failing Refugees." *Christian Century* 137, no. 24 (Nov. 18, 2020) 7.

Marzouki, Nadia. *Islam: An American Religion.* Translated by C. Jon Delogu. New York: Columbia University Press, 2017.

Masci, David, and Conrad Hackett. "Meditation Is Common across Many Religious Groups." Pew Research Center, Jan. 2, 2018. https://www.pewresearch.org/fact-tank/2018/01/02/meditation-is-common-across-many-religious-groups-in-the-u-s/.

May, Rollo. *Man's Search for Himself.* New York: Norton, 1953.

McCann, J. Clinton, Jr. *Great Psalms of the Bible.* Louisville: Westminster John Knox, 2009.

McGraw, Phillip C. *Self Matters: Creating Your Life from the Inside Out.* New York: Simon & Schuster, 2001.

McLaren, Brian D. *Faith after Doubt: Why Your Beliefs Stopped Working and What to Do about It.* New York: St. Martin's, 2021.

———. *Finding Our Way Again: The Return of the Ancient Practices.* Nashville: Thomas Nelson, 2008.

McLean, Terri Bocklund. *New Harmonies: Choosing Contemporary Music for Worship.* Bethesda, MD: Alban Institute, 1984.

Meachem, Jon. *The Soul of America: The Battle for Our Better Angels.* New York: Random House, 2018.

Meacham, Jon, and Tim McGraw. *Songs of America: Patriotism, Protest, and the Music That Made a Nation.* New York: Random House, 2019.

Means, J. Jeffrey, with Mary Ann Nelson. *Trauma and Evil: Healing the Wounded Soul.* Minneapolis: Fortress, 2000.

Memos, Roger C., dir. *Marsha Hunt's Sweet Adversity: A Life of Acting and Activism.* Los Angeles: Indie Rights, 2015.

Mendenhall, G. R. "Call, Calling." In *The Interpreter's Dictionary of the Bible*, edited by George A. Buttrick, 1:490. New York: Abingdon, 1962.

Mercadante, Linda A. *Belief without Borders: Inside the Minds of the Spiritual but Not Religious*. New York: Oxford University Press, 2014.

Merritt, Jonathan. "Why Christians Need the Church: An Interview with Lillian Daniel." *Religion News Service*, Aug. 13, 2013. https://religionnews.com/2013/08/13/answering-the-spiritual-but-religious-an-interview-with-lillian-daniel/.

Metaxas, Eric. *Bonhoeffer: Pastor, Martyr, Prophet, Spy*. Nashville: Thomas Nelson, 2010.

Metev, Denis. "How Much Time on Social Media?" Whatagraph, 2021. https://whatagraph.com/blog/articles/howmuchtime. Site discontinued.

Metzl, Jonathan M. *Dying of Whiteness: How the Politics of Racial Resentment Is Killing America's Heartland*. New York: Basic, 2019.

Michalson, Carl. "Authority." In *A Handbook of Christian Theology: Definition Essays on Concepts and Movements of Thought in Contemporary Protestantism*, edited by Marvin Halverson and Arthur A. Cohen, 24–28. Cleveland: World, 1963.

Migliore, Daniel L. *Faith Seeking Understanding*. Grand Rapids: Eerdmans, 1991.

Milam, Pamela. "How Religion and Spirituality Affect Our Health." Spirituality and Health, July 2, 2014. https://www.spiritualityhealth.com/articles/2014/07/02/how-religion-and-spirituality-affect-our-health.

Miller, Herb. "Do We Help People Grow Spiritually?" Parish Paper, Sept. 2007. https://www.theparishpaper.com/back-issue/do-we-help-people-grow-spiritually.

Miller, Madeleine S., and J. Lane Miller. *Harper's Bible Dictionary*. New York: Harper & Brothers, 1961.

Miller-Idriss, Cynthia, and Susan Corke. "Parents Can Learn to Recognize and Respond to Extremism in Seven Minutes." *Des Moines Register*, May 12, 2021.

Miller-Wilson, Kate. "How Religion Affects Family Cohesion." Love to Know, n.d. https://family.lovetoknow.com/about-family-values/how-does-religion-increase-decrease-family-cohesion.

Mitman, F. Russell. *Worship in the Shape of Scripture*. Revised. Cleveland: Pilgrim, 2009.

Moore, Diane L. *Overcoming Religious Illiteracy: A Cultural Studies Approach to the Study of Religion in Secondary Education*. New York: Palgrave Macmillan, 2007.

Morrison, Toni. *Home*. New York: Knopf, 2012.

Muller, Richard A. *Dictionary of Latin and Greek Theological Terms: Drawn Principally from Protestant Scholastic Theology*. Grand Rapids: Baker Book House, 1985.

Nacoste, Rupert T. W. *Taking on Diversity: How We Can Move from Anxiety to Respect*. Amherst, NY: Prometheus, 2015.

Nangle, Joseph. *Engaged Spirituality: Faith Life in the Heart of the Empire*. Maryknoll, NY: Orbis, 2008.

Napier, B. Davie. *Song of the Vineyard*. New York: Harper & Brothers, 1962.

Nash, Robert J. *Spirituality, Ethics, Religion, and Teaching*. New York: Lang, 2002.

Nash, Robert J., and Michele C. Murray. *Helping College Students Find Purpose: The Campus Guide to Meaning-Making*. New York: Jossey-Bass, 2010.

Nash, Robert J., et al. *How to Talk about Hot Topics on Campus: From Polarization to Moral Conversation*. San Francisco: Jossey-Bass, 2008.

National Alliance for Caregiving, and AARP Public Policy Institute. "Caregiving in the United States 2015." AARP, June 4, 2015. https://www.aarp.org/ppi/info-2015/caregiving-in-the-united-states-2015.html.

National Alliance to End Homelessness. "State of Homelessness: 2021 Edition." NAEH, 2021. https://endhomelessness.org/homelessness-in-america/homelessness-statistics/state-of-homelessness-2021/.

Nelson, C. Ellis, ed. *Conscience: Theological and Psychological Perspectives*. New York: Newman, 1973.

Neusner, Jacob, ed. *World Religions in America: An Introduction*. Louisville: Westminster/John Knox, 1994.

Newburg, Andrew, et al. *Why God Won't Go Away*. New York: Ballantine, 2001.

Niebuhr, H. Richard. *Christ and Culture*. New York: Harper Torchback, 1956.

———. *Radical Monotheism and Western Culture*. New York: Harper & Brothers, 1960.

———. *The Responsible Self: An Essay in Christian Moral Philosophy*. New York: Harper & Row, 1963.

Niebuhr, Reinhold. *The Irony of American History*. In *Major Works on Religion and Politics*, by Reinhold Niebuhr, 459–589. Washington, DC: Library of Congress Classics, 2015.

———. *Man's Nature and His Communities*. New York: Charles Scribner's Sons, 1965.

Niles, Damayanthi. *Doing Theology with Humility, Generosity, and Wonder: A Christian Theology of Pluralism*. Minneapolis: Fortress, 2020.

Nord, Warren. *Religion and American Education: Rethinking a National Dilemma*. Chapel Hill: University of North Carolina Press, 1995.

Norris, Kathleen. *Amazing Grace: A Vocabulary of Faith*. New York: Riverhead Books, 1998.

———. *Dakota: A Spiritual Geography*. Boston: Houghton Mifflin, 1993.

Norton, Amy. "Early Findings Suggest Yoga Could Calm Your A-Fib." *Des Moines Register*, Sept. 6, 2020.

Nouwen, Henri J. M. *Reaching Out: The Three Movements of the Spiritual Life*. New York: Doubleday, 1975.

———. *The Return of the Prodigal Son: A Story of Homecoming*. New York: Image, 1992.

———. *The Wounded Healer*. New York: Image, 1979.

Nye, Joseph S., Jr. *The Future of Power*. New York: Public Affairs, 2011.

Oakes, Kaya. *The Nones Are Alright: A New Generation of Believers, Seekers, and Those in Between*. Maryknoll, NY: Orbis, 2015.

Oberholzer, Emil, Jr. *Delinquent Saints: Disciplinary Action in the Early Congregational Churches of Massachusetts*. New York: Columbia University Press, 1956.

Ogletree, Kelsey. "When You Become the Family Therapist." *AARP Bulletin* (Nov. 2020) 36–37.

Olsen, Charles M. *The Wisdom of the Seasons: How the Church Year Helps Us Understand Our Congregational Stories*. Herndon, VA: Alban Institute, 2009.

Osmer, Richard R. *Teaching for Faith: A Guide for Teachers of Adult Classes*. Louisville: Westminster/John Knox, 1992.

Osmer, Richard R., and Frederick L. Schweitzer, eds. *Developing a Public Faith: New Directions in Practical Theology*. St. Louis: Chalice, 2003.

Packard, Josh, and Ashleigh Hope. *Church Refugees: Sociologists Reveal Why People Are Done with Church but Not Their Faith*. Loveland, CO: Group, 2015.

Pagels, Elaine. *The Gnostic Gospels*. New York: Vintage, 1989.

Palmer, Parker J. *The Company of Strangers: Christians and the Renewal of America's Public Life*. New York: Crossroad, 1981.

————. *A Hidden Wholeness: The Journey toward an Undivided Life.* San Francisco: Jossey Bass, 2004.

————. *Let Your Life Speak: Listening for the Voice of Vocation.* San Francisco: Jossey-Bass, 2000.

————. *To Know as We Are Known: Education as a Spiritual Journey.* San Francisco: HarperSanFrancisco, 1993.

Palmer, Parker J., et al., eds. *Caring for the Commonweal: Education for Religious and Public Life.* Macon, GA: Mercer University Press, 1990.

Parachin, Janet W. *Engaged Spirituality: Ten Lives of Contemplation and Action.* St. Louis: Chalice, 1999.

Paris, Peter J. *The Social Teaching of the Black Churches.* Philadelphia: Fortress, 1989.

————. *Virtues and Values: The African and African American Experience.* Minneapolis: Fortress, 2004.

Parker, Pierson. "Disciple." In *The Interpreter's Dictionary of the Bible,* edited by George A. Buttrick, 1:845. New York: Abingdon Press, 1962.

Parks, Sharon Daloz. *Big Questions, Worthy Dreams: Mentoring Emerging Adults in Their Search for Meaning, Purpose, and Faith.* Minneapolis: Fortress Press, 2019.

————. "Home and Pilgrimage: Companion Metaphors for Personal and Social Transformation." *Soundings* 72, no. 2–3 (Summer/Fall 1989) 297–315.

————. "Household Economics." In *Practicing Our Faith: A Way of Life for a Searching People,* edited by Dorothy C. Bass, 43–58. San Francisco: Jossey-Bass, 1997.

————. *Leadership Can Be Taught: A Bold Approach for a Complex World.* Cambridge, MA: Harvard Business School Press, 2005.

————. "To Venture and to Abide." In *Developing a Public Faith: New Directions in Practical Theology,* edited by Richard R. Osmer and Fredericks L. Schweitzer, 61–78. St. Louis: Chalice, 2003.

Patel, Eboo. *Acts of Faith: The Story of an American Muslim, the Struggle for the Soul of a Generation.* Boston: Beacon, 2007.

————. *Interfaith Leadership: A Primer.* Boston: Beacon, 2016.

————. *Out of Many Faiths: Religious Diversity and the American Promise.* Princeton, NJ: Princeton University Press, 2018.

Patton, Howard G. "Love and Justice." In *Reinhold Niebuhr,* by Howard G. Patton. Religion Online. https://www.religion-online.org/book-chapter/chapter-5-love-and-justice/.

Pavlovitz, John. *A Bigger Table: Building Messy, Authentic, and Hopeful Spiritual Community.* Louisville: Westminster John Knox, 2017.

Peck, M. Scott. *The Road Less Traveled and Beyond: Spiritual Growth in an Age of Anxiety.* New York: Simon & Schuster, 1997.

Pelikan, Jaroslav. "Dogma." In *A Handbook of Christian Theology: Definition Essays on Concepts and Movements of Thought in Contemporary Protestantism,* edited by Marvin Halverson and Arthur A. Cohen, 80–82. Cleveland: World, 1963.

————, ed. *The World Treasury of Modern Religious Thought.* Boston: Little, Brown, 1999.

Pérez, Elizabeth. *Religion in the Kitchen: Cooking, Talking, and the Making of Black Atlantic Traditions.* New York: New York University Press, 2016.

Perkins, Stephanie. *Anna and the French Kiss.* New York: Speak, 2010.

Perkinson, Henry J. *The Imperfect Panacea: American Faith in Education 1865–1990.* 3rd ed. New York: McGraw-Hill, 1991.

Peters, David. "Shrink-Smart Small Towns: Communities Can Still Thrive as They Lose Population." Iowa State University Extension and Outreach, Nov. 2017. https://store.extension.iastate.edu/product/Shrink-Smart-Small-Towns-Communities-can-still-thrive-as-they-lose-population.

Peterson, Houston, ed. *Great Teachers.* New Brunswick, NJ: Rutgers University Press, 1946.

Phenix, Philip H. *Realms of Meaning: A Philosophy of the Curriculum for General Education.* New York: McGraw-Hill, 1964.

Philippe, Maria. "Children and Religion." Translated by Eliot Cole. Humanium, updated Sept. 2, 2012. https://www.humanium.org/en/children-and-religions/.

Piazza, Michael S., and Cameron B. Trimble. *Liberating Hope! Daring to Renew the Mainline Church.* Cleveland: Pilgrim, 2011.

Piediscalzi, Nicholas, and William E. Collie, eds. *Teaching about Religion in Public Schools.* Niles, IL: Argus Communications, 1977.

Pitts, Leonard. "Greed Is Only Greed; Too-Rare Generosity Is What's Good." *Des Moines Register,* Dec. 24, 2020.

———. "Small Wonder the Church is Shrinking." *Des Moines Register,* Apr. 4, 2021.

Platt, Suzy, ed. *Respectfully Quoted: A Dictionary of Quotations Requested from the Congressional Research Service.* Washington, DC: Library of Congress, 1989.

Poling, James Newton. *Deliver Us from Evil: Resisting Racial and Gender Oppression.* Minneapolis: Fortress, 1996.

Power, Samantha. *A Problem from Hell: America and the Age of Genocide.* New York: Basic, 2013.

Professor's House Staff. "Does Religion Have a Positive Impact on Family Values?" https://www.professorshouse.com/does-religion-have-a-positive-impact-on-family-values/.

Prothero, Stephen. *God Is Not One: The Eight Rival Religions That Run the World—and Why Their Differences Matter.* New York: HarperOne, 2010.

———. *Religious Literacy: What Every American Needs to Know—and Doesn't.* San Francisco: HarperSanFrancisco, 2007.

Purcell, Kristen, and Aaron Smith. "The State of Groups and Voluntary Organizations in America." Pew Research Center, Jan. 18, 2011. https://www.pewresearch.org/internet/2011/01/18/section-1-the-state-of-groups-and-voluntary-organizations-in-america/#overview-the-most-popular-types-of-groups-and-organizations.

Putnam, Robert D. *Bowling Alone: The Collapse and Revival of American Community.* New York: Simon & Schuster, 2001.

Putnam, Robert D., et al. *American Grace: How Religion Divides and Unites Us.* New York: Simon & Schuster, 2010.

Raman, Varadaraja. *Deus Ubiquitus.* New York: Outskirts, 2020.

———. "Worldviews." Lecture given at Iowa State University, Ames, IA, Oct. 30, 2019.

Raskin, Jamie. "Lessons I Learned from My Father." Institute for Policy Studies, Jan. 16, 2018. https://ips-dc.org/lessons-learned-father/.

Rasmussen, Larry. "Shaping Communities." In Dorothy C. Bass, ed., *Practicing Our Faith,* edited by Dorothy C. Bass, 119–32. San Francisco: Jossey-Bass, 1997.

Rasnaske, Eddie. *Using Your Spiritual Gifts.* Canada: AMG, 2004.

Reese, W. L. *Dictionary of Philosophy and Religion: Eastern and Western Thought.* Atlantic Highlands, NJ: Humanities, 1980.

"Religion and Health." Wikipedia, last edited Dec. 13, 2021. https://en.wikipedia.org/wiki/Religion_and_health.

"Religious Landscape Study." Pew Research Center, "Marital Status by Religious Group," July 31, 2020, https://www.pewform.org/religious-landscape-study/marital-stutus.

Rest, Friedrich. *Our Christian Symbols*. Philadelphia: Christian Education, 1954.

Reuters. "Number of Refugees Worldwide Has Doubled in a Decade, U.N. Report Says." *New York Times*, June 18, 2020. https://www.nytimes.com/2020/06/18/world/middleeast/united-nations-refugees-80-million.html.

Richardson, E. Allen. *Strangers in This Land: Pluralism and the Response to Diversity in the United States*. New York: Pilgrim, 1998.

Richo, David. *How to Be an Adult: A Handbook on Psychological and Spiritual Integration*. New York: Paulist, 1991.

Ricoeur, Paul. *History and Truth*. Translated by Charles A. Kelbley. Evanston, IL: Northwestern University Press, 1965.

Ritchie, Hannah. "How Many People Die and How Many Are Born Each Year?"

———, et al. "Coronavirus Pandemic (COVID-19)." Our World in Data, accessed Dec. 13, 2021; updated daily. https://ourworldindata.org/coronavirus.

Robinson, Anthony. "Follow Me." *Christian Century* 124, no. 18 (Sept. 4, 2007) 23–25.

Robinson, Marilynne. *Home*. New York: Farrer, Straus & Giroux, 2008.

Rohr, Richard. *Falling Upward: A Spirituality for the Two Halves of Life*. New York: Jossey Bass, 2011.

———. *Immortal Diamond: The Search for Our True Self*. New York: Jossey-Bass, 2013.

Root, Andrew. *Unpacking Scripture in Youth Ministry: A Theological Journey through Youth Ministry*. Grand Rapids: Zondervan, 2012.

Rosario, Isabella. "Catholic Worker House Opens in Ames." *Des Moines Register*, Jan. 17, 2021.

Rosling, Hans. *Factfulness*. New York: Flatiron Books, 2018.

Routley, Erik. *A Panorama of Christian Hymnody*. Edited and expanded by Paul A. Richardson. Chicago: GIA, 2005.

Rudolph, Frederick. *The American College and University: A History*. New York: Vintage, 1965.

Ruger, Sarah. "Science Gives Us Recipe for Civil Conversations." *Des Moines Register*, Feb. 23, 2020.

Rupp, George. *Commitment and Community*. Minneapolis: Fortress, 1989.

———. *Globalization Challenged: Conviction, Conflict, Community*. New York: Columbia University Press, 2006.

Russo, Charles J. "Does Religion Have a Place in the Diverse Marketplace of Ideas?" Canopy Forum, Sept. 2020. https://canopyforum.org/2020/09/14/does-religion-have-a-place-in-the-diverse-marketplace-of-idea/.

Sacks, Jonathan. *The Dignity of Difference: How to Avoid the Clash of Civilizations*. London: Continuum, 2002.

———. *Not in God's Name: Confronting Religious Violence*. New York: Schocken, 2015.

Saliers, Donald E. *Worship and Spirituality*. 2nd ed. Akron: OSL, 1996.

Sandel, Michael. *The Tyranny of Merit: What's Become of the Common Good?* New York: Farrar, Straus & Giroux, 2020.

Sanders, Scott Russell. *Staying Put: Making a Home in a Restless World*. Boston: Beacon, 1993.

———. *The Way of Imagination: Essays*. Berkeley, CA: Counterpoint, 2020.

Scheer, Greg. *The Art of Worship: A Musician's Guide to Leading Modern Worship.* Grand Rapids: Baker, 2006.

Schenck, Rob. *Costly Grace: An Evangelical Minister's Rediscovery of Faith, Hope, and Love.* New York: Harper Collins, 2018.

Schickler, Paul E. "Finding Common Ground, with Civility, Creates Unity." *Des Moines Register*, July 9, 2021.

Schmalzbauer, John, and Kathleen A. Mahoney. *The Resilience of Religion in American Higher Education.* Waco, TX: Baylor University Press, 2018.

Schmidt, Stephen A. *A History of the Religious Education Association.* Birmingham: Religious Education, 1983.

Schmiechen, Peter. *Defining the Church for Our Time.* Eugene, OR: Cascade, 2012.

———. *Words Unspoken: An Invitation to Christian Faith.* Eugene, OR: Cascade, 2012.

Schochet, Leila. "Five Facts To Know About Child Care in Rural America." American Progress, June 4, 2019. https://www.americanprogress.org/article/5-facts-know-child-care-rural-america/.

Searcy, Nelson, and Kerrick Thomas. *Activate: An Entirely New Approach to Small Groups.* Grand Rapids: Baker, 2014.

Seligmann, Brad. "Making Space for All: The Importance of Physical Spaces for RSSIs." Convergence, Aug. 26, 2020. https://convergenceoncampus.org/making-space-for-all/.

Sentient Media. "Food Insecurity: What It Is and What Is Causing It." Sentient Media, Dec. 4, 2018. https://sentientmedia.org/food-insecurity/.

Sheehy, Gail. *Passages in Caregiving: Turning Chaos into Confidence.* New York: Harper, 2010.

Sherrill, Lewis Joseph. *The Struggle of the Soul.* New York: Macmillan, 1958.

Sirchio, Bryan J. *The 6 Marks of Progressive Christian Worship Music.* Bloomington, IN: Author House, 2012.

Sitwell, Edith. *Taken Care Of: The Autobiography of Edith Sitwell.* New York: Atheneum, 1965.

Sloan, Douglas. *Faith and Knowledge: Mainline Protestantism and American Higher Education.* Louisville: Westminster John Knox, 1994.

Smart, Ninian. *Dimensions of the Sacred: An Anatomy of the World's Beliefs.* Berkeley: University of California Press, 1996.

———. *Worldviews: Crosscultural Explorations of Human Beliefs.* 3rd ed. Upper Saddle River, NJ: Prentice Hall, 2000.

Smith, Christian. *Religion: What It Is, How It Works, and Why It Matters.* Princeton, NJ: Princeton University Press, 2017.

Smith, Christian, with Melinda Lundquist. *Soul Searching: The Religious and Spiritual Lives of American Teenagers.* New York: Oxford University Press, 2005.

Smith, Christian, with Patricia Snell. *Souls in Transition: The Religious and Spiritual Lives of Emerging Adults.* New York: Oxford University Press, 2009.

Smith, Huston. *Why Religion Matters: The Fate of the Human Spirit in an Age of Disbelief.* San Francisco: HarperSanFrancisco, 2001.

Snyder, Timothy. *On Tyranny: Twenty Lessons from the Twentieth Century.* New York: Duggan, 2017.

Soboroff, Jacob. *Separated: Inside an American Tragedy.* New York: Custom House, 2020.

Sparks, Paul, et al. *The New Parish: How Neighborhood Churches Are Transforming Mission, Discipleship and Community*. Downers Grove, IL: IVP, 2014.

Spong, John Shelby. *Unbelievable: Why Neither Ancient Creeds nor the Reformation Can Produce a Living Faith*. New York: HarperOne, 2018.

———. *Why Christianity Must Change or Die*. San Francisco: HarperSanFrancisco, 1980.

Standish, N. Graham. *In God's Presence: Encountering, Experiencing, and Embracing the Holy in Worship*. Herndon, VA: Alban Institute, 2010.

Stasha, Smijanic. "The State of Homelessness in the US—2021." Policy Advice, Apr. 22, 2021. https://policyadvice.net/insurance/insight/homelessness-statistics/.

Statista Research Department. "Estimated Number of Homeless People in the United States from 2007 to 2020." *Statista*, Mar. 23, 2021. https://www.statista.com/statistics/555795/estimated-number-of-homeless-people-in-the-us/.

Steere, Douglas V. *Prayer and Worship*. Reprint, Richmond, IN: Friends United, 2000.

Stern, Jessica. *Terror in the Name of God: Why Religious Militants Kill*. New York: Ecco, 2003.

Stewart, Katherine. *The Power Worshippers: Inside the Dangerous Rise of Religious Nationalism*. New York: Bloomsburg, 2019.

Stewart-Sicking, Joseph A. *Spiritual Friendship after Religion: Walking with People While the Rules Are Changing*. New York: Morehouse, 2016.

Stoppa, Tara M. "'Becoming More a Part of Who I Am': Experiences of Spiritual Identity Formation among Emerging Adults at Secular Universities." *Religion & Education*, 44, no. 2 (2017) 154–79.

Sue, Derald Wing. *Microaggressions in Everyday Life*. San Francisco: John Wiley, 2010.

Sulloway, Frank J. *Born to Rebel: Birth Order, Family Dynamics, and Creative Lives*. New York: Pantheon, 1996.

Suttanta, Sigālovāda. *Dialogues of the Buddha*. Translated by T. W. Rhys Davids. Vol. 3 of *Sacred Books of the Buddhists*. New York: Oxford University Press, 2016.

Sutton, Christine McMahon. *Stop and Smell the Garbage: A Caregiver's Story of Survival*. Self-published, 2012.

Suza, Walter. "Many Children in the United States Are Denied Their Right to Food." *Des Moines Register*, June 6, 2021.

———. "Too Little, Too Late." *Ames Tribune*, June 28, 2020.

Talbot, Mary Lee. *Chautauqua's Heart: A History of the Chautauqua Literary and Scientific Circle*. Rochester, NY: Mountain Air, 2017.

Tanzi, Alexandre. "Growth of Working-Age Adults Hasn't Kept Up with Graying America." *Bloomberg News*, June 27, 2020.

Tarabassi, Maren C., and Maria I. Tarabassi. *Before the Amen: Creative Resources for Worship*. Cleveland: Pilgrim Press, 2007.

Tarabassi, Maren C., et al. *Caring for Ourselves While Caring for Our Elders*. Cleveland: Pilgrim Press, 2007.

Taylor, Barbara Brown. *Holy Envy: Finding God in the Faith of Others*. New York: HarperOne, 2019.

———. *Learning to Walk in the Dark*. New York: HarperOne, 2014.

Thangaraj, M. Thomas. *Relating to People of Other Religions: What Every Christian Needs to Know*. Nashville: Abingdon Press, 1997.

Thurman, Howard. *Disciplines of the Spirit*. New York: HarperCollins, 1999.

Tickle, Phyllis. *Emergence Christianity*. Grand Rapids: Baker, 2012.

————. *The Great Emergence: How Christianity Is Changing and Why*. Grand Rapids: Baker, 2008.

Tickle, Phyllis, with Jon M. Sweeney. *The Age of the Spirit: How the Ghost of an Ancient Controversy Is Shaping the Church*. Grand Rapids: Baker, 2014.

Tillich, Paul. *Systematic Theology*. Vol. 1. Chicago: University of Chicago Press, 1951.

————. *Theology of Culture*. New York: Oxford University Press, 1964.

Tournier, Paul. *The Meaning of Persons*. New York: Harper & Row, 1957.

Turkle, Sherry. *Alone Together: Why We Expect More from Technology and Less from Each Other*. New York: Basic, 2012.

Tye, Karen B. *Basics of Christian Education*. St. Louis: Chalice, 2000.

United Church of Christ. *New Century Hymnal*. Cleveland: Pilgrim, 1995.

"United States COVID-19 Cases and Deaths by State over Time." Centers for Disease Control and Prevention, accessed Dec. 13, 2021; updated frequently. https://data.cdc.gov/Case-Surveillance/United-States-COVID-19-Cases-and-Deaths-by-State-0/9mfq-cb36.

Vanderwall, Howard, ed. *The Church of All Ages: Generations Worshiping Together*. Herndon, VA: Alban Institute, 2008.

Vogel, Linda Jane. *The Religious Education of Older Adults*. Birmingham: Religious Education, 1974.

Wachlin, Marie, and Byron R. Johns. *Bible Literacy Report II: What University Professors Say Incoming Students Need to Know*. Front Royal, VA: Bible Literacy Project, 2006.

Waggoner, Michael. "Religion and Spirituality in Public Higher Education." In *The Oxford Handbook of Religion in American Education*, edited by Michael D. Waggoner and Nathan C. Walter, 364–82. New York: Oxford University Press, 2018.

Waldman, Steven. *Sacred Liberty: America's Long, Bloody, and Ongoing Struggle for Religious Freedom*. New York: HarperOne, 2019.

Walker, J. Brent. *Church State Matters: Fighting for Religious Liberty in Our Nation's Capital*. Macon, GA: Mercer University Press, 2008.

Wallace-Wells, David. *The Uninhabitable Earth: Life after Warming*. New York: Duggan, 2019.

Warren, Tish Harrison. *Liturgy of the Ordinary: Sacred Practices in Everyday Life*. Downers Grove, IL: IVP, 2016.

Warshaw, Thayer S. *Abingdon Glossary of Religious Terms*. Nashville: Abingdon, 1980.

Wehner, Peter. *The Death of Politics: How to Heal Our Frayed Republic after Trump*. New York: HarperOne, 2019.

Weintraub, Karen. "Spirituality, Sense of Awe Seem to be Hard-Wired." *Ames Tribune*, July 9, 2021.

Westberg, Granger E. *Good Grief*. Fiftieth Anniversary ed. Minneapolis: Fortress, 2021.

Westerhoff, John H., III, ed. *A Colloquy on Christian Education*. New York: Pilgrim, 1972.

————. *Will Our Children Have Faith?* 3rd ed. Harrisburg, PA: Morehouse, 2012.

Westermeyer, Paul. *Te Deum: The Church and Music*. Minneapolis: Fortress, 1998.

White, James F. *Introduction to Christian Worship*. 3rd ed. Nashville: Abingdon, 2000.

Whitehead, Andrew L., and Samuel L. Perry. *Taking America Back for God*. New York: Oxford University Press, 2020.

Whyte, William H. *Organization Man*. Philadelphia: University of Pennsylvania Press, 2002.

Wild Goose Worship Group. *A Wee Worship Book: Fourth Incarnation.* Chicago: GIA, 2006.

Wilder, Craig Steven. *Ebony and Ivy: Race, Slavery, and the Troubled History of America's Universities.* New York: Bloomsbury, 2013.

Wilder, Thornton. *Our Town.* In *The Treasury of the Theater,* edited by John Gassner, 928–51. New York: Simon and Schuster, 1957.

Wilke, Harold H. *Creating the Caring Congregation.* Nashville: Abingdon, 1980.

Wilkerson, Isabel. *Caste: The Origins of Our Discontents.* New York: Random House, 2020.

Willis, Jim. *The Religion Book: Places, Prophets, Saints, and Seers.* Detroit: Visible Ink, 2004.

Witvliet, John. *The Biblical Psalms in Christian Worship: A Brief Introduction and Guide to Resources.* Grand Rapids: Eerdmans, 2007.

Wolf, Ernst S. *Treating the Self: Elements of Clinical Self Psychology.* New York: Guilford, 1988.

Wolfe, Thomas. *You Can't Go Home Again.* New York: Harper, 1940.

Woods, Robert, and Brian Walrath, eds. *The Message in the Music: Studying Contemporary Praise and Worship.* Nashville: Abingdon, 2007.

Woodward, Kenneth L. *Getting Religion: Faith, Culture, and Politics from the Age of Eisenhower to the End of Obama.* New York: Convergent, 2016.

Wren, Brian. *Praying Twice: The Music and Words of Congregational Song.* Louisville: Westminster John Knox, 2000.

Wuthnow, Robert. *Acts of Compassion: Caring for Others and Helping Ourselves.* Princeton, NJ: Princeton University Press, 1991.

———. *After Heaven: Spirituality in America Since the 1950s.* Berkeley: University of California Press, 1998.

———. *All in Sync: How Music and Art Are Revitalizing American Religion.* Berkeley: University of California Press, 2003.

———. *The Left Behind: Decline and Rage in Small-Town America.* Princeton, NJ: Princeton University Press, 2018.

———. *The Restructuring of American Religion.* Princeton, NJ: Princeton University Press, 1988.

———. *Sharing the Journey: Support Groups and America's New Quest for Community.* New York: Free Press, 1994.

Young, Josiah Ulysses, II. *James Baldwin's Understanding of God: Overwhelming Desire and Joy.* New York: Palgrave, 2014.

Zavada, Jack. "Monasticism: What Is Monasticism?" Learn Religions, May 15, 2019. https://www.learnreligions.com/what-is-monasticism-700048.

Zdero, Rad. *Nexus: The World House Church Movement Reader.* Pasadena, CA: William Carey Library, 2007.

Subject Index

Scripture Index

NEW TESTAMENT